Intimate Geopolitics

The Politics of Marriage and Gender: Global Issues in Local Contexts

Series Editor: Péter Berta

The Politics of Marriage and Gender: Global Issues in Local Context series from Rutgers University Press fills a gap in research by examining the politics of marriage and related practices, ideologies, and interpretations, and addresses the key question of how the politics of marriage has affected social, cultural, and political processes, relations, and boundaries. The series looks at the complex relationships between the politics of marriage and gender, ethnic, national, religious, racial, and class identities, and analyzes how these relationships contribute to the development and management of social and political differences, inequalities, and conflicts.

Intimate Geopolitics

Love, Territory, and the Future on India's Northern Threshold

SARA SMITH

RUTGERS UNIVERSITY PRESS

NEW BRUNSWICK, CAMDEN, AND NEWARK, NEW JERSEY, AND LONDON

Library of Congress Cataloging-in-Publication Data

Names: Smith, Sara, 1974– author.
Title: Intimate geopolitics : love, territory, and the future on India's
northern threshold / Sara Smith.
Description: New Brunswick, NJ : Rutgers University Press, 2020. |
Includes bibliographical references and index.
Identifiers: LCCN 2019019286 (print) | LCCN 2019980706 (ebook) |
ISBN 9780813598574 (hardcover) | ISBN 9780813598567 (paperback) |
ISBN 9780813598604 (pdf) | ISBN 9780813598581 (epub)
Subjects: LCSH: Geopolitics—India. | Geopolitics—Religious identity—India. |
India—Social life and customs.
Classification: LCC JC319 .S568 2020 (print) | LCC JC319 (ebook) |
DDC 320.1/20954—dc23
LC record available at https://lccn.loc.gov/2019019286
LC ebook record available at https://lccn.loc.gov/2019980706

A British Cataloging-in-Publication record for this book is
available from the British Library.

♾ The paper used in this publication meets the requirements of the American
National Standard for Information Sciences—Permanence of Paper for
Printed Library Materials, ANSI Z39.48-1992.

www.rutgersuniversitypress.org

Manufactured in the United States of America

For Sasha Kunzes

CONTENTS

SERIES FOREWORD

The politics of marriage (and divorce) is an often-used strategic tool in various social, cultural, economic, and political identity projects as well as in symbolic conflicts between ethnic, national, or religious communities. Despite having multiple strategic applicabilities, pervasiveness in everyday life, and huge significance in performing and managing identities, the politics of marriage is surprisingly underrepresented both in the international book publishing market and the social sciences.

The Politics of Marriage and Gender: Global Issues in Local Contexts is a series from Rutgers University Press examining the politics of marriage as a phenomenon embedded into and intensely interacting with much broader social, cultural, economic, and political processes and practices such as globalization; transnationalization; international migration; human trafficking; vertical social mobility; the creation of symbolic boundaries between ethnic populations, nations, religious denominations, or classes; family formation; or struggles for women's and children's rights. The series primarily aims to analyze practices, ideologies, and interpretations related to the politics of marriage and to outline the dynamics and diversity of relatedness—interplay and interdependence, for instance—between the politics of marriage and the broader processes and practices mentioned above. In other words, most books in the series devote special attention to how the politics of marriage and these processes and practices mutually shape and explain each other.

The series concentrates on, among other things, the complex relationships between the politics of marriage and gender, ethnic, national, religious, racial, and class identities globally and examines how these relationships contribute to the development and management of social, cultural, and political differences, inequalities, and conflicts.

The series seeks to publish single authored books and edited volumes that develop a gap-filling and thought-provoking critical perspective, that are well balanced between a high degree of theoretical sophistication and empirical richness, and that cross or rethink disciplinary, methodological, or theoretical boundaries. The thematic scope of the series is intentionally left broad to encourage creative submissions that fit within the perspectives outlined above.

Among the potential topics closely connected with the problem sensitivity of the series are "honor"-based violence; arranged marriage (forced, child, and so forth); transnational marriage markets, migration, and brokerage; intersections of marriage and religion/class/race; the politics of agency and power within marriage; reconfiguration of family, for example, same-sex marriage or union; the politics of love, intimacy, and desire; marriage and multicultural families; the (religious, legal, and so on) politics of divorce; the causes, forms, and consequences of polygamy in contemporary societies; sport marriage; refusing marriage; and so forth.

Sara Smith's *Intimate Geopolitics* is not only a good fit with the thematic scope of the series, it will certainly also become a landmark study for quite some time to come in research on the subtle and dynamic relationship between geopolitics, territory, body, and intimacy. In this thought-provoking and compelling analysis, Smith convincingly demonstrates why bodies and individual decisions on intimate bodily life—marriage, birth, contraception, and so forth—can acquire geopolitical agency and significance of their own; and how bodies can contribute to the construction and maintenance of territory by affecting demographic data, discourses, processes, and the imaginaries of possible demographic futures. *Intimate Geopolitics* brilliantly highlights how, in the Ladakh region of northern India, which is characterized by intense, historically rooted territorial conflicts, marriage and the reproductive capacity of bodies are often regarded as strategic and contested "symbolic sites" (to be monitored and ideologically controlled) in the course of geopolitical planning, maneuvering, and conflicts between various ethnic or religious populations. Smith's book offers a pathbreaking and insightful analytical framework for a deeper understanding of how bodily technologies of territory operate and how the body, demography, and territory intersect and shape one another; it also elegantly illuminates why these technologies and interplays matter for all of us.

—PÉTER BERTA
University College London
School of Slavonic and East European Studies

Intimate Geopolitics

1

Introduction

The last time I saw Fatima and Paljor together was many years ago. They asked me to take a photograph and posed close together, displaying affection in a way that any guidebook to the region would tell you is culturally inappropriate.[1] They loved to cook and prepared a small feast in their two-room flat on the edge of Leh Town while they bantered in a flirtatious manner that caught me off guard. Fatima and Paljor eagerly played host, coming in and out of the tiny kitchen with a seemingly impossible number of dishes. I sensed that this was a rare opportunity to share this kind of intimacy. During our interview, they teased each other over questions of religion and politics, and their affection seemed undefeatable. They made an attractive and well-matched young couple. Paljor was in his early thirties, Fatima in her late twenties; both were mid-level government employees. They enjoyed their jobs and were sincere in their desire to serve the far-off villages in which they worked—dreaming of setting up their own nonprofit. They even had a dramatic love story to relay as their courtship tale—along the lines of the classic Bollywood star-crossed lovers.

Fatima is a Shia Muslim, Paljor is a Buddhist, and their romance played out in the high-altitude Himalayan Ladakh region of Jammu and Kashmir State (J&K), only a few hundred kilometers from the disputed Line of Control that separates India from Pakistan (see figure 1). They had married in Delhi after years of secret courtship. But later that summer, I ran into Fatima near the Sunni mosque in Main Bazaar—the bustling heart of Leh Town where Tibetan dumpling restaurants, religious sites, shops, and vegetable sellers line the street below the old palace. I was getting out of our car when she sprang off the sidewalk. "Please tell Paljor: I'm pregnant, I want to be with him. Why is he ignoring me?" she pleaded, with panic and tears in her eyes. When I recounted this story at Paljor's house, his family insisted she could not be trusted. Fatima had converted to Buddhism to win their favor, but they told me that they had found objects for

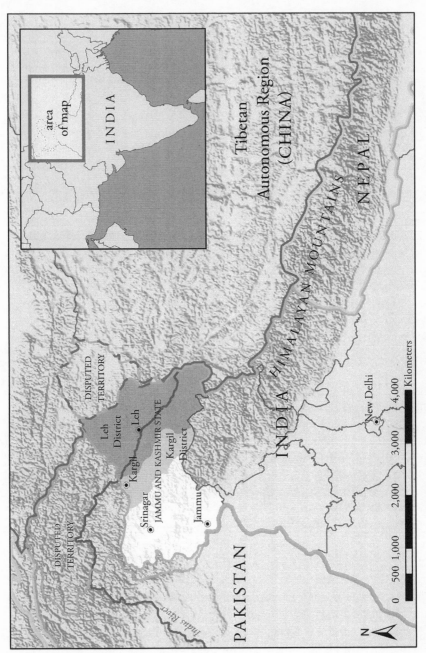

FIGURE 1 Context map of Ladakh, created by Timothy Stallman.

Shia prayer hidden in a closet. This cast doubt on everything that she had told them. Meanwhile, her family had continued to interfere in the marriage. Even Paljor seemed uncertain about Fatima's affections. I could never ascertain how he might have felt about Fatima's religious conversion or the possibility that she had loved him and also been unable to give up the religion of her birth. It was difficult for me to imagine that he did not sympathize with her. Along with his family, he expressed resignation at the karmic burdens that seemed to shape his fate.

Within one year, both Fatima and Paljor were ensconced within their own religious circles, after agreeing to new marriages arranged by their families. Fatima had an abortion and moved to a distant town in Kargil District. I have not seen her since that day in the Main Bazaar but was relieved to hear second-hand that she is content in her new marriage and now has a son. Paljor's subsequent hastily arranged marriage fell apart after a few years. Despite what I had heard about Buddhist–Muslim tensions, after seeing Fatima and Paljor interact over a matter of months, I had been convinced that they would overcome political pressures; this turned out to be naive and perhaps a projection of my own romantic and individualistic understandings of marriage. Their apparent happiness and ease in each other's company was no match for the dire geopolitical potentials associated with their union. As a sweetly serious and devout nineteen-year-old Sunni Muslim daughter of a Buddhist mother and Muslim father told me, such marriages—like that of her own parents—are impossible today.

Fatima and Paljor's love story unwound in Ladakh's Buddhist-majority Leh District; it cannot be removed from the geopolitical context. In 2019, as this book was being copyedited, Ladakh was slated to become a Union Territory (UT), breaking away from J&K. The struggle for UT is part of what made this marriage impossible. Caught between contested borders with Pakistan and China, life in Leh is geopolitical, that is, framed within the context of international conflict and struggles for territory. Religious identity is expected to shape voting patterns—hence the marriage between those of different religions and the relative growth of religious populations is anticipated to determine the region's political future. The colonial cartographic practices that carved up these mountains at Partition in 1947, according to the counting of bodies inscribed with religious identity, have rendered population numbers a persistent backdrop to territorial contests. What continues today is a sense of existential vulnerability for all religious and ethnic minorities. At partition, over 500 nominally autonomous princely states, including J&K, were left to determine their own fate, though with the understanding that sovereignty would be a difficult if not impossible trajectory.

Kashmir: hearing the word, outsiders most likely think of the armed struggle for independence centered in Srinagar and the valley and perhaps picture young men throwing stones, soldiers patrolling the city, or the rolling wooded hills and mountains that were once a staple of Indian cinema's dance scenes and the troubled object of India's love (Kabir 2009; S. Varma 2016). These visions of militancy and romance flatten Kashmir itself but also elide the diversity of J&K's residents, many of whom have different stakes in the future of the state and feel themselves to be ignored by the global media and by local and national politicians (Behera 2000; Duschinski et al 2018; Rai 2004; Robinson 2013; Zutshi 2003). J&K was India's only Muslim-majority state, but Jammu is a Hindu-majority region. Ladakh had always been left out of the state's name and frequently left out of discussions about the future (Aggarwal 2004; Beek 2000, 2004; Bertelsen 1996). Until 2019, Ladakh was a place you could not find on a map of India. Historically an independent kingdom, in 1979, Ladakh was broken into two districts, Leh and Kargil, each named for their capitals. Both districts are populated by India's religious minorities—Kargil by Shia Muslims (most Kashmiri Muslims are Sunni), with a small percentage of Sunni Muslims, Buddhists, and other religions, and Leh by Buddhists, with Shia, Sunni, Sikh, Christian, and Hindu minorities. The districts share cultural practices, such as language, food, and architecture, with neighboring Tibet due to histories of trade, commerce, and religious interaction—though Ladakh's language and cultural practices are simultaneously quite distinct.

In the 1980s and 1990s, Buddhist political figures began to increasingly invoke religious identity to call for greater autonomy from J&K. This occurred alongside the rise of the Bharatiya Janata Party (BJP) and Hindu nationalism across India and increased violence in Kashmir. Ladakh drew national attention during the 1999 Kargil War between India and Pakistan, which led to a military imperative to win "hearts and minds" along the border and the incorporation of the region into the national imaginary. In 2000, the Republic Day parade included a tableau of Indian soldiers on Ladakh's mountain border (Sultan and Goswami 2017).[2] This was followed with state actions to extend a "healing touch" to such border regions through welfare programs (Aggarwal and Bhan 2009; Bhan 2013; see also Sabhlok 2017). The research for this book centers on Leh District. Over the course of the last century, and in tandem with the development of independent India and the shifting forces of Indian nationalism, religious identity in Leh has become bound to a political struggle playing out through management of its demography.

When religion, population, and voting blocs are implicitly tied to territorial sovereignty, love across religious boundaries becomes a geopolitical problem. Contraception and family planning become geopolitical as well. Love and babies are folded into a struggle for political power through the management of territory—space—bounded for political ends. Who is reproducing? At what rate? Why? To their parents, children are love, labor, extension of a family name, care in old age, cuteness, and companionship; they are also the political future.

Children grow up to take on a religious identity, to be counted in the census, and to vote in elections. These become political questions tied to elections and the foundational idea that the fate of territory should be determined by demographics—manifest in the partition of South Asia, during which initial decisions about the border were made according to demographic characteristics. The region was cut in two: Muslim-majority West Pakistan and East Pakistan (present-day Pakistan and Bangladesh) and Hindu-majority India. This partition was one of the most momentous events in recent human history, with the migration of twelve million, deaths from interreligious and interethnic violence reaching at least the hundreds of thousands, and widespread sexual violence (Butalia 2000; V. Das 1995).

How could geopolitics be intimate? The struggle for territory is so masculine, so abstract; lines on a map, tanks in the distance, situation rooms and targeted strikes that defy state sovereignty—what do any of these have to do with marriage and its more mundane politics of family squabbles, care for children, and dinners with the in-laws? Even in its most abstracted forms, such as the cartographic delineation of territories on a map, territorial thinking is fundamentally tied to bodies on the ground in multiple and complex ways (Edney 1997, 2007). Generals and presidents who command the tanks and the air strikes have bodies, have masculinity to uphold (regardless of their own gender). Their lives are shaped by their own fear of death or humiliation, love of or indifference to children, desire for or aversion to intimacy. Marriage is likewise a geopolitical tool—how did the emperors and kings negotiate with or wage war on others? Sometimes on the battlefield, but at other times territory itself was expanded through strategic marriages. In some wars, rape as a weapon was military strategy (Hyndman and Giles 2004; Korac 2004; Mayer 2000; Morokvasic-Müller 2004;). Through conquest, the bodies of the colonized were gendered, managed, and violated, not as footnote, but as a central facet of how humanity and civilization were defined to undergird that imperial violence (Fanon 2008; Lugones 2010; Perry 2018; Simpson 2009, 2014; Spillers 1987; Wadi 2012). Here I will trace how marriage and intimacy are entangled in and shape territorial struggles in Ladakh. This entanglement defies scalar distinctions between body and home, nation and globe.

This is not merely a story about only one formerly colonized place or one set of cultural and political practices around marriage and family. My intention is not to locate intimate geopolitics in Ladakh or to deploy normative judgments on those who are caught up in these intimate struggles. Rather, globally taut and tight threads connect the bordering of land into oppositional territories and the bounding of bodies into collectives of family, community, national identity, ethnicity, race, and religion. The fraught model of state sovereignty that spread from Europe in the colonial era spoke territorial autonomy while impinging on the sovereignty of the colonized (Elden 2009; Pasternak 2017) and partitioned the world while pretending to discover pre-existing divisions (Lowe 2015). This speaking of sovereignty while undermining it is enmeshed in embodied life.

As I began this book, the 2016 United States presidential election and spiraling outcomes centered the performance of white masculinity and aggression as a key geopolitical story line to distract from the disenfranchisement of the poor: it held up and tore down the peculiar marriages of Hillary Clinton and Donald Trump, with profound geopolitical results (Gökariksel and Smith 2016). Since then, we have seen the intensification of a global turn to the right that seeks to transform vulnerable and minoritized people into a chimera of threat, only to further render them precarious to the point of death. In the United States, this right-wing turn fetishizes and fantasizes the white family through attacks on and dissolution of the safety and the kinship and care networks of minoritized Brown and Black people, Indigenous people, immigrants, Muslims, genderqueer people, and (in some cases) white women (Gökariksel, Neubert, and Smith 2019; Smith and Vasudevan 2017; Smith et al. 2019). Part of the political strategies at play in the turn to the right involved the use of demographic fantasies—oddly specific and feverish imaginaries of potential demographic futures, used to inspire fear and nationalist identity consolidation (Gökariksel et al. 2019). This book argues that geopolitics cannot escape the intimacy of bodily life and that marriage, family planning, and raising children are domains through which political and territorial struggles play out.

While Fatima and Paljor's story is bound to its local and historical context, the possibilities it contains allow for engagement with embodied and bodily ways of understanding territory. This book is inspired by feminists working in South Asia and among South Asian diasporic communities, particularly on partition's aftereffects in the body, the family, and the nation (Butalia 2000; V. Das 1995; Menon and Bhasin 1998; Nagar 1998). These stories about geopolitical love and territorial babies build on feminist geopolitics (Dixon 2015; Dowler and Sharp 2001; Gilmartin and Kofman 2004; Hyndman 2001, 2007; Secor 2001), and ethnographic or everyday approaches to the state (Anand 2017; Gupta 1995; Painter 2006). This work also builds on scholars of Ladakh who have carefully engaged with the ways that religious and ethnic identity and the state form become enmeshed in daily life (in particular, Aggarwal 2004; Aggarwal and Bhan 2009; Beek 2000; Bhan 2013; Fewkes 2009; R. Gupta 2011; Srinivas 1998). My theoretical premise is heavily informed by the ideas of the young women and men I have been interviewing over the past seven years, such as Namgyal Angmo, Fatima Ashraf, Tsetan Dolkar, Rinchen Dolma, Tashi Namgyal, Tsewang Chuskit, Stanzin Angmo, Faisal Qadir Abdu, Kunzes Zangmo, and many others, some of whom you will meet in chapters 5 and 6. The framing of this project around the intertwined heuristics of body and territory is due to the ways that people in Ladakh spoke with me about the political through its bodily manifestations and through the way that I heard space talked about, that is, as territory, as space that "has been acted upon" (Cowen and Gilbert 2008, 16).

Making Territorial Bodies in the Himalayan Threshold

Fatima and Paljor's story allows us to see that intimacy, love, and babies are sites at which geopolitical strategy is animated and made material. The possibilities engendered by their relationship (religious conversion, protests, or a Buddhist child born to a Shia Muslim mother) were read as threats to political stability, the purview not only of family circles but also of community leaders. How did romantic relationships and children come to be imbued with geopolitical tension? Part of the answer lies in South Asia's colonial legacy and partition. Partition links the bodily and the territorial in those moments when India is imagined as a violated woman's body or Muslim women's bodies are imagined as a fertile threat to India's national identity. In such moments politics relies on violence inflicted upon aggregates of gendered bodies during partition but also afterward in the rise of Hindu nationalism, and in subsequent religious violence such as the 2002 Gujarat riots (Bacchetta 2000; Butalia 2000; Chatterji and Mehta 2007; R. Das 2004; V. Das 1995; Krishna 1994; Rao 2010).

J&K began as a conglomeration of independent kingdoms cobbled together by conquest and treaty during the nineteenth century (for nuanced accountings of the history of the region, see Behera 2000; Bhan 2013; Kabir 2009; Rai 2004; Zutshi 2003). On the eve of India's independence, J&K was a downtrodden Muslim-majority region ruled by a Hindu prince, Maharaja Hari Singh. In a moment of chaos in October 1947, (newly) Pakistani tribesmen crossed into his territory, and the Maharaja quickly opted to call India for support. The first India–Pakistan war began. Wars, treaties, and failed negotiations have left this border a jagged and unruly "Line of Control." As Bhan (2013, 4) writes, the wars that followed "ensured that people's desires and aspirations to determine their political destinies fell by the wayside and Kashmir was reduced to a 'struggle' over precious territory between two warring nations." Aggarwal (2004, 1) elaborates on the Line of Control: "Drawn and redrawn by battles and treaties, the line is identifiable by traces of blood, bullets, watchtowers, and ghost settlements left from recurring wars between India and Pakistan," its broken form "symbolic of the rupture between the two neighboring nations as well as their troubled but shared histories." This line is such that people speak of "light" or "heavy" shelling as though it were the weather, a strange kind of storm that has left brothers and sisters separated for their lifetimes because they had settled on the wrong side. Bhan (2013, 5) recalls an army recruit explaining such shelling: "There is nothing to be scared about. These shells are constant reminders that Indians and Pakistanis send each other to announce that, guys, we are here on the border, so remain within your limits."

Leh District comprised the largest region in J&K in terms of area but was only a small percentage of its population. Ladakhis often express acutely that they are ethnic and religious minorities not only in India but also in the state. As you travel across Leh and Kargil Districts, you will find people who describe themselves in more specific terms: as Brogpas, as Shammas, as Changpas; each cultural lineage is now bristling and rubbing against other forms of marginalization that unspool across the mountains alongside the entrenchment of India's sovereign state form (see in particular Bhan 2013 for a nuanced accounting of what this means for the Brogpas of Kargil; Beek 1999; Srinivas 1998). Alongside this, increasing numbers of tourists, workers, and entrepreneurs from elsewhere in India and Nepal now are woven into the sense of change and dissolution. Discussions of the future of J&K explicitly or implicitly reference the politics of majority and minority religious identity, from its status as India's only Muslim-majority state, to the plebiscite that never occurred, to the Hindu Kashmiri pandits that fled the valley in the 1980s. Demographics are thus tied to discussions of whether J&K should rightfully be part of India, Pakistan, or its own independent entity. Ladakh is absent from these conversations, even as a large military presence and nationalist sentiment about the Kargil War in 1999 reveal its importance (Aggarwal 2004; Aggarwal and Bhan 2009; Sabhlok 2017). Population numbers matter here in concrete ways—as a factor in how politicians handle the territorial conflict over J&K State and as a determinant of electoral futures.[3] These relationships build to an intense and intimate enmeshment between each body and the territory within which that body resides or through which the body traverses.

In conversations and public forums, Ladakhis have consistently described their aspirations and fears as marginalized and their future as fraught. As long as their fate was tied to J&K, that future felt uncertain. Minority status was referenced when Ladakhis were absent from state-level lists of students admitted, soldiers recruited, and government posts. An amorphous sense of vulnerability and millennialist political narratives frame around the figure of the minority religious identity (claimed by both Buddhists and Muslims). I was told that contraceptive use would lead Ladakhi Buddhists to "die off," and community leaders and other well-educated middle-class Ladakhis would invariably frame their discussions of Buddhist or Muslim problems within a discourse of minority discrimination. These discourses are now entangled in the right-wing politics of Narendra Modi's India, which in turn is entangled in a global turn to the right that trades in fear of others, touching down in specific forms in different places: Islamophobia, xenophobia, racism.

What is territorial and bodily sovereignty in these conditions? Over years of research, I came to understand the pain and anguish experienced by Fatima and Paljor as the manifestation of a geopolitical conflict that had come to rest on the body itself. The logic of communalism as it emerged through colonial and nationalist frames (Pandey 2006) was crystalized by partition, and this logic worked its way through networks of political actors and narratives of nationhood into the bodies of the men and women who face the aftermath: national and bodily sovereignty enmeshed and compromised. Competitive political demography is grounded in a heteronormative and reprosexual (Friedman 2000; Warner 1991) understanding of desire, that is, an understanding that ties desire to heteronormative couples and anticipates the birth of children as a key facet of sexuality. In this book, I ask how geopolitics, the struggle to claim territory, is manifest in intimate daily life when women talk about contraception or when young people are scolded by their parents for flirting with the wrong person. The work of political actors to discourage contraception and intermarriage reconfigures the body by meshing it with territorial concerns, rendering it a geopolitical instrument in conjunction and conflict with a host of future-oriented bodily and embodied desires and hopes. In this way, they capitalize on the body's territorial capacity to take up space, reproduce, and be counted in elections and censuses. How and at what point does the materiality of the body, and the fear and desire embodied in it, refuse that reconfiguration?

Here I develop a framework for understanding geopolitical bodies, or the relationship between bodies, territory, and the future. I seek to populate territory, that is, to voice the embodied lives of territory, a conventionally masculine and abstract rendering of space, with the stories of those who live out or live through territorialization in heartbreak and in joy. The future emerges as an object of interest: points of concern and anxiety referenced are temporally placed in the time of children and grandchildren. I want to understand territory as a living entity; to provide an accounting of the embodied experiences of people whose lives have been rendered territorial through attempts to enlist them in the management of future territory through their own embodied life of birth and marriage; and to suggest a consideration of time, territorial futures, and intergenerational relationships in the geopolitical arena.

The Body-Territorial

The articulation of the body–territory nexus emerges primarily, though not exclusively in four enmeshed sites of tension in Ladakh, particularly around the reproductive capacity of the body: intimacy, intermarriage, reproduction, and youth—the management of the future through the next generation. The book begins from these sites, which are sketched here briefly through a handful of fieldwork moments, after which I will lay out a framework for theorizing intimate geopolitics beyond this regional context.

In the cold winter of 2008, I spent a few hours in a gathering of Buddhists and Muslims mourning a relative—it was the home of Yangchan, a Buddhist, whose sister had a long and happy marriage to a Sunni Muslim man. The sister and relatives from both sides of the family were lingering over tea, mourning, reminiscing, and engaging in casual chitchat. I sat in the corner with my aunt-in-law. I asked Farida, a stylish middle-class professional woman in her forties, about the unraveling of interreligious intimacies. Hearing the question "why aren't Buddhist–Muslim relations as strong as in the past?" the relatives teased her, in a mocking-serious way. Genuinely interested, they also inserted levity through exaggerated deference: "yes! Tell us!" Farida delivered this analysis, as her relatives nodded in agreement: "Since there is a lot of wealth, people compete. . . . With lots of money, with jobs, people aren't happy, and they make problems. In the past, what a great relationship. Everyone would eat together. No one would say *lakma* [leftovers, to be shared only by family]: neighbors would eat off one plate. Now those things have come. If the children who are yet to be born, if they study and they understand things, then things will stay nice. Otherwise, it seems like with education it has gotten worse." Women nodded approvingly.

Put yourself in this room of Buddhist and Muslim women of all ages on a chilly February afternoon, lingering for hours, talking about their children's education, their elderly relatives' health problems. These women are kin. They have shared food, kindness, and gossip, at countless *skidsdug* (happy-sad occasions, like births, weddings, and funerals). Yet they understand these relations to be in a process of dissolution that they are unable to prevent. Time, territory, and ties between people are fracturing and proceeding according to their own logics. Today there is the speeding up of time, the rushing out the door, the neighbor whose desire to exchange gossip or leftover momos from the night before now is an obstacle to reaching work on time. That neighbor's newly renovated home, the news of her child's admission to a top university: these bring a mixture of feelings. Who is the neighbor to us in these times? Who are our true kin? This is how intimacy feels as a territorial site.

Increasing distance between those who once and sometimes still considered themselves kin is caught in shifting economic fortunes and incorporation into formal labor markets. But this distance is also tied to the forbidding of historically common intermarriages that once challenged the fuzzy borders of religious categorization itself. In and around Leh Town, more than 80 percent of the women and men I spoke with during my research have relatives across the religious line, mostly within the previous two generations (a mother, father, aunt, uncle, or grandparent). Such marriages have become almost impossible since 1989, when a political movement for a Ladakh UT (which would spell greater autonomy from the state of J&K) turned to a Buddhist social and economic boycott of Ladakhi Muslims. UT was achieved in 2019, not in response to Ladakhi demands, but through the political machinations of the BJP, which had promised to integrate Kashmir in its election platform earlier in the year. Even in obtaining this desired outcome, Ladakh's fate was in the national scheme, incidental to other political projects. In the lead up to this event, rhizomatic relations that tangled the roots of Buddhists and Muslims were withering. Today's youth, the generation that came of age after this break, may constitute the last generation that can claim parents or grandparents with a heritage bridging religious identification. Despite many inquiries, and in spite of Buddhist allegations of ninety marriages since the boycott (Iqbal 2017), I could not find successful examples of intermarriage after 1991, with one exception discussed in the conclusion. The policing of intermarriage indicates a new arborescent structure of nation and family—that is, one in which marriage reaches down and up the generations without breaching the borders of religious identity, rather than tangling and mingling in once ordinary but now retrospectively subversive ways. The newness of this separation is most plainly evident in the widespread links through intermarriage that render most families hybrid within a few generations. A Buddhist man in his thirties laughed throughout his story of visiting a remote village known for families in which Buddhists and Muslims still live under one roof:

> I finally arrived at a house, and asked for the mother and father, and met a kid, and asked him what's the name of his father. And he said my father's name is Ghulam [a Muslim name]. And I said, "Where did your father go?" And he said, "My father went to the *gonpa* [Buddhist monastery or temple] to make offerings." [laughter] I really felt like slapping him. I thought he was playing a joke on me. Or I did not understand. I said again, "where did your father go?" and he said, "he went to the gonpa to make offerings, he just left!" Then finally, he brought his mother, and I asked the mother, "where did the father go?" And she also said, "he went to the gonpa to make offerings."[4]

Unless there is a turn in how intermarriages are viewed, the generation of young people growing up today, and their children, will know fewer and fewer of these family interactions—this is indicated even in the preceding story, as the narrator's laughter indicates absurdity. As one generation gives way to another, and grandparents pass away, what becomes of the entangled past? These connections were felt, embodied, and made through practices of food and family. These practices are ephemeral unless they are carried down into the future by young people, now themselves striving to make it in a new world. When I asked parents in their forties and fifties today what they would do if their child wanted to marry someone of another religion, almost without exception they replied that they would prevent such a marriage with force if necessary. When I asked Nilza, a middle-aged Buddhist mother of three whom we will meet again in chapter 2, what she would do if her child married a Muslim, she told me in an offhand manner, "I would beat them and bring them back." What makes such comments striking is that they are made by those who are themselves entangled in families with interreligious heritages and in interreligious friendships. In central Leh

District, the majority of those I spoke to had relatives across the Buddhist–Muslim line and yet believed that today intermarriage must be prevented. Nostalgia for intimacy between those of different religions is described as a hopeless nostalgia, a nostalgia for a way of being that is now blocked by time itself.

And yet each year there are cases of broken hearts and interreligious couples that flee over the Himalayas in the summer—a season for intermarriage, when the mountain passes are open—to marry in distant cities. These actions cannot be explained without reference to impulses that elude capture in the discursive realm. When I asked young women why they had chosen to elope or to marry a particular person, words often failed to describe what had happened: "I just liked him," they would say; or "because of the letters he sent me"; or, in reference to what they knew of my life, "you should know how it is; like me you also had a love marriage."

Romance as a site of tension is tied to the struggle to manage the reproductive capacity of the body, the third site of tension. Beginning in Leh in the 1980s, the availability of the IUD and tubal ligation created new ethical questions that did not come to fruition until reproductive bodies became politically charged in very specific historical ways with the rise of population politics at the turn of the twenty-first century (Ginsburg and Rapp 1995; Towghi and Vora 2014; Vora 2015). While women continue to use family planning, and both Muslim and Buddhist fertility rates in and around Leh Town remain relatively low, the women that I spoke to grapple with family planning as a moral and political question and often suffer in the process. They struggle to reconcile religious injunctions against family planning with economic imperatives, particularly given the current emphasis on private schooling for families with any sort of cash income. In addition to the economic pressures, women emphasize the role of the body itself in shaping their decisions. Kunzang, a Buddhist, is using the IUD to space her children, finding it impossible to have more: "I am a government employee, and when I went to my job I had to take this little one [to work] when I was still breastfeeding him." This necessity does not mitigate her moral judgment:

AUTHOR: In Buddhism, does it say anything about not having children?

KUNZANG: What! Do they say? Of course! They say it is a big sin. They say to have as many children as you can, otherwise you are going to be reborn in hell.

AUTHOR: What about spacing your children?

KUNZANG: That is also a sin. They say you shouldn't do anything.

AUTHOR: Who says that?

KUNZANG: All the *rinpoches* [respected Buddhist monks who are often reincarnations of bodhisattvas].

AUTHOR: Do most listen to that and then not use family planning?

KUNZANG: What? How could anyone listen to that? They just think for themselves and they use methods.

It is in answers like that of Kunzang that we find a complex interplay between the needs of the body, the economic needs of the family, and the ethical and geopolitical demands being placed on their bodies. The materiality of the body itself, the emotional and economic demands of family life, and the cultivation of modern subjectivities each smash up against ethical and territorial pressures to have many children. Women navigate this charged landscape with subtlety, grace, and sometimes pain.

Tension around intimacy, intermarriage, and reproduction lead to an emergent and pivotal role for youth. Young people are the embodiment of the future, including the future of territory itself. This means incitements to discourse around the category of youth itself as a site of concern and policing, as well as the assertions of young people themselves for the possibilities of both hopeful and dystopian futures.

Intimate Geopolitics as a Theoretical Frame

As the generative, reproductive capacity of bodies is understood to shape the composition of future populations, and this future population is expected to determine the future of territory, so this understanding in effect makes bodies into a territory to be struggled over—understood to "belong" to a particular religion, protected from unruly love, dressed to represent religious identity, managed with the future in mind. The story of Fatima and Paljor reveals critical links between territory, the body and its desires and needs, anticipation of the future, and emergent subjectivities. From the tightly woven strands that link territory to the individual body, and aggregates of bodies marked with political meanings to particular political effect, I have been working to develop an intimate geopolitics of the body–territory relationship. What does it mean to inhabit a geopolitical body—a body charged with geopolitical potential? How is marriage implicated in geopolitics? How do intimate relationships and decisions about reproduction shape the political and geopolitical future, and how does the knowledge of this process affect the subjectivities of those who participate in it?

Elsewhere this co-constitutive relationship is just as important but takes on different forms: in France, Switzerland, and the Netherlands, we see it in tensions over women's right to veil and the perceived threat to (white, Christian/secular) ethno-territory that thus plays out on the proxy of women's bodies that are also understood to be reproductive threats to that territory (Bialasiewicz 2006). Demographics flit in and out of view and then take center stage in political performances of walled borders. In China and India, questions are asked about the future of a largely male population resulting from a widespread preference for sons over daughters. Intimate geopolitics also have an entrenched colonial legacy—from the management of intimacies between Dutch colonizers and the colonized in the East Indies (Stoler 2002), to anti-Black provision of reproductive health services in North America and elsewhere (Bridges 2011; Briggs 2003), to the reorganization of gender in the Americas (Lugones 2016), to the negotiations of entangled native citizenship (Dennison 2012; Simpson 2014). Each of these cases is about the management of the territorial future through the management of the body, with the brunt of the pressures falling upon women's reproductive capacities.

I begin here from six interconnected frames—ways of thinking about material bodies and cultivated subjectivities as geopolitical entities. These frames highlight the excesses of territory—the way that territory seeps over into the intimate practices of the body—as well as the excess of the body—the way that the body acts upon territory.

First and perhaps most intuitively, the individual body and bodies as a collective can become ideological or symbolic territory. This theme is well developed in the scholarship of South Asian feminists and in work on embodied nationalism. This research explores how representations of the body, often the body of a woman, serve as a proxy for the national body, thus rendering these bodies vulnerable to both spectacular and mundane violence (Bacchetta 2000; Chatterji and Mehta 2007; V. Das 1995). We cannot understand territory without understanding the violence and acts of inscription that take the body as their site (my understanding of these processes is also informed by Perry 2018; Sharpe 2016; Simpson 2009; and Weheliye 2014). Women's bodies become a proxy site of territorial struggle. The devastating sexual violence of partition hinged upon the symbolism of women's bodies as proxies for the nation (Bacchetta 2000; Butalia 2000; V. Das 1995; Ramaswamy 2010). In the United States, the violence inflicted upon Black men's bodies in lynching was likewise a vicious means of defending an imagined white nation through violence shored up by an idealized vision of white womanhood interlinked with economic benefits accruing to white people through racial capitalism (Collins 2004; Crenshaw 1991; Hodes 1993; Nast 2000; Wells 1997). In Ladakh, the body as proxy has been manifest in a mundane policing of dress and comportment in subtle ways; however, there have been isolated incidents of the spectacular. The most notable of these was the public shaming of a Buddhist woman living with a Muslim family during the social boycott, after the breakup of her marriage to a Muslim man. In this oft-repeated story, which we will return to, her long hair was chopped off in the courtyard of the Buddhist temple, and her body becomes a proxy for Buddhist women as a population.

Second, bodies are the most intimate space and the instrument through which we know the world; all knowledge is embodied and situated knowledge, and all bodies are spatial (Longhurst 2001; Moss and Dyck 2003; Nast and Pile 1998). Geopolitical bodies are phenomenological bodies (S. Ahmed 2004; Scheper-Hughes and Lock 1987): sites through which geopolitical strategy is lived and made palpable. Geopolitical strategy is experienced when state actors and sub-state groups seek to produce territory through the instrument of the body. Feminist geopolitics and its associated scholarship indicate the value of approaching the geopolitical from the starting point of those who experience its embodied repercussions (Dowler and Sharp 2001; Gökariksel 2012; Hyndman 2001; Legg 2014; Mountz 2010; Pain 2015; Secor 2001; Williams and Massaro 2013). The geopolitical can also engender new subjectivities and ethical requirements—particularly in concert with emergent technologies that change what the body can do; we see this in Leh with new ethical questions and demands caught up in the possibility of "planning" a family.

Third, there is a physics of bodies. Bodies are sticky, fleshy-messy, dancing, kissing entities; they clump together; they spin apart; they cry in empathy; they spit in anger (S. Ahmed 2004; Grosz 1994; Katz 2004; Longhurst 2001; Nast and Pile 1998; Saldanha 2007, 2008; Tyner and Houston 2000). Bodies are always in relation to other bodies, with affective, sometimes unpredictable, sparks that do work in the world. Bodies are unbounded. In his luminous study of race in Goa's rave culture, Saldanha pursues this unboundedness through the ways that whiteness as a machinic assemblage is comprised of not only bodies but also substances and qualities of light. In Leh, fragile and contingent assemblages involve fluids from breast milk to blood, described as forming affective ties that manifest as a particular terrain—potentially resistant or vulnerable to territorialization. In subsequent chapters, these will emerge and submerge as breast milk shared between brothers and as distinctions between human beings killing one another and nations going to war.

Fourth, bodies comprise disciplined and managed populations, choreographed and marked in order to disaggregate them into populations in a hierarchy of humanity (racialized, gendered) that undergirds all other power structures (Foucault 1978, 2003; Legg 2005; Perry 2018; Sharpe 2016; Weheliye 2014; Wynter 2003). State tools of visibility and enumeration underwrite these territorial forms of governmentality (Appadurai 1996; Foucault 1991; Hacking 1990; Scott 1998). The composition of aggregates of bodies produces particular territories: the possibility of engineering territory through bodies is the premise upon which the chilling logic of ethnic cleansing and eugenics is built. Stoler (2002) has helpfully worked through how Foucault's (e.g., 1978; 2003) insights can shed light on the colonial project. In her reading, the colonial project relies on particular forms of managed intimacy, and this management of intimacy has significant territorial implications.

These conceptual frames have been elaborated on in literatures from feminist studies to political geography to history, and they help us begin to understand the ways that the body–territory nexus is configured. The next two themes arise more from conversations with women in Ladakh than from the literature, though in retrospect I could see their resonance with those sketched out above.

Fifth, and central to the case of Ladakh, beyond our first point of bodies as inscribed territories, bodies themselves exceed their own bounds to create territories. This happens through the population of those territories with particular political subjects but also through the ways that a refusal to be instrumentalized for territorial purposes can have political effects. In 2008, when a member of the Ladakh Buddhist Association described the "population problem" to me as the organization's top objective, he was alluding to the body's territorial power through its geopolitical strategy. When a Buddhist woman agrees that Buddhist women should have more children but then tells me that due to poor health she is unable to comply with this dictate, she indicates the degree to which her body plays a role in the geopolitical. Though she is asked to turn her body into an instrument for the capture of territory, she refuses (Simpson 2014). In refusing, she turns to the materiality of the body itself—indicating her participation in the discourse of geopolitical territorialization but excusing herself from participation in its material practices and their associated costs. Similarly, when the woman described above was paraded through town with her hair cut off, it is not enough to understand this body as a passive territory. As interpreted by Nargis, her childhood friend, this incident led her to abandon Buddhism and to marry a Muslim man. Telling the story, Nargis plaintively inhabited her friend's voice, asking: "How could I remain, after they did this to me?" In this voicing, I understand her embodied experience itself as playing a role and exceeding the symbolic role, as its defense grounds her resistance.

Finally, bodies comprise a crucial link between the territory of today and the territories of the future. Parents, religious leaders, and politicians look to the future with hope and anxiety. This is clear in the millennialist language suggesting that Buddhists are going to "die out," or, in an anonymous flyer circulating in spring of 2008, reading, "Countless birth doors have been closed, we are at the end of time." I elaborate on this with the concept of generational vertigo, the sense that the fate of this territory is unknown and is manageable only through the young bodies that will populate that territory, determining its demographic composition and its political future. Anxiety and hope around young lives coalesces as young people are understood to be "on the cusp" (Anagnost 2008; Chua 2014; Gergan 2014, 2017). While the young populate this future territory, the embodied past of affective relationships, both immanent and ephemeral, passes away with the people who knew different ways of being together. As this process takes shape, those no longer young place blame for conflict and violence on the youth—but young people often resist this characterization. In 2010, in collaboration with the Ladakh Arts and Media Organization, I ran a

FIGURE 2 Photograph taken by the "Emo Boys" in a 2011 workshop at the Ladakh Arts and Media Organization Center.

participatory photography project with Ladakhi youth. Comprised of the young Buddhists and Muslims described by their elders as conflict-prone, these young men and women worked well together and spoke hopefully about the future. Of five teams of young people, three teams took photographs linked specifically to the relationship between people of different religions. Two teams took photographs similar to that of the self-named "Emo Boys," who captioned the photograph of the Buddhist temple and Sunni mosque to read "We want peace today and in the future also" (figure 2).

These six themes suggest the need to populate claimed and bounded, or territorial, space, with the lives that comprise its substance. Young people are faced with the prospect of being read as territorial selves and territorial bodies and will either further or refuse that territorialization in their day-to-day lives, struggling to make sense of how their lives intersect with contested territory and geopolitical projects. Territory has been experiencing resurgence in geography and related disciplines (Delaney 2005; Elden 2009, 2010; Moore 2005; Storey 2001), as scholars have pointed to its sometimes hidden centrality in current geopolitical trends, unraveled its historical origins (Elden 2010), and traced its presence in everyday life (Moore 2005). Here I take a different tack, following the lead of feminist scholars attending to the ways that bodies are racialized and sexualized as part of nationalist projects (Anthias and Yuval-Davis 1992;

Bacchetta 2000; Bialasiewicz 2006; Collins 1999; Fluri 2011, 2014; Perry 2018; Puar 2007; Weheliye 2014). I extend this attention to the realm of territorial practice. This is not to dispute that the discursive and legal framings of territory are vital to our understanding of it and its functioning, as Elden (2009, 2013) in particular has cogently argued. It is rather to build on the arguments of feminist geopolitics (Dixon 2015; Dixon and Marston 2011; Dowler and Sharp 2001; Hyndman 2001, 2007; Secor 2001). Here, I have tried to relay how territory is spoken and lived into existence.

Methodological Strategies

The research that informs this book begins from approximately twenty-seven months of ethnographic work in Leh between 2004 and 2010 and in the summers of 2011 and 2013–2019. This includes approximately 120 semi-structured interviews with residents of Leh and surrounding villages, interviews with religious and political leaders, and a 2008 in person survey of 198 women about their lives and reproductive histories. I conducted these surveys and interviews, though I was accompanied for a handful of interviews by my husband, Tonyot, or another relative and for about half of the 2008 interviews by a research assistant. Additional interviews and ethnographic work conducted between 2011 and 2019 are described below. I also refer to four youth projects: a 2008 oral history project, a 2010 photography project organized with the Ladakh Arts and Media Organization, and two more recent year-long participatory photography projects with Ladakhi young people, also organized in collaboration with the Ladakh Arts and Media Organization.

This work is more broadly informed by my time spent in Ladakh since 1999, especially two years spent living mainly in Leh between 1999 and 2002, but also in subsequent summers. My marriage to Stanzin Tonyot, a Ladakhi from a Buddhist family, has profoundly shaped this work. This positionality enabled, enriched, and hindered my research—another complex and sometimes fraught reflection of the geopolitics of marriage. My marriage absorbed me into the rhythms of a Ladakhi family and taught me how to fit in to a household: how to sit, what kind of shoes to wear to town, how to talk to a baby, when to refuse tea, how to be helpful at dinner preparation, all the small things I did to become family, not realizing these were also fieldwork skills until I was sitting in a stranger's kitchen. All the while, I was ensconced in a home full of love and care and patience for an unruly and awkward daughter-in-law. This research is unimaginable without that un-repayable generosity, without the ways that I (unknowingly at the time) benefited from blending in, from speaking Ladakhi learned in a kitchen, picking up a specific and identifiable village accent such that strangers would say, "ah, your husband's family is from Sham!" and came to feel at home. My research was facilitated in particular by my mother-in-law, Dolma Tsering, whose work as the former director of the Women's Alliance of Ladakh and as a schoolteacher meant that she had an extensive network and was kind enough to introduce me to many people. As a feminist of her own making and an advocate for all women, Dolma tirelessly supported my work, even when she might disagree with my analysis. Similarly, my sister-in-law Stanzin Angmo, and our aunts, Eshay Angmo and Tsewang, and cousins like Jigmet Laskit, Stanzin Yangdol, and Stanzin Legsmon generously made introductions and gave me advice at all stages of the research. These gifts have always felt too much, too undeserved, that I could never be worthy to receive them.

At the same time, Leh is a small town, and Leh District is likewise a small place in its own way. It is common for people to recognize me and identify me as part of a Buddhist family. I introduce myself to hear, "I know you, I danced at your wedding," or, "you were married years ago, why haven't you had a child yet?" I have been greeted on the street with "Ah, it's the Ladakhi *bahu* [daughter-in-law]!" by a Muslim community leader who had teased me about beginning an interview with him before telling him who my in-laws were (something revealed when we had tea and chitchatted on a break). This made it all the more important for each interview to be a two-way process in which information is exchanged and not just extracted. I learned after a few interviews that I should disclose more about myself up front—something that had initially seemed arrogant or awkward. In particular, I faced the problem of being read as politically Buddhist, distinct from simply participating in religious life, having a Buddhist marriage, and so forth. Revealing aspects of my identity either dismantled or armed defense mechanisms in ways that I learned to notice. In all these ways, I was trying though often failing to work toward ethical ways of being in the field (Nagar 2014). This posed ethical problems, and I struggled to destabilize expectations about my positionality through frank conversations about the Buddhist–Muslim relationship in Ladakh and about the ways that these political processes were familiar from similar ones in the United States.[5]

What would become this research began in 2004 as part of my master of arts fieldwork. This preliminary work was comprised of twenty-nine interviews, primarily with Ladakhi leaders and scholars, which led me to the larger project. The second component of this research was conducted over eleven months in Leh and surrounding villages in two periods—mid-June to mid-August 2007 and mid-December 2007 to mid-September 2008. During this time, I conducted a survey on reproductive decisions, choices around marriage, and opinions about religion and religious conflict. I surveyed a sample of 198 women, stratified by age and religion. I engaged sixty-five of these women in longer interviews about their lives and how their experiences relate to political events. When feasible, I discussed some of the same questions with men in the villages or neighborhoods—these comprise ten additional interviews. I interviewed thirteen political, religious, and association leaders, including the heads of religious organizations, women's organizations, and active politicians. I also did two participatory oral history projects. I conducted all interviews and survey interviews myself but was accompanied about half the time by my insightful and enthusiastic research assistant, Hasina Bano, from the Maski house in Chushot. A young mother who taught at the same school as my mother-in-law, Hasina was an ideal research assistant: smart, witty, charming, and curious. Hasina helped me make contacts, particularly in unfamiliar villages. She assisted me greatly by suggesting follow-up questions, engaging me in discussion between interviews, and buoyed my spirits by expressing surprise and delight at our findings. Hasina's insights helped me to refine questions, and she interjected when I worded things badly or misunderstood an answer.

The survey was intended to develop a broad sense of the logic of fertility choices. I asked how women made marriage and fertility choices, about desired family size, and about families crossing religious lines. I did not expect these surveys to reveal "the truth" about fertility practices and marriage; however, they provided partial knowledge of the complexity of factors implicit in these choices. For example, I suspected that there was a significant degree of interrelationship between Buddhists and Muslims. The survey was invaluable in eliciting this kind of contextual data to destabilize the idea that there are two Ladakhi communities. Surveys could not explain what fertility and marriage decisions mean to individuals in a politically charged context. For this, I engaged in oral histories asking what kinds of discussions happen around family planning and marriage decisions and what cultural and political factors come into play. How do individuals feel about having children? Do they see their own lives in a different light than that of their parents? What kinds of pressures do they face or imagine in relationship to their religious identities, if any?

I worked toward the co-production of knowledge, often failing along the way. It is an ethical imperative to be open about the meaning of my questions, about the intent of my work, and about my own position in Ladakh. Carrying the possibility of being interpreted as politically "Buddhist," I had to explain the purpose of my research clearly and often to reveal as much about myself as I asked. I answered countless personal questions about my marriage, my use of contraception, my plans for having children. The other main challenge was to find ways to destabilize expectations of me not only as a white foreigner but as a daughter-in-law of a well-known family. I did this by visiting Muslim areas where I did not have prior contacts with Hasina or by expressing affirmation, opening the door to my own positions—in this context, the myth of the neutral researcher would have been particularly unhelpful.

The third component of this research has been my continued engagement and return trips to Ladakh every summer for two months, with the exception of 2012, when our daughter, Sasha Kunzes, was born. In these return trips, I have increasingly worked with young people; interviewing them and hearing them talk about photographs, as we make connections between Ladakh's past and the future they will create. This work, which has built toward a new project on young people and the future in collaboration with Mabel Gergan, has included sixty-five new interviews, several workshops, and two exhibitions held at the Ladakh Arts and Media Organization (LAMO). All of this work with young people at LAMO was enriched by the insights of Monisha Ahmed, Tashi Morup, Rinchen Dolma, Mabel Diskit, and Rigzin Chodon. This research is woven into the last third of the book and is partly driven by a conscious desire for a different kind of research project in which those who I speak with will also be interested in reading and engaging with what I write. As I sat down to write this book, it was only when I imagined sharing my ideas with young Ladakhi college students and asking for their feedback that words began to land on the page.

Plan of the Book

This book is comprised of six chapters building toward a reframing of territory as a lived, embodied, and temporal entity and a conclusion that pushes beyond Ladakh. I begin from the premise that bodies play an active role in making territory, as well as bearing the brunt of territorial struggles. This argument is initially developed through cases revolving around the regulation of reproduction (in chapter 2) and marriage (in chapter 4). I further the argument as the book progresses, through a shift from love, marriage, and reproduction toward a focus on how young people are managed as a site of anxiety tied to territory. In this chapter, I have introduced the central questions: What is the relationship between bodies and territory? How can incorporating life into territory change our understanding of body politics and how we think of defined and defended space? These questions matter not just for Ladakh, but for countless other sites through which embodied and reproductive life serves both as a target for territorial and geopolitical struggle and as a site at which these struggles are refused.

Chapter 2 builds on this argument by tracing the ways that Ladakhi women theorize and cope with political demands made on their reproductive bodies and their families and thus traces the tight and tense linkages between territory and the subtleties of contraception and motherhood. In the early 2000s, a new set of ethical and geopolitical demographic moves began with letters sent to doctors asking them to restrict access to family planning technologies, explicitly anti–family planning campaigns among Buddhists in rural areas, pressure on doctors at Leh's main hospital to discontinue sterilization surgeries, and the promulgation of new interpretations of Buddhist doctrine that condemn contraception (Aengst 2008; Gutschow 2006; Smith 2008, 2012). The future of the district is understood to be demographic in nature, that is, if one group's birth rate is such that the demographic composition of the region shifts, that is expected to shape the political future of the district. These territorial concerns intersect with this religious framing and attendant ethical questions; thus, the reshaping of territory is inseparable from the reconfiguration of subjectivity.

Chapter 3 traces the ways in which territory came to matter by following the steps through which political questions took on particular embodied and material forms in Ladakh. This chapter places the events of the book within Ladakh's changing landscape of new religious architecture, changing religious ideals, and shifting politics. As global and national understandings of what it means to be Buddhist and what it means to be Muslim began to gain circulation, in the local context, the relationship between Leh's Buddhist majority and its Sunni and Shia minorities began to change. Beginning in the 1930s, political and religious leaders were organizing with territorialized ideas of religion in mind (Beek 2000, 2004; Bertelsen 1997). In 1947, the Ladakh Buddhist Association (LBA) suggested that Ladakh be governed directly by India, stating, "We are a separate nation by all the tests—race, language, religion, culture—determining nationality" (Beek 1998, 38). By the late 1980s, after decades of struggling to obtain Ladakh's autonomy from the state of J&K, the LBA took advantage of the national political climate engendered by the outbreak of insurgency in Kashmir and the national rise of Hindutva (Beek 2004). The LBA deployed a new, very embodied, political strategy (Aggarwal 2004; Beek 2000, 2004; Behera 2000; Bertelsen 1997; Srinivas 1998), raising the stakes in Leh District by petitioning for autonomy based on religious difference by using a localized politics of exclusion. Pointing to oppression, neglect, and spatial injustice in the distribution of development funding, the LBA declared that Ladakh was a fundamentally Buddhist region, oppressed by the Muslim majority in the state, demanded a semi-autonomous hill council, and called for a social boycott of Ladakhi Muslims. Chapter 3 describes how enforced restrictions on interaction came to mark most Ladakhis as members of one of two antagonistic political entities.

Chapter 4 picks up from this base to trace the sites through which politics became entrenched in the intimate—from dinner parties to love affairs—and how the intimate is tied to international geopolitics. This chapter centers around three nodes: intermarriage, the intimacies born of a history of intermarriage, and the regulation of these marriages in contemporary Ladakh. The unraveling of intimacy has been achieved in tandem with a barrage of subtle shifts—increasing differentiation in dress, styles of weddings, and regulations around food. On occasion, young people I spoke with expressed surprise on learning that Sunni Ladakhis used to dance at weddings, and a number of young women mentioned clothing styles—particularly jeans—as a mark of difference between Buddhist and Muslim young women (for a thoughtful reflection on how women Islamic scholars in Ladakh are thinking about Islam in relation to these local changing traditions, see Fewkes 2018). Buddhists turned away from polyandry (multiple husbands) in the mid-twentieth century. Religion began to require different things. While welcomed by many as the shaking off of old superstition, lax practices, and ignorance, these changes also entail a new strictness in defining religious identity that may exacerbate interreligious tensions (Aggarwal 2004; Pinault 2001). How did this context shape movement between homes and over thresholds of various kinds?

Chapters 5 and 6 turn to youth as the embodiment of the territorial future and the disciplining of young people's desires through retrenched gender and sexual norms. These chapters center first on how young people become a vector for concern about the future and the ways this becomes a means to play with time and territory, folding them and disassembling linear narratives in order to tell a story about Ladakh that has personal and political salience. Young people themselves then speak about their aspirations and yearning for a future that weaves a sense of "tradition," that they revere into new ways of being together.

The conclusion bringing together the themes of the book, their relevance for other cases and political geography, and an exploration of the relationship between territorial claims and narratives about the future. What are the links between the temporal and the territorial, and how is territory imagined beyond the life span of those who strategize its trajectory? In the conclusion, I delve into the ways that the young become the focus of concern through the ways that they represent the future and touch on young people's aspirations and the potential for counter-geopolitical spaces that resist politicized religion.

An Unmapped Future

On August 5, 2019, a few weeks before I received copyedits for this manuscript and a few days after Tonyot, Sasha, and I left Ladakh for the summer, the Kashmir Valley awoke to a communications blackout, to "infrastructural war" (Varma 2019). With landlines, cable television, and mobile networks interrupted, a president's order suspended Article 370 and the Jammu and Kashmir Reorganization Act was passed in legislature. It was announced that the state would be split into two Union Territories: Jammu and Kashmir would become a Union Territory with legislature, and Ladakh would become a UT without legislature. Kashmiris outside the valley feared for the safety of those inside, unable to call or communicate with their loved ones. Seeing the news unfold we began calling Ladakh almost immediately, wondering if we could get through. Within about an hour we managed to call home—these communications restrictions were not in place in Ladakh. In the weeks since the reorganization of the state, the little news out of Kashmir has been distressing—reports of families waiting for weeks to communicate outside of the state, arbitrary arrests, particularly of young men, and mobility restricted due to checkpoints and blockades. Varma (2019), writing within the

FIGURE 3 In 2019 these stickers could be spotted in Leh. This one is on the wall near the Polo Ground.

valley, has described Kashmir as now a "zone of permanent, limitless war," with an additional 40,000 security forces now stationed in the state in addition to the usual 400,000 (see also Bhan et al. 2019; Chandhoke 2019; and Ali et al. 2019).

When news of the reorganization of J&K reached Ladakh, most residents of Leh District were elated. My social media feeds began to fill with celebration and commentary on the historic nature of the decision, and a rally popped up in Main Bazaar (Abraham 2019). Jamyang Tsering Namgyal, an up-and-coming BJP Lok Sabha member from Leh, declared, "Today is a historic day for the people of Ladakh which always faced discrimination and step-motherly treatment from successive governments in the past in funding shares and employment" (Abraham 2019). Concerns flurried around the abrogation of 370 and around the provision of UT without legislature even in the first few days. Article 370 had allotted special status to the state, and this prevented nonresidents from buying property. The rare comments of concern on social media and in a public forum held a few days after the announcements asked if this would mean further demographic change, as the opening up of restrictions might result in a land rush in the newly configured state. A handful of younger voices on social media asked whether Ladakhis might be suspicious of autonomy coming just as the country moves further to the right, while others expressed gratitude to the young political activists of the late twentieth century who began the movement for autonomy. Gamble and Davis (2019) point to the ways that Modi has worked to pull Buddhists into the Hindu-Nationalist fold, and warn, "It is unlikely that the links created between India's new 'model minority' Buddhists and the majoritarian BJP will be as favorable as the Buddhists hope." Political parties in Kargil District called for a strike, though it is unclear how broadly this was supported beyond the capital.

The struggle for UT was central to what unfolds in this book. This summer, shopping for a birthday present for our daughter, Tonyot pointed out a sticker reading, "free Ladakh from Kashmir," in the alley leading up to the polo ground (see figure 3), and as I took a photo I remembered the blurry newspaper image I had seen from the early 1990s agitation, in which women in *sulma* [local dress] hold up a sign reading "Ladakh Shall Not Remain Colony of Kashmir." It is disorienting to see so many things happening at once. As I have written in chapter 3, Ladakh's incorporation into the state of J&K was facilitated through the domination of kings and colonizers, not through affinity with the Kashmir Valley or with Jammu. The inclusion of Ladakh in J&K has meant endless logistical obstacles for ordinary Ladakhis who often have to travel for exams, government promotions, and other bureaucratic challenges. The reorganization is assumed to portend more government jobs in the new UT, less territorial uncertainty, and more autonomy for Ladakh. As I write, rumors are suggesting that Ladakh will be announced as a new tribal area, strengthening the powers of the hill councils. As the news unfolds it is hard not to see what Stoler (2013) has referred to as imperial ruination. In this "imperial debris," sovereignty continues to be in relation to the colonial enterprise, such that Ladakh is now freed from a set of spatial relations that was only imposed through imperial cartographic practices. As Ladakh obtains greater autonomy the aspirations of Ladakhis are still obscured in the national conversation, which continues to focus on the future of the Kashmir Valley. Through writing this book, what has given me inspiration is the generation of young people growing up today and dreaming of a different set of relations to one another across forms of difference. As I look to this new chapter in Ladakh's history, my hope is that their dreams will be realized.

2

Birth and the Territorial Body

In the middle of a long conversation about politics in Leh Town, Nilza caught my attention with a story about her neighbor. "One day," she began, "a little boy showed up at my neighbor's gate." The boy was three or four years old, and I can picture the story she wove for me—a boy pointing through horizontal wooden slats. He is staring at a *dzo*, a common docile farm animal—the result of cross-breeding a yak and cow.[1] The boy calls out indignantly, "that's my *dzo*, and that's my house. I wanted to return, but the gate was closed." This scene lodges vividly in my mind, cast in familiar colors: a bright blue sky, the pink cosmos and orange marigold flowers that might be planted by such a gate, the sandy soil and distant blue mountains. But Nilza is already interpreting these images for me, using the figure of the boy to drive home the point that she's been making to me across multiple interviews—about the chaotic and mixed-up nature of the times we live in and the mistakes we may be making through our selfishness. This boy at the gate, she tells me, is not from Leh Town. He is from Changthang, a day's drive to the east and almost at the border with Tibet. Two generations ago, farmers from Leh and Sham (western Ladakh) would trade barley, apricots, walnuts, and other goods for the fine pashmina wool and salt collected by Changthang's nomads and villagers. Raw pashmina still travels from those plains to be processed and turned into expensive shawls in factories farther away in Kashmir. For Nilza, the boy's origins in Changthang signal that he is relatively poor and at a disadvantage to children born in Leh.

This boy, Nilza explains, should have been born in her neighbor's home, but the young wife had decided to limit her family size after having two children. The wife's father-in-law had passed away a few years before and now was returning in the form of the child at the fence, calling out a lament: that he wanted to return, but "the door was closed." The way Nilza sees it today, family planning introduces complications and chaos into the cycle of reincarnation, and the

26

daughter-in-law has made a selfish choice with significant consequences (for more on the complications of family planning and reincarnation, see Adams 2005). Rebirth in human form is precious: this is the form in which you have the best chance of accumulating merit through prayers and pilgrimage, and this is the form in which you can understand the teachings of the Buddha. To be reborn in a land like Ladakh, where there are practicing Buddhists and *rinpoche*—reincarnated monks who may be incarnations of bodhisattvas—is even better as you have more opportunities to develop your spiritual practice. But how will human rebirth be affected by the use of contraception like IUDs, often referred to as copperT in Ladakh and tubal ligation (permanent sterilization or having your "tubes tied")?[2] Nilza is practical, resourceful, and funny and has made me blush on many occasions with her penchant for unexpected dirty jokes. She is an advocate for women's voices and decision making, and none of this should strike me as incompatible with her condemnation of this daughter-in-law as selfish and the father-law as a victim of injustice, trapped, for this life, in the wrong body, but somehow it is hard for me to reconcile. Perhaps it is because I know Nilza as someone confident in her own decisions, and she is condemning herself through this story. When she was this young woman's age, she also had a tubal ligation to limit her family size to three. At that time, in the early 1980s, this was not a spiritual concern. It was rather a practical medical decision made with the advice of the doctor and her family.

Birth is the remaking of the world in multiplicitous ways. It is a circulation of life through bodies and incarnations. It is the continuation, or disruption, of a lineage of ancestors, becoming more rooted in a place, becoming dispersed, or carrying a place to distant lands. Will the remaking of the world proceed along the existing tracks and passageways? Will parents raise the children they desire? Or will the birth of children bring chaos and disruption? In remaking the world, birth also gets caught up in geopolitical discourse and practice. Birth itself is geopolitical (Bialasiewicz 2006; McKinnon 2016). As the world is remade through birth, does it resemble the one that we now inhabit? Or does demographic change mean that we collectively give birth to a world that looks quite different? These questions are taken up in other languages and valences across contexts. In 2017, in Charlottesville, Virginia, 200 miles from where I wrote this book, a crowd of white supremacists chanted, "You will not replace us, Jews will not replace us." The previous year's election rhetoric was largely based in imagery promising a revanchist nationalism that returned the United States to a different demographic time, in order to "Make America Great Again." This is a different language of difference, but an undercurrent travels across these contexts: the twinned ideas that bodies themselves carry a geopolitical charge and that an unrecognizable future must be avoided.

When Nilza described her concerns in relation to the spiritual realm, her reasoning struck me as unusual. When concerns about contraception were broached, it was most common for Buddhists to describe them as a question of competitive demography, with the assumption that Muslim Ladakhis were eschewing contraception in favor of larger families. I wish I could remember the moment I realized that despite discourses of difference between Buddhist and Muslim women, their concerns regarding family planning, children, and the future were nearly indistinguishable, and that I had absorbed the idea that there must be difference and thus been looking for it. Women from all faiths told me:

> They say it's sin if you use family planning, but isn't it also sin if your children aren't given proper education and food?

> Nothing will happen to the parents [if you have many children] but for the children things won't turn out well. The children won't have a happy life.

> Our own bodies, they don't have the ability to have a child one after another. If you have a child every year, you yourself won't survive.

> We waited between children: if you have them quickly, the mother's body will become weak, and the next child to be born will also be weak.

Nilza's story leads us to ask: when contraception is used to alter the circulation of beings, will children be born in the wrong places? Or, as another woman asked me, what if they cannot find human rebirth at all? These concerns flow among fears that these children might also love the wrong people and forget their own language and the religion of their parents. Will our small practical decisions and attempts to care for our family turn out to have been selfish and wrong-headed? Places are remade each generation, and the birth of a generation thus remakes the world anew. But what if fewer children were born, and those born were sent to the wrong homes? Ideas about reincarnation, morality, and the body are brought together to do political work, but political work is also the work of the body itself. Flows of time, ideas, bodies, and souls are entangled through attempts to fix and cohere bodies in place, time to a predictable pattern, and place to territory. In another interview, Nilza had told me she had heard that only wealthy, highly educated Muslims use family planning but that most of them eschew it completely. This chapter describes how decisions about contraception are pulled into the realm of the geopolitical, how women cope with this politicization, and how this confounds the boundary between corporeal flesh and bounded political space. In a temporal echo, this story points to the body as a point at which the timelines of family, individual, and territory converge, and decisions made affect all three. Thus, its focus is the life stories of women and men coping with and re-theorizing the body (whether through original interpretations of religious doctrine or reappropriation of doctors' medical explanations of their state of health) as they make family planning decisions in a context of heightened tension.

Muslim fertility looms large in Nilza's frame of reference now, because reproduction has been caught in the pervasive territorial strategies competing for this contested region. This is also filtered through national discourses on Muslim fertility that have been picked up as demographic fever dreams centering Muslim fertility as a threat (Gökariksel et al. 2019; P. Jeffery and Jeffery 2002; Johnson-Hanks 2006). Political discourse in Ladakh today describes Leh District as vulnerable to fragmentation and loss of sovereignty. In conversation and daily life, Ladakh emerged as a territorial chimera. A few weeks before I received copy-edits for this book, this terrain shifted. After October 31, 2019, this place will be visible on the map of India as the Union Territory of Ladakh. Through the years of conversations that structured this book, this seemed like an impossible goal, and instead, Ladakh was a place that you could not bound precisely; it was not marked on any map as a jurisdiction. But still somehow there was a place called Ladakh that emerged when someone said, "we Ladakhis love to gossip," or "our young people are forgetting their own language." Ladakh as a place is called into being when someone mentions they are flying or driving over the roads to go to Delhi or elsewhere, saying they are going to *Gyagar* (India), or *angwa* (over there), referring to people from lowland India as *downpa*, or "the people from down [there]." There is slippage between Ladakh as a space and Ladakh as comprised by people. Talk of "our *yul*," a word that could mean country, homeland, village, or kingdom, easily slips into talk of "our youth," or "our women." There is also a pervasive sense of vulnerability, whether expressed in concerns about tourists and other outsiders in Ladakh (described as bringing materialism and loose sexual morals) or about time spent outside Ladakh—a time understood to be risky for the youth who study in Indian cities such as Delhi, Chandigarh, and Jammu. It is in this sense of vulnerability that ties between spaces, bodies, and subjectivities emerge, as a dizzying feeling of confronting the unknown, the threshold, the precipice. Here, the territorial meets the temporal, as stories about Ladakh's vulnerability bring past and future together to question how action is taken now reflects the past and shapes the future.

Countless Birth Doors

The same summer I had been speaking with Nilza, an anonymous letter circulated in Main Bazaar. Beginning "Evil eye has struck. Leaders are paralyzed. Temples are locked. Buddhists are at a loss. Unity has been destroyed. Leaders have become the enemy. Union Territory has become a dream. Ladakhis have become donkeys," the letter goes on to list catastrophic conditions involving politics, culture, and Leh as a place—from loss of unity to pollution and hopelessness. Accusing Ladakhi politicians of clinging to the influence of outsiders, the letter goes on to speak of divisions among Buddhists ("They say, 'I heart you Drukpa [dragon],'" they say, 'I heart you Serpo [yellow],'" referring to two main

Tibetan Buddhist sects sometimes known as red hat and yellow hat) and then ties these catastrophic trends to fertility and natural destruction. "Countless birth doors have been closed. Buddhists are going to be finished. We're at the end of time. Glaciers have melted away. Untimely floods have come. Grasshoppers have eaten half the country. Lamas and monks are mixed in all kinds of things. The knife is at our throat and we are blaming each other for murder. Religion has been harmed. Hey Buddhists, think about it. Still you have time to think. One day you'll have to leave this place. One day you will have to convert to another religion."

Here, fears over the future of Buddhists slip into existential anxieties about the land itself (glaciers and floods commonly discussed as harbingers of climate change in Ladakh), and the letter ends with the threat of exile and conversion. Demographic strategy became explicit in the Ladakh Buddhist Association actions in the first decade of the 2000s through measures such as awareness campaigns about the religious and political repercussions of using birth control and attempts to ban tubal ligation at Leh's Sonam Norbu Memorial Hospital. Gutschow (2006) reports that health workers in Zangskar have had trouble stocking contraceptives such as IUDs and condoms. Anecdotal evidence in Sham and events in Nubra suggest that anti–family planning sentiment may be interfering with health workers' ability to make contraceptives available. These public actions reflect upon and draw on widely held Buddhist beliefs that Muslims do not use family planning (Aengst 2008; Smith 2008). The imaginary of aggressive Muslim fertility references national and global tropes: what R. Jeffery and Jeffery (2005) have termed "Saffron Demography" at the national level and what Bialasiewicz (2006) describes as new moral geographies of birth, bodies, and "demographic-reproductive menace" within a global imaginary.

The millennialist language of the letter reflects the uncertainties that have engendered pro-natal actions. Buddhist and Muslim women now frame their decisions in accordance with new moral narratives in circulation. The decision to have a tubal ligation, once something "everyone was doing," is now justified through explanations of compromised or vulnerable bodies, limited incomes, and the need to produce modern, well-educated children.

The explanations women currently employ for their use of family planning suggest that this need to justify family planning is leading to shifts in the technology used—away from tubal ligation toward use of the IUD to limit births rather than to space them. For most women I spoke with, tubal ligation was the preferred method to limit family size, discussed as safe, effective, and foolproof. Aside from tubal ligation, women referenced the IUD, or "copper T," but also mentioned instances of contraceptive failure or complications from IUD insertion. Out of 198 women I spoke with about contraception, only one was using birth control pills and one was using condoms (something she was clearly embarrassed to explain).

One offhand exchange between Fatima and Paljor is lodged in my mind. Explaining to me the concern about their interreligious marriage, Paljor had said Shia Ladakhis had large families and that her community would resent her having Buddhist children. Fatima had laughed and responded, "oh, you think we have ten children each?" She then reminded us that she was one of three children—the same family size as Paljor's family. And yet, as I mentioned earlier, when I spoke with Shia and Sunni women about family planning, perhaps because I was so embedded in Buddhist social worlds, I was struck most of all by how similar their concerns were to those of Buddhist women: how to prepare children for an unknown future by sending them to private schools and providing for their needs, how to care for their own bodies and cope with health issues related to or exacerbated by giving birth, and how to care for children while balancing work and other family demands. Among those with whom I spoke, I found similar rates of contraceptive use and comparable family sizes amongst Shia, Sunni, and Buddhist Ladakhis, with slight differences in older generations.

Buddhist, Shia, and Sunni women have all heard that some forms of family planning go against their religion, and they struggle to balance family needs with ethical demands. The relationship between religion and contraception is described contextually. Despite the stories about differential fertility, my 2008 survey found very similar fertility practices among most women in and around Leh Town (see table 2-1 and table 2-2).[3] Aengst (2012), working from a very

TABLE 2-1
Survey Participants

Religion and residence	Number of survey participants*	Average age
Buddhist Leh residents	48	47
Shia Leh residents	22	37
Sunni Leh residents	35	41
Total Leh residents	105	42
Buddhist rural residents	20	41
Shia rural residents	36	39
Sunni rural residents	31	41
Total rural residents	87	40

*This refers only to those to whom I asked a standard set of survey questions. These are all women. Around fifty of these women were requested (and were generous enough) to spend an hour or so with me answering more in-depth questions about their lives.

TABLE 2-2

Mean Number of Children (among Ever-Married Women)

Age range	Religion	Mean	Number of participants
Ages 18–39	Buddhist	2.00	24
	Sunni	1.72	32
	Shia	1.25	28
	Total	1.64	84
Ages 40–59	Buddhist	2.94	17
	Sunni	2.83	23
	Shia	3.57	21
	Total	3.11	61
Ages 60 and above	Buddhist	4.50	18
	Sunni	3.67	6
	Shia	4.60	5
	Total	4.34	29
Total	Buddhist	3.03	59
	Sunni	2.33	61
	Shia	2.46	54

different sampling methodology (collecting data at the district hospital), found even slighter differences and lower fertility than my survey suggests. In fact, her survey found that in Leh District, 89 percent of Muslim women were using contraception compared with only 78 percent of Buddhist women. This is unsurprising as her survey was collected at the hospital and thus likely included more women still in their childbearing years, while mine included more older women who had not had access to family planning. There is a strong preference for smaller family sizes. While women disagree on whether spacing children by using an IUD is acceptable, all the Buddhist women with whom I spoke describe tubal ligation as a sin. Women marshal a variety of theoretical, theological, and empirical arguments to defend their own personal choices: health, professional reasons, quality of children versus quantity, and the discourse of modernity. Most of all, they stressed the pressure to provide a private school education for their children. The majority of women, regardless of religious identity, state their desired number of children, and the ideal number of children, as two to three.

Nilza's story about the nameless young boy is entangled in her own life. In the late 1980s, Nilza had survived a difficult labor, almost dying during the birth of her third child. Her relatives pleaded with her at the hospital—why not have the surgery that would prevent future births? She had three children now—two daughters and a son—and as a farmer, she had little disposable income. After this difficult birth, she should take care of her health: another pregnancy might be dangerous—why take the risk? Persuaded, Nilza asked the gynecologist, who had taken such good care of her in the hospital, to perform a tubal ligation. With just three children to care for, Nilza and her husband had sent them to good private schools, started side businesses, and live comfortably in their new but traditionally styled home with a big garden and cute little dog. Nilza is respected as a leader among women in town and spends time doing volunteer work and caring for her grandchildren. It would seem that her life had all gone according to her wishes and plans.

When Nilza tells the story of her own tubal ligation, and she has told me this story three times, it is a lament: "I didn't know, I didn't know at the time," she reiterates through the telling. In the 1980s, family planning was becoming popular in Leh and was being promoted by the government as well (though not in the coercive ways recorded elsewhere in India). Access to reproductive health care reached this region late—in the 1980s, Leh received its first dedicated obstetrician-gynecologist, Dr. Padma Lhadol, much beloved by Ladakhi women, who credit her with saving the lives of women and their babies and providing them with services that changed the course of their lives.

When family planning first arrived in the region, it was quickly embraced as word spread about its possibilities. Dr. Lhadol provided services in a careful manner considering local circumstances. Dr. Lhadol, for instance, knew that women from remote regions like Changthang—the higher altitude region bordering Tibet, from which the boy in Nilza's story travels—had relatively high infant and child mortality, so even when these women requested tubal ligation, she asked them to first use the IUD until their children were over the age of five and then to return for tubal ligation when their children were past this most dangerous period. Speaking about the introduction of reproductive health and obstetric services in Leh, women used the most honorific language that they could to emphasize the service of Dr. Lhadol in saving the lives of women and babies—though this was also reference to her position as a member of a *skutags* (aristocratic) family. In our conversations, even those women who now believe family planning should be curtailed cannot bring themselves to criticize her as they have stories of how she has intervened in their own or their friends' and relatives' difficult births. During my 2008 research, a letter had been sent to the main district hospital requesting doctors to restrict access to tubal ligation, and sentiments against the practice were running high, but I still did not encounter criticism of Dr. Lhadol as a very public figure who had been at the forefront of enabling family planning in Ladakh. Even while Nilza expresses concerns about widespread Buddhist use of contraception and links this practice to Dr. Lhadol's efforts (mentioning that this might have been part of the Indian government's directives), she praises Dr. Lhadol effusively. She tells me, "No woman has died in childbirth with Dr. Lhadol present." Spalzes, of the same generation as Nilza, told me in the space of a few breaths that "The Muslims have really increased," and that some people criticize those who provide contraception, but that most women were glad to have family planning services available. Everyone of Nilza's generation knows of women who died in childbirth or had complicated deliveries or babies that died young. Jamila, for instance, tells her story as though it were unexceptional:

AUTHOR: Is your life easier now or when you were young?

JAMILA: It's easier now. When I was young we didn't have the ability to eat good food and drink. At the same time, we didn't have a lot of disease, but now there are all kinds of disease.

AUTHOR: Did you give birth in the hospital?

JAMILA: Aiy [a cry of lament], I gave birth at home, we were also kind of without money. I gave birth at home and many of my children died. Four of my children died. There was nothing, no hospital, nothing.

AUTHOR: Died as children?

JAMILA: Yes, born. One when they were three.

AUTHOR: When did you get married?

JAMILA: When I had my first child I was only fifteen. My mother died young, so they sent me as a bride when I was very young.

AUTHOR: So you had arranged marriage?

JAMILA: Yes, at that time, that was the way we all went.

AUTHOR: Which is more common?

JAMILA: Nowadays, the girls all go by themselves, they have talked to the boys and decided themselves.

This life, of arranged marriage, unfettered reproduction, and home births, with all their attendant risks, is the milieu in which women like Nilza took to family planning. Even if this was not their own experience, it was the experience of their older sisters or mothers, and the embodied experience or the missing but remembered mother or aunt who had died in childbirth is central to how these generations of women talk about family decisions. Sometimes that translates to praise for doctors who provide the service that they believe should not be used; other times that translates to fears for young babies and children and young women's decisions. I remembered this when I returned to Ladakh with our own daughter at ten months and received a deluge of advice meant to protect her from harm, requests to put another sweater on her, keep her out of the wind and cold, and to have another child, as to invest all one's love and care into just one child is risky.

Nilza's family planning decision was a pragmatic one, and at the time she did not make a connection between her Buddhist religion and the procedure. Now, along with many women, Nilza has heard that family planning is "the worst sin," that Buddhist use of contraception will lead to the eventual decline and perhaps disappearance of the Buddhist population, and that Muslims do not use contraception. Nilza has heard from Buddhist politicians and religious leaders that Muslim Ladakhis will become the majority through rapid reproduction and thus gain electoral and political control of Ladakh. Inundated with these messages and reflecting on her decision, Nilza now bitterly regrets her mistake and told me that she has confessed to *konjok*[4] and prayed over it. Nilza's daughters and daughter-in-law are spacing their children by using an IUD, so that they are not born too close together. Nilza worries they will keep their family size too small. She has advised them to have a minimum of three children. She worries about broader changes: that wealthy families treat their children as "precious" and do not let them do ordinary farmwork, thus ensuring the death of traditional Ladakhi practices in that household. It is not, however, that she wants Ladakh to remain fixed in time.

While some folks lament a perceived rise in love marriages (versus arranged marriages), Nilza thinks it is wonderful. She and her husband are not close—they function well as a team in providing for their family, but they do not share the same interests, and she finds him aloof, disinterested in her passions and concerns. Contrary to some women who suggested young people these days were impulsive, divorcing and marrying with ease, she thinks there are now fewer divorces since women and men have chosen their own spouses. But Nilza's marriage is peripheral to how she sees herself. Nilza is confident and outgoing. She has a large social network and spends her spare time doing community organizing around religious, gender, and environmental issues. She is largely satisfied with her life, particularly her community service and leadership among women, and describes her own trajectory from farm girl to mother of three educated professional children as a success story. Nilza's son and two daughters went to school, and Nilza's entrepreneurial spirit fed her interest in a range of activities that bring in additional income. Combined with her husband's salaried work, Nilza's standard of living is high, and her house is spacious and modern in the popular style, which incorporates a brand new refrigerator, counter for food preparation, and gas range, with nods to older Ladakhi homes (ornately carved wooden shelves for displaying large pots used for weddings, a woodstove decorated with Buddhist symbols).

At the end of our last interview about these matters, her daughter-in-law comes back from town with her two young children in tow. She is stylishly dressed, confident, but polite and deferential to Nilza: she matches Nilza's description of an ideal daughter-in-law. Something in her manner made it hard for me to imagine this practical young woman would make the decision for her fertility to go unchecked and risk disrupting their smoothly functioning household. Despite her life's trajectory, geopolitical body talk impinges on Nilza's sense of self and peace of mind, causing her to agonize and suffer for a decision made at a vulnerable moment twenty years ago. Nilza at once perpetuates a territorial body project that shapes how she sees herself as a person but also celebrates Buddhist–Muslim harmony (she herself has Muslim relatives, friends, and neighbors). In this way, and in a context in which "living has been rendered problematic" (Lakoff and Collier 2004, 419), the geopolitical reaches into the body and becomes part of intimate decision making and subject formation. When Nilza reflects on her past choices, even though she is happy with her family, she feels remorse over her decisions—they cannot be disentangled from the religious and political messages that frame them, just as Fatima and Paljor's marriage faltered when they were unable to carry the geopolitical weight it entailed in addition to the normal stresses of two people making a life together.

Circulation, Temporal Flows, and Fixity

The father-in-law born in the wrong body is, for Nilza, a deviation from the way things should have been. In turn, this reoriented flow of life was disrupted by the circulation of a contraceptive technology, tubal ligation, which was first performed in 1880 in Toledo, Ohio, to block eggs from traveling through the fallopian tube to be implanted in the uterus. The development and spread of reproductive technologies emerges from a complex mess of convergent and contradictory impulses: governmentality manifest in the neoliberal and eugenic approach to managing population as a resource, women's and men's desires to disentangle sex from reproduction, the market for technologies that allow people to plan their families, development rhetoric and funding encouraging small nuclear families (Hartmann 1995; Pigg and Adams 2005; Rao 2004; Qadeer 2005). Even as contraception has been crucial to women's and men's abilities to manage their bodies, safety, and futures, it has been enmeshed in its uneven distribution, its forcible imposition on specific segments of society racialized as undesirable (Briggs 2003; Roberts 2014), or its Malthusian underpinnings (Chatterjee and Riley 2001; Ginsburg and Rapp 1995; Hartmann 1995). These undercurrents haunt its history through representations of places like India as containing an excess of life that then need not be cared for, signaled most intensely perhaps in the "Victorian Holocausts," in which the British allowed famine to reign unchecked in India, asserting it would improve the population (Davis 2002).

In Nilza's telling of the boy at the gate and of her own reproductive history, these flows and blockages are enmeshed in the interpretation of religious doctrine. But they are also entangled in the fixing of bodies to territory in the 1947 partition of India, itself the outcome of colonial modernity's drive to categorize, compartmentalize, and map, which led to the drawing of lines according to the percentages of Hindus and Muslims and then the subsequent complications of places that could not be so easily resolved. In the kitchen over homemade bread, or in the polo field where politicians make speeches, these circulations and efforts to fix and territorialize people and land take shape in conversations about birth control and the future.

Over cups of sweet tea and cups of salty tea with butter slowly melting on top, Buddhist women, especially those in their forties, fifties, and sixties, spoke to me of the future, of their choices, and those of their daughters. Yangdol, a forty-five-year-old Buddhist mother of three, stated this vulnerability most clearly and explicitly in terms of electoral politics, telling me that while Buddhists have used family planning, Shia Muslims have not. She insists, "Among the Shia Muslims, if you look in Kargil and Chushot, even now they have eight or nine children each." Not hinting or mincing words, Yandol goes on to reference speeches by rinpoches in which she learned that "our Buddhists are getting fewer, and then our Hill Council, in the future it will be run by Shia Muslims." Yangdol is grateful for the Ladakh Buddhist Association (LBA) intervention and the clear message to Buddhists: "you should think. Up to four, or up to six, or up to five, let them be born. Don't sterilize after two."[5]

Diskit also supported the pro-natal movement, even traveling to rural areas with a group of twenty women to implore women not to use family planning, saying that women of her generation had used it willingly out of ignorance and thus had the responsibility now to discourage other women from making the same mistake. Diskit insisted, "the Muslims, they totally don't do it [use family planning], not at all. And for that reason, their population is growing. Their population is really big now." She continued: "Now they say, in Turtuk, from one house, they had thirty grandchildren. Now, our Buddhist population is going to be cut off. In the past, the [Sunni Muslims] were few, but now there are many."

When Diskit was speaking, I recognized Turtuk as a village of around 3,000 in Nubra Valley on the border with Pakistan. Later, the specter of Turtuk would become a refrain in my research, as when I mentioned to those engaging in Buddhist pro-natalism that most Muslim women I spoke with enthusiastically used family planning and I would hear in response, "but you haven't been to Turtuk."

This public campaign against birth control has attempted to limit access to family planning and shifted the discourse about family planning, but whether this will result in the rejection of family planning is difficult to predict. Some Buddhists, like Dolkar, a forty-year-old Buddhist mother of two girls, believe family planning practices are changing:

DOLKAR: Some talk about Buddhists and Muslims and say that Buddhists have had fewer children and as a result our population is smaller. With that in mind, some are now having more children.

AUTHOR: Really, they say that?

DOLKAR: Since Baltis don't use family planning, they just let them all be born, so they have had so many children and their population is really growing.

AUTHOR: Do you think that is really having an impact? Do you think that some women hear that and then have a lot of children?

DOLKAR: There are those who do. Older Buddhists are saying don't use family planning, just let your children be born. Later, something is going to happen with our Muslim population. . . . Those who are thinking about our religion are having children, like four or five.

Chatting in an upstairs guest room with two young Shia women doing handicrafts for a side income, I found that nuances of religious interpretation were evident. Both Sunni and Shia women seemed to me to be quite pragmatic in negotiating religious concepts and family planning. There were far more similarities than differences in how women talked about the use of contraception—describing it as a practical decision made in conversation with their spouse and reasoning through religious discourses with confidence. Women often told me that families would make practical choices regardless of religious discourses; only two or three hedged on women's absolute autonomy in this regard. While most described decisions about family planning as largely the woman's choice, or a joint decision, a few suggested, for instance, that a mullah's wife might face pressure not to use family planning if her husband had publically spoken against it. The only time this came up as more than a hypothetical aside was in conversations with these two young women—who spoke as much to one another as to me, while they sewed in the warm sunny room. When I asked about family planning, they looked to one another, both agreeing that most women they knew used contraception for practical reasons. One went on to describe her husband as a "mullah-type" in English but added that she would do what she liked if he expected her to avoid contraception, turning to her friend for affirmation of this decision, which she seemed to be making right there in the room. In other cases, it was women's own interpretation of religious doctrine that gave them pause about the range of reproductive technologies; however, as with Buddhist women, this was usually directed toward abortion, about which most women had reservations across religious and generational lines.

In other interviews, however, the sense of vulnerability emerges with less explicit sense of the political and a more millennialist undertone. In my interview with Jamyang, a Buddhist monk active in programs to strengthen interreligious harmony, a sense of inevitability is clear:

> In Ladakh, the Muslims are growing, Buddhists are feeling insecure, but in no way can we now balance it. We have to accept the reality. The Buddhists, no matter how much they feel insecurity, this cannot be prevented. We Buddhists can never stop the growth of the Muslim population. We can never. No one can. A miracle cannot stop. No one can stop it. . . . So, in Ladakh, yes, Buddhist people have difficulties, and the future of the Buddhists, it is not good. Every year, the Muslim population will grow, the Buddhists will go down. What to do? . . . They may not have a very strong intention to increase their population in Ladakh in order to suppress the Buddhists, but it is growing unintentionally because of their traditional beliefs and all those things. So, it seems really difficult, if the Buddhists feel insecure, or they want to balance through some, how do you say, aggression or these things, we should not. It will never succeed.

In the summer of 2008, I was wrapping up a year of research and struggling to take on the interviews I had saved until the end—those with political and religious leaders. I had spoken with people in this role four years prior and then had started this research segment by speaking mainly to those who did not hold leadership roles in political or religious organizations (though certainly many of them were community leaders in their villages). Before wrapping up fieldwork, I needed to speak with those in leadership roles. Perhaps I should not have been surprised by the opening comments of the LBA representative I spoke with that summer. I had been dreading the interview as I found talking to officials so much more difficult than casual chats about family life over tea and biscuits. I began the interview remembering advice I had been given—that politicians would stick to talking points. I asked a neutral first question: what are your organization's aims and objectives? The answer was unambiguous: "our top priority is population." The representative was generous with his time and gracious in answering my questions, but I found the conversation frustrating. When I told him that women say they cannot afford large families, he told me that Ladakhi Buddhist women had grown too proud to send their children to government schools—that instead they wanted private education. If they would be willing to send their children to government schools ("which are fine!" he added), then they could afford to have more children. For this reason, there had been tours out to the villages to encourage women to give up family planning.

This answer galled me—the families I had spoken with were betting their futures on education, with even relatively poor farmer families scrimping together money from here and there with their children's futures in mind. This concern cut across class, with everyone feeling the pinch. While poorer families struggle to send their kids to private tutoring in Leh and to college in Jammu, middle-class families wish they had the money to send their children outside of Leh to attend private schools in Delhi and elsewhere from the age of ten. They pressure their children to study and do well, even as they privately express concerns that this pressure to excel is to blame in young people's suicides, which are understood to be on the rise. In the LBA representative's answers, I heard a profound disconnect or intentional dissonance from middle-class life in Leh (which I knew him to be part of) and the struggling-to-get-ahead low-income families, where mothers and fathers took on extra work as coolies on the roadside to save for their children's education. These parents were not acting out of pride or vanity but out of intention and hope that their children have happy, safe lives free from backbreaking or degrading physical labor. The men and women who spoke to me about their children would vehemently protest the notion that government and private schools are equivalent, and we can read into this sentiment the consolidation of class power: a Leh resident with economic and social capital suggesting that government schools are good enough for poor or rural people.

This kind of talk about women's fertility links identity, sovereignty, and territorial control. Members of both the LBA and the LBA Youth Wing, historically important in the movement to gain autonomy (described in chapter 3), now mention the "population problem" as their most critical issue. In this locus of power, women's bodies are a critical site through which territorial sovereignty can be defended. The conditions of possibility that engender this linkage are the colonial techniques of governance divide-and-rule, that culminated in partition, the ongoing struggle for J&K, and a continual sense of vulnerability in the region felt by both residents and the politicians in the government of India. Alongside these are the assumptions that territory must be linked to majority and sovereignty (religion, linguistic, ethnic)—that is, body counts can determine sovereignty. Where this logic runs into trouble is in the bodies themselves, which are not only political instruments but also where we experience the material constraints, hopes, dreams, and fears that make up our everyday lives. Traveling through and disrupting this work of territory, which is the work of delineating, pinning, measuring, and claiming, are multiple forms of circulation and flow.

The circulation of new technologies and practices, tubal ligation and IUD, engender new ethical questions. Women place various contraceptive technologies on a spectrum from most to least sinful or politically problematic: abortion is marked as the most sinful practice, and spacing births using the IUD is the least sinful practice. There are at least three forms of circulation in this story.

The first is the disrupted circulation (of souls) from one body into another. The second is the circulation of new practices and technologies, implied to have arrived from outside, the tubal ligation or IUD, and their potential to close (birth) doors. The third is the circulation of new interpretations of Buddhist doctrine that complicate bodily practices and place new expectations on the bodies of women making decisions about childbearing. These circulations rub up against or are understood through the context of a drive to fix and bound Leh District as a territory. What if birth results in an unrecognizable future? What if the world that we birth does not reflect us?

Nilza's story allows us into the material and bodily ways that the desire to fix bodies and territory plays out—it cannot be removed from its geopolitical context. Political struggles for rights and sovereignty in Leh are always already geopolitical, that is, framed within the context of international conflict and struggles for territory. Population persists as a backdrop to the territorial conflict over Jammu and Kashmir State, and these logics of calculation frame daily life such that stories about reincarnation and cesarean sections are haunted by political concerns in ways that blur the lines between religious and political motivations for action. Political narratives about the meaning of majority, talk of a Jammu and Kashmir plebiscite to determine the territorial future of the district, and the wielding of power by local politicians via vote blocs often mobilized around religious identity, these each build to an intense and intimate relationship between bodies and territory.

Buddhist concerns about family planning are indexed in a number of ways: the disruption of the cycle of reincarnation, a rejection of small family sizes as a means to success because all children come with their own luck, the equation of family planning with killing a person, the characterization of human life as precious and too valuable to prevent, the idea that limited family sizes mean a decline of monks and nuns, and finally the territorial concern that suggests a loss of demographic majority in the district will mean that the local government will be run by Muslims.

Closed Birth Doors and Modernity

Though religious and political leaders might suggest that women could simply choose to avoid family planning altogether, the way that women talked through these decisions suggests a more rugged terrain. In their responses to my questions, I sometimes felt they were building a case, helping me and themselves to understand not why they made their decisions but why these were the only possible decisions. Though family planning was largely understood as being compatible with Islam, it was also sometimes discussed in relation to morality. Bilqis is Shia, forty years old with one child. She differentiated between abortion (forbidden) and using an IUD to space children (acceptable if you have any kind of health issues): "We can't just let them be born—if we don't put a gap that is damaging to ourselves . . . if you have a child every year, we ourselves won't survive." Though she had heard people say that sterilization was "like killing a person," on the contrary, "looking at today's conditions, how could you avoid it? Now it's also difficult to get a job. If you have twelve children, you won't even be able to clothe them and keep them clean. Even taking care of two children, it reduces women to tears." Amira, another Shia woman of the same generation, had been married twice and had five children. She never used family planning, preferring to follow God's will, but suggested that women who were frail ought to use contraception. She placed her opinions in the context of political rhetoric: "At the minimum, two or three. One is not ok. Three is perfect. Then if something happens, it's ok. After that, if you do the operation, that's fine. How could you have more than three today? Nowadays those Botos [Buddhists], all the Botos are saying, 'have children! Have children! Let's increase.' Our people, we're not doing that. What do I know? They say that however many you have, they will come with their own fortune." Angmo, a mother of six surviving children and a Buddhist of the same generation as Amira and Bilqis, asked me: If someone had more than three children, "how would they get an education? How would they be able to provide clothes? Tasty, good food, how would they get it?" For Angmo, it does not seem that there is a choice to be made; rather, "These days, it's chaotic, it's the time itself. It's happening like that. . . . If you have a lot of children, the children themselves won't turn out well." Women describe a complicated combination of economic pressures and bodily fears that lead them to use family planning despite religious injunctions or political incitement. Angmo relates to me:

ANGMO: The doctor scolded me, "You're a farmer, so you work so hard, and then every two years you're having another child?" and I said, "thank you, please do something about it." And then she did it. I was in the hospital for one day and then I left. I did the operation. Having given birth to seven boys, really!

HER FORTY-YEAR-OLD NIECE: Having two, I just feel like it will kill me, it's so much trouble.

ANGMO [TO HUSBAND IN THE DOORWAY]: Don't come in! She's asking me questions!

AUTHOR: Then, between those children, did you put gaps?

ANGMO: I didn't put gaps, and at that time they didn't have the thing to put gaps [that is, an IUD]. But it just kind of happened that there were gaps. There are those who take care and intentionally put gaps, but we're farmers, we don't know anything about that. All we know how to do is how to work. About children—even when I was pregnant, I wouldn't realize I was pregnant, after three or four months, then I would realize.

Angmo's pragmatic description of her family planning decisions in the early 1990s described a time when there was not yet a need to defend this choice. Angmo tells us, "These days, it's chaotic, it's the time itself," and as others describe their choices, they are placing themselves within both a geographic and a temporal context, sometimes using the word "modern" to describe themselves and their lives. Like Jamyang, the monk interviewed above, they evoke time as a force, a wave washing over them, affecting every decision, even as they also make conscious choices and defend their decisions. The insistence that family planning is necessary today arrives not as a statement but as a question: how could you not? Yangzes, using an IUD to limit her family size, had heard the speeches of women like Nilza, telling women, "let your children be born . . . you don't need to send your children to private schools, you can also send your children to government schools." When I asked her opinion, she replied, "What will I do with many children? We don't have a lot of income." In this heightened geopolitical context, residing in a state of not knowing, asking rather than stating, can become, if not a political strategy, a tactic for sidestepping or negotiating geopolitical pressure.[6]

Modernity is linked to the pro-natal campaign, as education and a deeper understanding of Buddhism is invoked as a reason to eschew family planning. And yet modern life is also described as requiring contraception. In explaining their choices to me, women depict themselves as caught between desire to provide their children an expensive private education, healthy food, and decent clothing and the religious and political injunctions that call for them to avoid contraception. They describe their position as an impossible one. In the words of Sonam, a young Buddhist woman, "They say not to use family planning. That's what they will keep saying, but it is impossible. If we don't block it, we will end up unconscious, overwhelmed.[7] Whatever they say about it in religion, we still have to do it."

The linking of women's bodies and sexuality to territory and the use of contraceptives has been taken up by ordinary women and men who espouse the rhetoric of territorial demographics as a means of maintaining sovereignty. The territorial reading of the body is summed up by Diskit, a proponent of the pro-natal movement who reads the history of contraception in Ladakh as one of demographic aggression, fear, and failure: a moral geography of births (Bialasiewicz 2006). But if territory and the future are vulnerable and contingent, so are bodies. Women told me of miscarriages, mothers and aunts who died in childbirth, and of failed attempts to use less politically charged forms of contraception. On the road leading out of Leh Town, toward the eastern villages and then south to Manali and lowland India, a neighborhood of houses built only a few decades ago is called the "housing colony." This neighborhood is largely occupied by those who moved to Leh from the villages or who have a need to rent rooms as they have no land in Leh. One might find a well-constructed house with a family who has lived there for many years—these spaces are transformed when you step from the dusty alley into their gated yard to find flowers and a small vegetable garden. But you might also find more challenging circumstances— economic migrants renting two or three rooms, choosing to live in Leh perhaps so that their children can attend better schools, or one older sister somehow managing to care for her siblings, working a low-level job, preparing rice and dal each night as they study. On Sundays, they will rush home to the village if they can and return with village gifts: hand-sewn bags of roasted barley and apricot kernels or, in summer, an old plastic bag full of the best gift—fresh apricots, juicy and irresistible. Parents or grandparents will send local flour, but the schoolkids will ask for rice instead. In a small set of such rented rooms, one woman described with frustration her experiences as a mother. She had tried to avoid tubal ligation. She had given in after the death of her sickly third child, who had been conceived when she was using an IUD. After two pregnancies with her IUD in place and a number of health problems, she felt justified in turning to sterilization. Using family planning does not necessarily mean women believe it is the morally appropriate choice, but it is sometimes the only choice in a contingent world in which they have to consider their bodily health, the pressure to educate, and the felt need for happy children. Another woman in similar circumstances told me she had an abortion when her IUD failed. The tone of her voice made me feel that she both hesitated to tell me this but also felt that she must; she wanted me to understand that she had made this choice in constrained circumstances and only after contraceptive failure.

Ordinary Life and Love in Extraordinary Times

Jigmet is a schoolteacher, employed in a government job that requires her to be transferred to a new village every three years. She and her government servant husband have built a home in Leh, but she is rarely able to stay there for more than two or three weeks during holidays. She is usually posted a day's drive away in one or another village. Of course, she describes this as just an ordinary kind of inconvenience—sometimes she misses her family; other times she loves the quiet of village life, which allows her to go for long walks in the evening away from the chaos of life with her two young children, who remain back home with her husband. Curious, unpretentious, and down-to-earth, Jigmet easily makes friends in each new place. Jigmet and her husband have the middle-class life to which many rural Ladakhis aspire. They both have stable government jobs with benefits. Their children attend English-medium private school, where they also have classes in Hindi/Urdu and Ladakhi. The two boys are encouraged to study each afternoon and do well in school, though they run off to watch Doraemon on television, play video games on their parents' phones, and ride bicycles around the neighborhood as much as they can manage. Jigmet indulges them and brings

them treats when home but also wonders about their future. Jigmet is not someone who had children just because that is what is expected; she has loved kids
since she herself was a child—the kind of child who would end up caring for the
younger neighbor kids when their parents were busy.

Jigmet married in her late twenties. She had not met anyone she wanted to
marry. When family members suggested some of her guy friends, she wrinkled
her nose in disgust, saying it would be like marrying a brother. Her parents had
arranged introductions to a few people who had not interested her at all: after
meeting them she would complain, "he looks like someone's uncle" or "he was
wearing these giant white shoes," small points that indicated deeper questions
of compatibility. But then an acquaintance started asking friends and family
about her. A few conversations turned into more serious inquiries between relatives. Jigmet was happily pregnant within a year of the marriage and then used
an IUD to delay a second birth when she felt ready. She and her husband are comfortable and practical parents who enjoy being goofy with their kids, though
they are still strict about studying.

A light-hearted and easy-going parent Jigmet is a devout Buddhist who prays
regularly and reads books on mindfulness in her spare time. For her, religion is
not at odds with her straightforward approach to family life:

> All of [religious leaders] are saying that we should have like . . . I don't
> agree with them, actually. If you have 10 or 12 children, they were just born
> and they will get education and they will get everything according to their
> own karma. But what do you think? Like during the time we give them
> education, what happens if we can't give them what they demand? It will
> be difficult during that time. . . . For higher education they need lots and
> lots of money. At that time we can't say, "It's karma, it's all karma, you
> will go according to your own karma." How can we say that? If he or she
> may like to go in a medical stream for education, like that they will need
> lots of money. But how can we say, "it will go according to your own
> karma?" We have to give them whatever they demand.

Her own childhood was on the cusp of the current moment of intense
competition—so she easily got a government job but not necessarily the kind of
prestigious one her parents had hoped for. What kind of life can she envision
for her boys, in the unforeseeable future? Jigmet tells me:

> In the past there was not so much competition, like we have. In the past
> all the family worked in agriculture. . . . But at present, with more and
> more development, everybody wants money . . . everyone is busy with
> money, money, money. In the past, children didn't have as many demands.
> Today, when they grow up, when they are teenagers, they just say, for
> example, "I want a motorbike, all my friends have motorbikes and I don't

have one so I need one," and things like that. So, I think, we have to meet
their demands, and we have to make our family smaller, so we can be sure
we can give our children whatever they want.

Jigmet asked later in the interview if those who propounded pro-natalism would
care for the children born to mothers giving up contraception. From an older
generation, Muhammad, now a grandfather, spoke in similar terms. On the roof
of his house, wife and daughter listening in, Muhammad spoke to me about
family planning. He began with a phrase that caught me off guard the first time
I heard it: like many Ladakhi Muslims, he uses a phrase that appends a Buddhist
religious term, *konjok*, onto the Urdu term for God, *khuda*. *Konjok* refers to the
Buddhist "triple gem," the Buddha, the Dharma (teachings), and the Sangha (the
community of followers):

MUHAMMAD: *Khuda konjok*, however many he will give you, that is great. . . .
But now the government has explained to us, and everyone understands,
that there are a lot of people now. That being the case, having two or three
children, that is nice. Otherwise, how will you educate them? Abi-le [his
wife] had one boy and five or six girls, with all those, how will they get
educated?

AUTHOR: So if you have nine or ten?

MUHAMMAD: They won't get an education. . . . We say you have to give them
each the same. Now, for instance, look at me. I am a father with five or six
girls. I have to give them each the same, carving up everything. For those
who have a lot of land, they will get a lot. If you only have a little land, each
one will only get one field. If they don't get much land, how will they take
care of their children?

In interview after interview, Buddhist and Muslim women who indicated
that they were against family planning suggested that the attempt to produce
high-quality, healthy, well-educated children was futile, because each child
would arrive with their own *sode* (luck, fortune). For Buddhists, this implied that
the good and bad deeds performed in previous lives were accumulated in the
child and would affect their lives more than any influence the family might have.
For Muslims, bringing your own *sode* was a way to state that everything was in
God's hands, or "written in the lines on your forehead." Women often told me
that no matter how many children were in a family, their fates would be determined by this *sode*. Women who had completed their fertility used this theory
to explain why contraception should be avoided, but women who had yet to complete their fertility repeated it with doubt: "they say every child comes with its
own *sode*, but everything is so expensive these days." For Buddhists, the dystopian political future of Buddhist decline is mirrored in the disruption of the cycle

of rebirth, as those waiting to be born are "blocked" from the birth doors that they were meant to pass through.

Like the politicians and popular narratives described by Megoran (2008) in Uzbekistan, Buddhist activists summon a sense of constant and territorial danger to encourage Buddhist women to produce children who will territorialize Buddhist political identity onto the district. But the bodily nature of this act is where they run into problems. Can abstract territorial strategy and millennialist visions compete with the flesh and blood concerns of those who open or close "birth doors"? And is it possible to imagine a counter-geopolitics, in which individual and family choices negate or at least contest these divisive politics? The very palpability of embodied geopolitics makes it a site of potential resistance to strategies that instrumentalize the body. Thus, asked if women of her generation will comply with the pressure to avoid family planning, Jigmet's mother, Tsewang, a fifty-four-year-old Buddhist mother of three, herself ambivalent, observes the simple impracticality of politically motivated suggestions to refrain from birth control:

> Her generation will say, and Jigmet is also saying, "If we have a child, that child will need a good education, if we have five or six children, there's not enough money for their education. If they don't get a good education, if they get a haphazard education, they won't get a good job, and then they are not going to have a happy life. If they say, for no reason, 'have children, have children,' are the rinpoches going to take care of those children? [laughing] Are the rinpoches going to give us money when our children can't get jobs?"

The contrast between the specter of Buddhists being "finished" and Jigmet's more mundane concern for her child's education reveals an important, visceral tension between the body as a site of territorialization and the body as a site of lived experience and emotion. In its reproductive capacity, the body is an almost inevitable target for geopolitical strategy—it has the potential to create certain kinds of territories through giving birth to many children or few.

The impossible is used to argue that avoiding family planning is not an option, and this is supported with bodily evidence or biomedical knowledge provided by medical practitioners:

PADMA: Look, I had seven children! [laughing] I have given birth to seven children. First, I gave birth to a dead child. I tried to use the IUD, but I couldn't. It wouldn't work for me, it wouldn't stick. Finally, I just did tubal ligation. Otherwise, what? I would have had ten or eleven or fifteen. I would still be having children, what? [laughing] That's how it is. I swear. This thing called woman, how can she not give birth? Isn't that how it is?

Plenty of women keep having children *lobi-lobi* [one per year]. I am like that. Some people are like that, and they keep having children even as they get old. [My friend] was like that. She gave birth to a dead child, and she died a year later. She died young.

Nilza expressed regret over her past actions. Jigmet pointed to the impossibility of bearing many children. Padma's rhetorical question hangs in the air: "This thing called woman, how can she not give birth?" Using logic and emotion, our conversations themselves ran in a strange kind of circle, tracing how things both impossible and mundane are asked and accomplished: giving birth to many children, balancing demands of motherhood and work, integrating new contraceptive technologies into moral frameworks, and feeling the pull of childhood friendships and received political realities that present themselves as inevitable.

Conclusion

As the stories of men and women coping with territorial incursions into their intimate lives indicate, territorial narratives do not play out in a vacuum; they meet with the complications of emotions and economic calculations, fears, hopes, and apprehensions. The geopolitical case for having more children (that is, anxiety about Buddhist decline and electoral change) aligns with broader fears of being abandoned in old age and thus the impulse to have more rather than fewer children. These are both entangled in the economic concerns that children bring. The border between these two reasons for having children was blurred in a few interviews: grandmothers and grandfathers wished for more grandchildren, mentioning both empty houses and a potentially empty territory. Care for oneself in old age and care for cultural practices here mingle and tangle. Thus, one woman in her fifties told me:

> That is like this. Nowadays, each woman only allows one or two children to be born, totally. They are not having children because they are thinking about their happiness right now, at this moment. They are thinking to make themselves happy, to be happy they are not having children. They're thinking about their own happiness, the mother's happiness. They're not thinking about the other thing. Then when their children are grown, after that, when they are old, then the mother will be happy, at that time, if she has a lot of children. There might be those who won't care for her, but then if she has many there will be some who do care for her. Otherwise, if there is only one or two children, or if each woman only has one child, if that child doesn't care for her, then what will happen? If she has a few children, maybe if the girl doesn't care for her, the boy will, or if he doesn't, one of the other ones will.

Political geography is not only "discursive, technological and economic, but also . . . a collectively embodied process of affects, prejudices, anticipations and negotiations" (Saldanha 2008, 323). As individuals are caught up in the animation of geopolitical projects, love, fear, anxiety, and pain come to play a role; political and territorial projects relying on the participation of bodies can be thwarted—not through intentional resistance but through the materialities of "life itself" (Rose 2006). The intimate space of the body cannot be completely extracted from the territory of the district, as the potential of the fertile body to extend itself into territory makes it a target. It is not that the body is a microscale embedded within or shaped by geopolitical forces from above; the body is the site where the geopolitical is produced and known. This is true no less for politicians, for those who make decisions to drop bombs or open borders, to fund family planning and reproductive services or to defund them. A few women commented on the small family sizes of those who were now promoting large families. And even as they sent a letter to the hospital requesting that the doctors restrict abortion and limit tubal ligation, some political actors must have wondered how this letter might be received by doctors who had cared for the wives of the signatories.

Use of the body as a territorial instrument is an effort to remake territory to match the political representations of antagonistic communities that have been deployed, by populating that territory with citizens arranged in hostile and exclusive voting blocs. This intensifies the difference (as majority Buddhist) that marks Leh as distinct from J&K and thus serves as a means to protect the district from any renegotiation of the state's sovereignty. With a crucial link, then, between religious identity, sovereignty, and the subject, the imaginary of national identity is made and remade, produced, refused, cast aside in a thousand actions and reversals. National territory is made in part by the claiming of bodies, but the materiality of the body, and the hopes and dreams that individuals have for their families, makes the body a rugged terrain. What this brings to bear on our understanding of territory is that the body, collectives of bodies, and their material circumstances can become a component of strategy and an unpredictable terrain that may eclipse rhetorical strategy and efforts to materialize new territories through the body.

As territory is always being bounded, so too the materialities of the body escape strategic demands. The question becomes: how will these bodies shape the geopolitical future? This question is especially salient for today's generation of young people: their choices about love and family will continue or disrupt the current geopolitical trajectory and determine whether and how Buddhists and Muslims can shape a future together.

3

The Queen and the Fistfight

Territory Comes to Life

> See, in olden times, there were matrimonial relations between the royal
> families of Baltistan and Leh. King Jamyang Namgyal married with Gyal
> Khatun, and their son was born Sengge Namgyal. Sengge Namgyal is con-
> sidered one of the best, one of the ablest, kings of Ladakh. . . . Like Ashoka
> in India, Sengge Namgyal is very popular in this region. (Hassan, inter-
> viewed in 2004)

When I asked Hassan to tell me about politics, he began with the seventeenth-
century story of Gyal Khatun. Gyal Khatun's Ladakh was on the just before the
colonial era and existed as an independent kingdom on trade routes linking
present-day Pakistan and Afghanistan to the west with Tibet and Mongolia to
the east, subject to incursions from both directions. When Hassan told me of
Princess Gyal Khatun, however, he did so to tell me the story of the twentieth
century: of his childhood, when it was not a problem to have married someone
of a different faith, and the story of how that changed. Collective memory is
evoked to tell the story that is necessary today (Blunt 2003; Legg 2004, 2007, 466;
Mills 2006). Gyal Khatun's father ruled the chiefdom of Skardu, now across the
Line of Control separating India and Pakistan. In interviews I spoke with those
who had never seen their brothers or sisters after finding themselves on the other
side of this line. The Ladakh of collective memory is a place that you cannot find
on a map. In August of 2019, the reorganization of the state of Jammu and Kashmir was announced, and from October 31, 2019, Ladakh will hold a place on the
map as a Union Territory, separate from Jammu and Kashmir (though contested
borders with China and Pakistan still blur the edges).

Ladakh is no longer ruled by kings. From 1979 to 2019, Ladakh was comprised of Leh and Kargil Districts, which were subdivisions of the Jammu and
Kashmir State. From 1995, each had been administered by their own Ladakh

Autonomous Hill Development Councils. These two districts were themselves partitioned in 1979 from the larger kingdom that had become a district in the state. Residents of Leh District often speak of the district as though it were Ladakh, raising the hackles of Kargilis, who point out that Kargil is also Ladakh, because the older district encompassed both Buddhist-majority Leh and Shia-majority Kargil, to the west. At the state level, Leh and Kargil were governed by the chief minister and Legislative Assembly. The two districts are represented in the national Lok Sabha by one member of Parliament. J&K was made from the historical regions of Gilgit, Baltistan, Jammu, Kashmir, and Ladakh, although each region also contains ethnic, linguistic, and religious diversity. Kashmir Valley's five million residents are mostly Sunni (with Hindu, Sikh, Shia, and Christian minorities, whereas Jammu's 4.5 million residents are predominantly Hindu, with Muslim and Sikh minorities. Ladakh's two districts combined are evenly split between Buddhists and Shia Muslims, with a smaller population of Sunni Muslims, Hindus, and Sikhs in Leh Town. The state's official language is Urdu—a strange compromise, as it is the native language for none of the state's three regions, where Kashmiri, Dogra, Gojri, Pahadi, Ladakhi, and other local languages are spoken. Gilgit, Baltistan, and parts of Kashmir have been under the administration of Pakistan since 1949. This diverse collection of regions was tied together by conquest, treaty, and imperial sale during the first part of the nineteenth century, a jigsaw puzzle loosely assembled through pieces of paper assigning ownership to a succession of kings. From late October until May the roads into Ladakh are blocked by snow, and the region is accessible only by plane.

Ladakh's territory has been ambiguous in the living memory of all Ladakhis. Until 2019, it was a division of J&K but has been missing from the state's name.[1] The northeast boundary is disputed between India and China, and the northwest boundary is the Line of Control separating India and Pakistan. Maps of the region differ depending on what country the map was made in, and many come with disclaimers warning that the boundaries of the map have not been authenticated. This region is paradoxically a small, out-of-the-way place and a crucial geopolitical location meaningful for Indian control of the state and nationalist imaginaries (Aggarwal 2004; Beek 2000, 2001; Bertelsen 1996; Sabhlok 2017). Ladakh comprised two-thirds of the state but 3 percent of its population; Leh District alone comprises India's second largest district, at a little over 45,000 square kilometers, and has the lowest population density in all of India, at around one person per square kilometer. Every local political campaign in Leh District promised of development and achieving Union Territory, that is, on the demand to gain autonomy from the state of Jammu and Kashmir and be in a direct relationship with the national government. As in so many places entangled in colonial histories, the words that people use—*Ladags*, Ladakh—did not make it onto the map, which is a reflection of sovereignty practices. "Ladakh" has been, until recently, missing from the official map, from the name of the state, and often from policy discussions (Fewkes 2009), even as it spirals lushly through the touristic gazing imagination and centers people's own identification as Ladakhi. Every political action, every politician's campaign is in some way framed in relation to these points of difference, injury, and marginality (W. Brown 1995; Povinelli 2002).

Shifts underfoot are spoken into a cohesive narrative by those living through geopolitical days in which land becomes territory through the emergence of a sovereign state. This chapter traces how people talk about the connections now unseen that once linked Ladakh to distant lands; how the discourse of injury, communalism, and minority status came to be understood as political currency; and the enmeshed ways that the history of a small place is also the history of a larger story. In telling this story, ordinary women and men describe themselves as bit players who are part of a changing landscape in a changing time. They describe purposeful actions in relation to their own lives and choices but abdicate that sense of agency when it comes to their ability to stop the passage of time, the territorialization of land, and the fragmentation of interreligious relationships, saying, "times have changed" and "this is how politics work."

How do ordinary people make sense of what has become of the ground beneath their families' feet? In recalling their own histories, and the histories of their place, they turn to moments where they felt this ground shift underfoot, and they tell the stories that help us understand those shifts. They tell the story of a Muslim queen in a Buddhist palace, giving birth to a mighty ruler; they tell the story of a messy political struggle that made sense to politicians but that was initiated when a fistfight broke out in the main bazaar. They recall moments when people rose to the occasion—an elite Buddhist leader declaring that Muslims would be hurt only "over his dead body"—or they recall sudden and inexplicable betrayal—Buddhist prayer flags thrown in the dirt, smoke rising from houses burning downhill. In all these ways, in Ladakh we can read patterns of colonial violence extending and fracturing up through the Himalayas and eastward, from the playing ground of the "Great Game." This violence renders bodies into territory and implicates each person in a paradoxical Westphalian sovereignty that unfolded from Europe until it had encompassed all the world in some form, expanding the logic of sovereignty and autonomy through the stripping of sovereignty and autonomy of non-Europeans (Elden 2009). These logics enact territory from abstract and undifferentiated space (Beek 1996); they are not always described in political and legal terms by those living on this now-mapped land, but they are felt, and it is that feeling of transformation that I have worked to record here.

The Queen and the Place Not Found on a Map

European explorers and travelers of the colonial era described Ladakh in the Orientalizing imaginaries (Said 1979) that we expect. A 1926 book, *In Himalayan Tibet* (Heber and Heber 1926), has a frontispiece reading: "A record of 12 years spent in the topsy-turvy land of Lesser Tibet with a description of its cheery folk, their ways and religion, of the rigours of the climate and beauties of the country, its fauna and flora." Travelers' tales describe its remoteness and emphasize its difference, giving it an otherworldly aura that continues in its representations today, both for foreign and domestic (Indian) tourist audiences. Lonely Planet describes Ladakh as having "almost supernatural landscapes" and goes on to portray "Spectacularly jagged, arid mountains" that "enfold this magical Buddhist ex-kingdom." Ladakh is woven into drone-view "Incredible India" videos of the palace, horse racing, and archery, with the tag line "Jammu and Kashmir, where time stands still."[2] In the most widely circulated book about the region, *Ancient Futures: Learning from Ladakh*, Ladakh is depicted as a remote and isolated place from the past to which we should return, a past in which everything was returned to the land, nothing was wasted, and families helped each other so that no one went hungry (Norberg-Hodge 2000).

These representations sit uncomfortably with histories that I had always heard in Ladakh from grandmas and grandpas, histories that are nuanced by fractures of wealth and gender. Yes, everyone had more time to sit outside and drink salty butter tea, and the barley fields were harvested not by individual families but collectively. I have also been a part of harvesting, which is both lovely and festive and a sweaty backbreaking labor that requires you to maintain a hunched squatting position and keep up with the pace of a row of others as you work across the field with your short-handled sickle. You drink and eat delicious sugary and salty tea and food or drink *chang* (barley beer) to stave off dehydration and exhaustion. At the same time, you sing and feel a sense of accomplishment and community when you haul too-heavy bundles of barley on your back to the place where they will dry. You make your bundle a little more than you can carry, because if each person puts a little more than he or she can bear, overall you will make fewer trips. Later you will thresh and winnow while you call for the spirit of the wind. Humming the words "spirit of the wind, please come to my broom," I can feel the breeze and see the fading late afternoon sky. Today it is more common that those who can will hire migrant labor from elsewhere in India, pay them a cash wage, and provide simple meals, rice, dal, pickle, sweeter and stronger tea than your own family drinks. If it was your friends, family, and neighbors, you would have not only fixed substantial meals but you would insist they eat as much as a person can.

The grandpas and grandmas who talk of the past do wax romantic about harvesting and winnowing songs, picnics and parties that last for days. But they also speak of being in debt to the wealthy families and having no choice but to work off these debts in other people's fields. They speak of taxes, of owing grain to the monasteries, and of eating the discarded barley from making beer in order to get by when they had diminished their sacks of grain and the new harvest would not be ready for months. Mothers speak mournfully of babies lost in difficult labors or in epidemics, of mothers and sisters lost in childbirth. A romantic and isolated mountain kingdom Shangri-La appeals to a Western audience. It can also be a relief for a Ladakhi audience that has learned from interactions with non-local Indians and foreign tourists that they come from a backward and tribal place. Yet when grandma and grandpa begin to elaborate, a much more complicated story comes into view.

As Fewkes (2009, 1) writes, even today, "Ladakh is often simultaneously discussed as a remote, 'tribal' area and a key national border of India." In contrast to Western and Indian imaginaries of isolation and remoteness, however, oral histories, most anthropologists, and local historians today describe Ladakh of the late nineteenth and early twentieth century as a crossroads or entrepôt. Grandparents and great-grandparents speak of boots that arrived with Uighur traders, of Mongolians in the market, of tax officers from the king who were merciless, and wealthy families who were generous or tricky, depending on your own position to wealth. Their geography is one of dusty roads that connect the world. A young woman from Shyok tells me that her grandmother taught her words and phrases in Uighur. Once upon a time, a man had traveled to Shyok as a trader, met a beautiful woman, and settled down in the village. That woman gave birth to Spalzes's mother and told Spalzes tales of her husband's travels. When Spalzes participated in an oral history project with Rebecca Norman and me at the Students' Educational and Cultural Movement of Ladakh in 2008, she knew immediately that what she wanted to do was to record her grandmother's memories of the Uighur language. Many traders from Kashmir settled and married in Leh Town. Along with other hybrid Muslim identities (Central Asians who settled and married Ladakhis), their descendants are sometimes called "Argon." Much of the Sunni population of Leh District today falls into this category.

This world of embodied connection is now reoriented, but this archive of history remains in family histories and collective memory. Van Beek argues that "Ladakhiness does not exist as a stable or uniform set of characteristics, forms, idioms, or practice" (Beek 2003, 286; see also Fewkes 2009). For Fewkes, understanding social life in Ladakh today must begin with understanding its historical connections. The feeling evoked by these tales is never one of isolation but rather is of a small cosmopolitan place deeply connected to many other small cosmopolitan places. Those old routes crossed what are now militarized borders, and this land imagined as trails that might bring camels, leather boots, or a husband is now reconfigured. Borders travel through the material of daily life and are enacted not only at the border itself but also in contradictory ways through bodies and landscapes across Leh District and in Leh Town as well (Aggarwal 2004; Aggarwal and Bhan 2009). Remembrances of fluid interreligious relationships still saturate family trees, but the generation of tangled branches is now aging, and new connections across those religious lines are not being formed. You may still find smuggled Chinese thermoses and blankets in the market, but most paths and connections are by paved roads, airline flights, and the Internet, and the land itself is part of the project of state territory, which seeps into the bodies of those who stand upon it. Shifts are also visible in architectural geopolitics that animate the landscape far from the border itself—recent renovation of Buddhist and Muslim religious structures at the center of Leh Town has been described in these geopolitical terms as a "nuclear buildup," mimicking the nuclear one-upmanship of India and Pakistan (Smith 2013). Enumerative politics implicate embodied life as, in Mountz's terms, borders are redefined at the limits of the body (Mountz 2010, 2011).

In the early years of the seventeenth century, Gyal Khatun was assigned to care for the Ladakhi king, Jamyang Namgyal, a Buddhist, when he was her father Ali Mir's prisoner. She married Jamyang Namgyal, became pregnant, and obtained her father's approval (the order of these events is unclear) and returned with Jamyang Namgyal to Leh with a retinue of Shia maids, musicians, and others (Halkias 2011; Petech 1977). Despite antagonism between Ladakh and Baltistan, including raids on monasteries, once Gyal Khatun arrived, she kept her faith, and mosques were built for her in Leh and Shey. Gyal Khatun gave birth to Senge Namgyal, Ladakh's most celebrated king, a Buddhist like his father. Famous for her beauty, inscriptions regarding her describe Gyal Khatun as an incarnation of Jetsun Dolma, "White Tara," the consort of Chenrezig or Avalokitesvara (the bodhisattva of compassion). She is a reference point for Buddhist–Muslim relations, and her story was referenced as signal of the possibility of coexistence (as embodied in her adherence to Islam and support of Buddhism and her Buddhist son who became king). It is also deployed as an origin story by some, who point to her retinue's arrival bringing Shia Muslims into the region, though both Shia and Sunni Islam spread in Ladakh before this and also through diverse points of connection (Bray 2013; Dollfus 1995; Fewkes 2009; Petech 1977; Sheikh 1995). These were Balti Muslims, which meant they also shared linguistic ties (Balti and Purig are also dialects of Tibetan). Some residents and local historian Abdul Ghani Sheikh suggest that the queen's retinue was the origin of the series of Shia Muslim–majority Chushot villages along the Indus River southeast of Leh and the village of Shey (Sheikh 1995).

When Gyal Khatun married Jamyang Namgyal, the Mughal Empire had extended its rule across much of India (though not Ladakh), with local kingdoms paying tribute in taxes and military support, and the British East India Company had been given permission to trade within the Mughal Empire in 1617. One hundred and fifty years later, the British would install the first governor of Bengal and begin collecting taxes, beginning their 200-year colonial project. On their departure in 1947, the lines that would become nations were drawn in three weeks by a British lawyer who had never been to India. As a nominally independent "Princely State," the king of J&K was to determine its fate.

When I ask Ladakhis about relationships in the past, they regale me with stories of Buddhists and Muslims who "ate off one plate," were like "one person," or "were like brothers." The stories of beautiful Gyal Khatun, bringing musicians and giving birth to a mighty king, are quite different from those of Fatima and Paljor and from cautionary tales told about women who waste away back home with family after the end of an interreligious love affair. It is not that people "were one." In fact, they went to war, demanded conversion, raided monasteries. But the ways religion marked the body and the mechanisms of power connected to space have been transformed. In intervening centuries, land became territory, and territory took on a life of its own, a life that impinges upon the body, seeps into it, and leaves a geopolitical charge. People moving through this space, meeting, eating together or not, marrying or not, carry this charge with them and grapple with it in daily life. They are carrying their ancestors' hopes and fears or their families' expectations, but alongside these, they are holding the life of territory, the struggle to maintain it through a vision of governance that links bodies on the ground to blocs of voters to political agency. The symbolism of eating from one plate both undergirds the narration of past connection and becomes a point of contention, as Buddhists point to events at which Muslims have separate plates for non-Muslims or do not wish to eat food prepared by Buddhists as one practice that prevents living together.

Thus, in a newspaper article published in 2000, a member of the youth wing of the influential Ladakh Buddhist Association accused the J&K administration of conspiracy: "Any Muslim government servant marrying a Buddhist girl is immediately rewarded with juicy postings." Visiting LBA headquarters in 2008, my first question was a request for the LBA's objectives, and I was told, "Our top priority is population." In 2015, the language of "love jihad" entered Ladakh when a letter was from the LBA sent to Prime Minister Narendra Modi alleging intentional wooing and conversion of Buddhist women in Zanskar (the primarily Buddhist region of Kargil District) (Ul-Qamirain 2015). "Love jihad" is a narrative that emerged in 2009 in Kerala, which portrays Muslim men as "Jihadi Romeos," seeking to convert Hindu women to turn them into "love bombs" (Das 2010). In 2017, another marriage between a formerly Buddhist woman and a Muslim man resulted in formal complaints, police reports, and strikes. Today a marriage between a Buddhist and a Muslim is a political problem, not a means of conflict resolution.

Minorities of Minorities: "Free Ladakh from Kashmir"

On October 4, 2018, Mabel Gergan and I were texting back and forth on What-sApp, trying to figure out the meaning of videos and Facebook posts showing young people running down the deserted Main Bazaar while loud noises that could be shots or smoke bombs sounded. In the grainy footage, we see a running monk, a boy picking up a stone and throwing it at the police. Comments on the videos sprung up quickly below: "This is why we need Ladakhi police, not Kashmiri!" A few days before, two young women had been harassed by men in the bazaar. Complaining at the police department, they had learned that the men were themselves police. Community organizations sprang into action, including all major Buddhist and Muslim organizations and women's organizations. A demonstration was held demanding accountability, and, unsurprisingly, women led the way, shouting "Shame, Shame!" as they marched through the street. The circulated videos show an altercation between Ladakhi young people and the police, and the comments below the posted videos signal common narratives, with the conflation of Kashmiri police with Kashmiri shopkeepers, demands for Union Territory, and even a reference to "Kashmiri Dogs." Comments allege that Ladakh is treated as a colony of Kashmir, that many police are from the outside and do not treat the locals with respect. Alongside these forms of analysis, others plea that each act be taken in isolation, that things not get out of hand, that Kashmiri police not be conflated with local Muslim Ladakhis and shopkeepers. These comments reveal the sense of grievance and feeling of occupation, even as other comments reference the shock of seeing a scene that is expected in Srinagar (rock throwing youth, retaliating police) but not in Leh. On November 1, 2018, Ladakhi students took to the streets again, this time to criticize the state government for inadequate education facilities.

In discussions over the fate of "Kashmir," the Kashmir Valley is the focus of anxiety and debate, but Ladakh's fate is folded into these discussions and caught up in this future, even as it is erased and Kashmir drives the imaginary of the region. Ladakhis are rendered invisible (Aggarwal 2004; Beek 2000; Behera 2000; Gutschow 2006); yet, as a borderland, Ladakh is crucial to nation building, as evidenced in its depictions in film and in nationalist performances such as Sindhu Darshan, the annual pilgrimage to the Indus begun in 2000 (Aggarwal 2004; Aggarwal and Bhan 2009; Beek 2004). "Borders are never to be found only in border areas" (Paasi 2011, 63); they refract through distant sites, in unfamiliar architectural styles that spring up like mushrooms in the street you have known all your life, in split-second decisions to go to the corner shop owned by someone of your own religion. The work of the border thus exceeds the marked and unmarked boundaries between nation-states and "marks some bodies as legitimate and others as out of place" (C. Johnson & Jones 2011, 61). In this exceeding of the border, the "cartographic anxiety" (Krishna 1994) of postcolonial nation building is brought to life, and the colonial geopolitical imagination that simultaneously fixed nations, territories, and the boundaries of self shapes intimate relations (S. Chaturvedi 2002). This anxiety creates the Kashmir Valley as a love object that is desired but can never flourish (Varma 2016) and a Ladakh whose sovereignty is subsumed into this haunted national relationship.

How did a world of mountains, roads, connections, and royal marriages become a world of vote banks and minority politics? When I speak with politicians or those in leadership roles, minority language insistently inserts itself. Thus, a chorus of senior Sunni and Shia Muslim leaders tells me: "By every yardstick, the Muslims are the disadvantaged minority community in India"; "Many Muslim girls have married Buddhists. But being the minority, they have become, we have become speechless"; "The minority is always in loss. Whether it is America or Europe or the Southeast Asian countries. Isn't it? They have to compromise with the majority on every piece." And a Sunni Muslim lawyer elaborates: "It's very strange. If you are in Leh, Buddhists are in the majority. If you enter Kargil, Buddhists are in the minority. Then if you go to Srinagar, Muslims are in the majority. Then if you go to Jammu, Hindus are in the majority. If you go to Rajori, Paunch, the Muslims are again in the majority. So there is a system, the combination of the population is such that no one can claim that we are in majority or we are in minority. Jammu and Kashmir is a Muslim majority state."

And yet, for Buddhists, shifting to the scale of J&K reveals a very different optic: every list of people selected for government posts, police positions, or other state-based positions is a list of almost entirely Muslim names, and the 1947 integration into India did little to alleviate the uneven power relationships. Ladakh escaped domination by a Hindu king only to be ignored by a new (Muslim-majority) government based in Srinagar and Jammu. The inclusion of Ladakh in the state of Jammu and Kashmir was a relic of the colonial era that has colored daily life. I ask Tsewang, a secular-minded Buddhist in his thirties, about animosity:

TSEWANG: The rumor, as you have seen in this "Why UT for Ladakh," is that although Muslims are a minority in Leh District, they get more of the government jobs.

AUTHOR: Have you seen that to be true?

TSEWANG: I don't know, I don't have the facts, but even if you observe, you can see, if you just go around in the government places here, most of them are either Baltis or Muslims. Buddhists even if they are, they are usually lower places and stuff. I mean in government jobs, I don't mean in politics. Like J&K government.

AUTHOR: J&K government, not local government.

TSEWANG: Yes, state government.

AUTHOR: Why would that be?

TSEWANG: Ladakhi Buddhists think it's because of Muslim states favoring Muslims in Ladakh. I don't know how the Muslims see it.

In another interview, a senior Buddhist politician frames the 1989 agitation in relation to these same dynamics:

> The state government was run by the very big Jammu ministry, sixty ministers. Not a single Ladakhi, not a single Buddhist. And the atmosphere in Kashmir was quite Islamic. And they did not advance any funding to Leh. There was more funding to Kargil, there was less funding to Leh. And, every file going to . . . there were quite a lot of things, going around. There was something, some very great deciding force . . . so, you had to, explode, fighting what was going on against you, all around . . . there was a great pressure, forcing us to get out of Ladakh. It was a sort of conspiracy by the Kashmir government. How do you say, they were going to create some sort of Islamic nation.

AUTHOR: In the state [of J&K]?

PALDEN: Yes, in the state. There was pressure. And the Hindus . . . but the Ladakhis, they are more brave than the Hindu people. So, Ladakhi Buddhists exploded. It was, the 1989, it was totally against Muslims. It was against an Islamic nation. They saw the Muslims before them, therefore in Leh itself, so, it, it was not totally some sort of anger against the local Muslims. It was a wider anger against the Muslim nationalist outlook of people, you know. So, then it exploded in a big way. People were ready to sacrifice everything. So, what we did, our, the people who were responsible, they diverted, they thought we should use this energy for a political end. And that political, it is basically against the Islamic nation.

Palden, sympathetic to his own Muslim friends and neighbors, perhaps unintentionally conflates Ladakhi and Buddhist identity when he says, "Not a single Ladakhi, not a single Buddhist." But the frustration that he expresses, even though it was not against local Muslims, comes to be manifest locally. In a later interview, I asked a Sunni man why he thought anger had been directed against local Muslims, if the cause of the political discontent was the actions of the state government. He responded with a saying, "If you cannot break the big black bean, break the little round pea."[3]

Both Buddhists and Muslims draw on the concept of minority–majority relationships: playing with scale, framing space in such a way that they are sometimes majorities and sometimes minorities. This is language that emerges from the belly of the Westphalian nation-state ideal as it traipses through formerly small places that are now parts of very large places mapped and counted, in which you must find your way to political agency by working for a version of peopleness (van Beek 2000, 2001). Buddhists sometimes explained their position as a minority within the state of Jammu and Kashmir, while Muslims represent themselves as a minority within the district and the Indian nation-state. Akbar tells me: "We also, we as Muslims, we also think and understand that the government should always honor the aspirations of the Buddhists, they are also a minority in this state. But we are also a minority. We do not get anything from the central government, the state government, or the local government. The Muslims are the worst hit and the worst discriminated against. Even here, you will not find any well-paid people in the whole system. The Buddhists are wholly in control of the local administration."

In this context, Muslims also raised larger issues for Muslims in India, such as nation-wide discrimination, Hindu nationalism, the Gujarat riots of 2002, and low percentages of Muslims in government jobs in India, topics that were on the radar of the young college students (regardless of religion) who will speak up later in the book, but which were not mentioned by most politically involved Buddhists I spoke with. Muslim community leaders describe being "speechless," fearful, or powerless within Ladakh, which necessitated strategies of appeasing the Buddhist majority, "flying below the radar," and not objecting if Muslims converted to Buddhism. Yet, Buddhists also feel the same sense of vulnerability, like Spalzes, a Buddhist woman in her seventies, who says: "Now everyone say that we have to be united, and we have pretended that we are united, but I just wonder if we can really know the true intentions of the Muslims. . . . They are advancing and doing all kinds of things, but we Buddhists just say, 'compassion and love,' and we do not progress. . . . We Buddhists procrastinate, and we are lazy." These concerns about the "true intentions" echo commentary on events from Partition to the present but were heightened during the 1989–1992 agitation, when spaces of religious worship became imbued with suspicion. Hasina, a Sunni Muslim woman in her fifties, extended forgiveness to Buddhists who had gotten wrapped up in violence and told of how violence was avoided in her hometown of Sakti:

> They were told that in Gonpa Soma, Muslims had destroyed everything, had broken all the statues and left nothing. Someone lied to them. . . . My husband's father was in Anjuman at that time. Then at that time they all went to Sakti. Everyone came with axes and saws. Our aba-le [her father-in-law], he was a contractor, so he had a lot of workers. He took them all out there. He said, "Don't do this. We are going to be together. Don't do this thing. You all go to Leh and see for yourselves. See if they mean it." . . . He stayed there and he said, "If their necklaces have been broken and torn down, then do it to mine. If their hands are cut off, then cut my hand off and throw it to the ground. You all go. I will stay here. If you go, you will

all find out. This is not something to start a demonstration." Then their anger subsided, and they felt ashamed. And then they didn't kill anyone.

Hasina went on to say, "if we had stayed in *mohabbat* [love, affection], that would have been better. . . . What they did was bad, they did worse than was necessary. Where do they expect us to go? We were born here, in this *yul*, this earth, this land, from here, where will we go?" *Yul* can mean village, place, or nation. In this ambiguity, it recalls scalar modes of thinking that elude the fixity of state borders. *Yul* here seems to indicate a place of belonging—whether that is at the scale of the village or the kingdom.

In a few generations, then, Ladakh as a place moved from being a collection of villages in relation to, and under domination by, small kingdoms, and tied to a cosmopolitan world of Central Asia through trade routes, and then through the foundational rupture of Partition, into a mapped and bounded place with an electoral system that both promises representation and accountability and inescapably links demography to political power. What is the feeling of this transformation? How does it feel to inhabit a body upon land that is becoming territorialized by state processes? This mesh of lines, districts, and contested sovereignties is the spiraling out of the ways that the idea and materiality of the sovereign state touched down through imperial practices that both normalized and undermined sovereignty as a necessary feature of governance. The subcontinent is enmeshed and entangled in the history of empire itself.

What Brought Us to This Precipice? From Kings to Councils

The centuries leading up to the formation of India and Pakistan as independent states may now seem to have been teleologically aligned toward that end, but of course there were many twists and turns, and the present conjuncture was never foretold. As Beek (2001) has argued, the division of Ladakhis into political blocs described in terms of religion was never inevitable—indeed, the past century has seen many instances of schisms between Buddhists, for instance, during the 1960s and 1970s split of the Congress Party.[4]

Before coming under the control of the Jammu Raja, in the nineteenth century, Ladakh was an independent kingdom, reaching its high point in the seventeenth century, under the reign of Sengge Namgyal, whom Hassan describes in the opening to this chapter as Ladakh's Ashoka. For centuries, Ladakh was oriented toward Tibet and Central Asia, an entrepôt through which the *pashm* fiber that is used to produce pashmina passed, as well as salt, barley, apricots, and other goods (Rizvi 1996). Ladakh's fate was tied to that of Jammu and Kashmir slowly over the course of several centuries. In the seventeenth century, Deldan Namgyal, Sengge Namgyal's son (Gyal Khatun's grandson), lost some of the territorial gains of his father, and Ladakh's sovereignty began an incremental

decline. Faced with threats from the northeast, Deldan Namgyal requested protection against the Tibetan army from the ruler of Kashmir, a vassal of the
Mughals (Aggarwal 2004). Assistance was given but resulted in the 1648 Treaty
of Tingmosgang between Ladakh, Tibet, and the Mughal Empire. This treaty put
in place trade regulations on pashmina, requiring exclusive rights to go to Kashmiri traders. Aurangzeb, the Mughal emperor, required a Sunni mosque to be
built in Leh in 1666, which remains beneath Leh palace today. This treaty was in
effect until the mid-nineteenth century, when desire to control the pashmina
trade and for the British to have a buffer frontier in its Central Asian competition with the Russians drove incursions into Ladakh. Maharaja Rangit Singh had
expanded his Sikh Empire from his base in the Punjab, eventually extending it
to Kashmir in 1819. He made a gift of Kashmir to his general, the Dogra Raja,
Gulab Singh, a Hindu descendant of Rajputs who had settled in Jammu. Gulab
Singh's general, Zorawar Singh, conquered Ladakh in incursions beginning in
1834, and the Ladakhi king became a vassal of the Dogras, forced to pay tribute.
Tibet signed the Treaty of Leh in 1842, acknowledging the Dogra kingdom's control of the region. In Leh, our home is just a few minutes' walk from the sandy
brown fort of Zorawar Singh. The fort is now maintained by the military, with
stray dogs resting in the dusty moat and the Indian tricolored flag fluttering
while teams practice polo in the field nearby. I have never seen or heard of Ladakhis visiting the fort in years of living in its shadow.

When the British defeated the Sikhs in the Anglo-Sikh War, Gulab Singh
turned against his former benefactors and agreed not to help the Sikh Empire
in exchange for his own princely state. Thus, at the Treaty of Amritsar in 1846,
Jammu and Kashmir became one of the largest of the 562 princely states and
included Ladakh because of the Dogra incursions in the prior decade. Princely
states were part of the British strategy of indirect rule in which local rulers were
granted some measure of autonomy in return for acknowledgment of the British crown. British officers and British representatives of the Dogra Raja were thus
stationed in Leh.

Under the rule of the Gulab Singh and his heirs, "Ladakh experienced
unmitigated autocratic rule. A succession of maharajas, nurturing ties with a
small group of Hindu pandits in the Kashmir Valley and a more extensive network of Dogra kinsmen in Jammu, willfully trampled on the rights of their subjects" (Jalal 2002, 351–352). Ladakhis often felt the pressures of this rule through
the power wielded by large landholding families, who lent grain to the poorer
classes, and the aristocracy, the *skutak*, through high taxes, and through the
begar system of enforced labor, that required villagers to provide portage and
other labor to government officials (Aggarwal 2004; Beek 1996; Rizvi 1999). Ladakhis have bitter memories of Dogra rule and of the excesses of the aristocracy
and royal intermediaries of the time—many interviewees mention by name the
tax collectors they encountered in the early twentieth century or heard of from

their parents. The period of Dogra rule is what some Buddhist politicians and historians turn to in order to explain Buddhist resentment against Muslims: in their account, during this time the employees and those who profited from the rule were mainly Muslims, who were more likely to read and write in Urdu and have links with Srinagar.

In the 1930s, popular uprisings in Kashmir challenged Maharaja Hari Singh's rule (Behera 2000). A Young Men's Muslim Association was formed in Jammu in 1930 around the same time that Sheikh Mohammad Abdullah established a group in Srinagar. July 1931 saw twenty-one protestors killed by the maharaja's troops in Srinagar. The Glancy Commission was set up to investigate, and thus, November 13, 1931, marks the first time Ladakh was formally represented in the state, by a delegation of three Kashmiri pandits and one Ladakhi Buddhist, Sonam Norbu. Sonam Norbu remains a hero, and his name is on Leh's hospital. The other men were Shridhar Bhatt, Shridhar Kaul, and S. N. Dhar, who founded the Raj Bodhi Maha Sabha in 1932 (Beek 1996). Beek's careful analysis points to this time as a key moment initiating the representation of Ladakh as a (Buddhist) community, in this case by a layperson with no official authority (Beek 1996, 212). As Beek suggests, the logic of the commission and the delegation's interaction with it suggested a kind of "peopleness," assuming that religion could define a distinct community, whose political interests could then be represented on that basis, and through this process, the community could be developed, even though "Ladakhis themselves played hardly any role at all" (Beek 1996, 219). This moment was a catalyst for the formation of the Ladakh Buddhist Education Society in 1934 and the 1938 formation of the Young Men's Buddhist Association. Following the Glancy Commission, the Praha Sabha (state assembly) was formed and later the king of Ladakh was designated to represent Ladakh.

As described by Beek, these political events occurred side by side with increasing efforts to classify and codify through census categories. This period saw the consolidation, then, of what Beek (1996, 92) has described as the transformation of Ladakh "from Space to Territory," a process that gained steam over the course of the nineteenth century through the codification of land rights, royal and colonial rights to collect revenue, and surveys performed by the Dogras and the British. Beek (1996, 100) argues that "In the eyes of the British surveyor and politician, space was just that: empty and homogeneous, and hence needed to be marked. In the Ladakhi/Dogra (feudal) officials' view, space was meaningless except when marked through subjects, religious, or strategic considerations."

In the 1940s, the first steps toward demographic politics occurred with the ban on polyandry and primogeniture (the practice of the eldest brother inheriting all farmland). Until that time, it was common practice among Ladakhi Buddhists for one woman to marry two or more brothers. This was practical. The arid desert nature of the region means all farmland is limited—it must be cultivated through careful irrigation from glacier-fed streams. Maintaining one home without the need for new households in subsequent generations kept the need for new cropland in check. In this way, the family's land was not divided; instead, the wife and her two to four husbands cultivated the land together. Additional sons were sent out to join monasteries or otherwise find their fortune. Women would marry into other households or remain at home as celibate nuns. In households without sons, the eldest daughter would have a husband brought in from outside, and property would pass through her. In the 1940s, the ban on polyandry and primogeniture was couched in the language of modernity and realignment with global Buddhist practices; these bans also had a strong undercurrent of demographic strategy, in that they encouraged a proliferation of households (one for each child that married) (Beek 2000; Bertelsen 1997; Gutschow 2006). Polyandrous marriages were banned in 1941 under the Buddhist Polyandrous Marriages Prohibition Act but continued in practice until the 1980s, as evident by many marriages still in existence.

Partition

The 1947 Partition of the subcontinent into India and Pakistan meant that this religion–body–territory schema was written into the states and citizens themselves (Bangladesh was East Pakistan until its own independence in 1971). The logic of Partition was for contiguous districts with Muslim majorities to become Pakistan, and districts with Hindu majorities to become India, while the fate of the nominally independent princely states was to be decided by their leaders. Feminist scholars working in South Asia have eloquently documented the ways that this formula resulted in the subjugation of women's rights and sovereignty to their symbolic value, as their bodies became contested territory (Butalia 2000; V. Das 1995; Menon and Bhasin 1998). As Veena Das (1995) has argued, beyond the initial violence that occurred during the population transfer between the new states, in the months and years following Partition, the fate of the abducted women—those who had been kidnapped and subject to rape and more ambiguous cases in which women expressed a desire to stay with those who had been represented as their enemies—was a further elaboration on the territorialization of women's bodies and agency, as these women's fate became part of a collective and national urge for redemption in ways that obscured their own desires. Today, this is echoed in representations of the Kashmir Valley as a distressed damsel in need of rescue, which is understood by others as occupation (Kabir 2009; Rai 2004; S. Varma 2016). In the decades since Partition, echoes of this formulation have arisen in the political use of sexual violence (see, for example, Bacchetta 2000; Oza 2001). As Oza (2007, 166) observes, women become a target in part because they "embody the site of regeneration and culture."

In 2004, I spent an afternoon with Tonyot interviewing three men about the time around Indian independence. The interview began as a conversation with Nazir, a Sunni man in his seventies, but as he talked about his close relationships with Buddhist neighbors, two neighbors happened to stop by and join the conversation.

NAZIR: We had these rumors that we would be killed or something. My grandmother was a Buddhist but was married to my family. There were rumors that the Muslims would be killed. So some of the families took my grandmother and hid her at a Buddhist house. There was a Buddhist *patawari*. He said, "Whoever comes, that person has to kill me before he does anything to that grandmother." Think about it, what kind of people were there at that time, how nice were they? Kalon [the minister] and Goba [village head] patrolled the Muslim houses in the nighttime to make sure that no one was harassing them. Although nothing happened, there were some rumors. But because we had such a good relationship and such good leadership, there was peace.

NAMGYAL (BUDDHIST NEIGHBOR): In 1947 in Punjab, Sikhs killed Muslims and Muslims killed Sikhs, and then army from Karsha came, and they said, "Let's kill the Muslims," but the Kalon and those people, they did not let anything happen. There were some Sikhs who killed Muslims, and some Muslims who killed Sikhs. But nothing happened to the Muslims here because of the Kalon and others.

NAZIR: They said, "You cannot do this here." Most of our relatives—we are all blood relations. The families in Leh, the good families, the heads of those families, like the Kalon, and Shangar, they told Prithi Chand, "You cannot do this kind of thing here, in Leh." Because of that, nobody so much as pinched us. Part of the reason is that the roots of many of the Muslims are Buddhist.

In another 2004 interview, Amid, a Sunni man in his sixties, also pointed to the role of the Kalon, a member of the Buddhist aristocracy: "Aba [father] Kalon and some other people said, "We have lived together for whole lifetimes with these Muslims, so you cannot do that [religious violence] here." Amid went on to describe the response of his Buddhist relatives: "We have many Buddhist relatives. . . . I remember that when the Pakistanis came all the way toward Leh, one of my Buddhist uncles from Alchi came to Leh and said, 'I was worried about my nephew and nieces!'" Hajira describes 1947–1948 Ladakh as a time of confusion but also solidarity, when both Buddhists and Muslims feared communal violence but took refuge with one another: "So, when the Muslims would run away, the Buddhists would take care of their belongings, and when the Buddhists would run, the Muslims would take care of their things. . . . If the enemy, whoever that was, did something, it would hit everyone, the bullet would not discriminate between a Buddhist or a Muslim."

Fistfights and Slaps: Living the Geopolitical

> I remember that there was a fight between two boys in the bazaar, that's
> what they say. And then something happened to a girl, and then it became
> a demonstration. How exactly it became a demonstration between Bud-
> dhists and Muslims, I don't exactly know. But the way it happened, every-
> one knew, and the children . . . it was very hard, it was a big struggle to
> get hill council. (Nilza)

In 1989, a fistfight broke out in Main Bazaar. This fistfight is described as a side-
show, a couple of young men fighting (maybe about a horse)—certainly not about
the sovereignty of Ladakh. And yet, somehow it is also the incident marking the
beginning of "the agitation," as it is often called, and one of the young men, Rigzin Jora, went on to become a major political figure during and after the agitation
for autonomy. In a 2008 focus group I conducted with young people, they describe
the fistfight in relation to oral histories they had completed with older neighbors
and family members:

KHADIJAH: The grandma we asked, she said that one Buddhist and one Muslim
got in a fistfight and everything started from there.

ABDUL: In the city, those youth got in a fight. One Muslim, and one Buddhist.
From there it spread.

LADOL: Is it good, then, that a fight between two people should spread like fire
all over Ladakh?

AUTHOR: How could it?

LADOL: Because fighting between two people often happens, but then there is
no such incidence where it spreads to everyone.

TASHI: They didn't say, they said they didn't really know. They only had heard
that it started between two people in Leh, but they didn't really know, they
just got the news later on. After that, they heard people saying that "we
should kick them out." They heard that the Muslim population is going to
grow and we'll be dominated by them. Thinking about that . . .

AUTHOR: In your opinion, what should we do to prevent these incidents from
causing the kinds of problems like happened in 1989?

RAHIMA: I think, that these days, people won't have time for fistfights, because
they are so busy with their own work. Then, but . . . we don't need to involve
politics in things. If someone gets in a fight, whether it's with a Buddhist or
a Muslim, their family, they should solve it themselves, peacefully, and outsiders shouldn't be involved, shouldn't interfere. Otherwise, because of that,
more talking will come and protests will come.

At the time of this fistfight, Hindu nationalism was taking hold in India with the increasing success of regional and then national parties. This culminated in spectacles such as the campaign to destroy the Babri Masjid in Ayodhya and an accompanying wave of anti-Muslim violence (Hansen 1999; Ludden 1996), which Bacchetta (2000) eloquently reads as an extension of the struggle for the landscape onto the body. This period also saw the deepening of separatist conflict in Kashmir with the beginnings of armed insurgency (Behera 2000; Bose 2009) and ramping up of Indian military presence. Events in the valley and the subsequent influx of Kashmiri economic migrants contributed to Ladakhis' sense of vulnerability and reinforced the knowledge that Ladakhis had negligible input in decisions made about the future of J&K (Aggarwal 2004; Beek 2000; Gutschow 2006). In this charged atmosphere, activists and the LBA made a strategic decision to portray their quest for autonomy within the state as the movement of a persecuted religious minority; they may not have anticipated the long-term effects (Beek, 2001). This followed a surge of violence against Ladakhi Christians in the late 1980s (Beek, 2004). While Ladakhis had advocated for greater autonomy since the 1960s and had received the support of Hindu nationalist groups each time, it was at this point, in the 1980s, that the call for autonomy was framed primarily in terms of religious difference and invoked first local Christians and then local Ladakhi Muslims as a proxy (Beek 2004). In 1988, a Buddhist woman married her Christian neighbor and converted, and a few months later, a bomb was set in their house, destroying a wall but resulting in no injuries. The Moravian pastor wrote to the government, arrests were made, tensions rose quickly, and demands were made to return fifty-two Ladakhi children studying at a missionary school in Srinagar. When protests broke out, the Kashmiri police came down violently. In an *India Today* article, Stagna Rinpoche is quoted describing these incidents as indicating a "great danger to Buddhism" (Devadas 1988). They also prefigured an increasingly tense relationship with the Kashmiri Police or "KP," who would the next year prove more adversarial, shooting three Buddhist protestors in 1989. At this moment, on the cusp of the agitation, leaders, including a pastor and Rigzin Jora, then an LBA member but soon to be a prominent politician, spoke in defense of Buddhist–Christian interreligious marriages, with Jora saying, "It's a matter of heart, no religion can come into it" (Devadas 1988).

Pointing to economic marginalization of Ladakh by the government of J&K, in 1989 the LBA declared that Ladakh was a fundamentally Buddhist region, oppressed by the Muslim majority in the state, demanded Union Territory status, and drew attention to this demand with a social boycott against Ladakhi Muslims, forbidding social and economic contact (Aggarwal 2004; Beek 2000). As negotiations with the central government unfolded, after the destruction of the Babri Masjid (which was condemned by the LBA) and calls by the Dalai

Lama, the boycott of Ladakhi Muslims was called off in 1992, just before the Hill Council was awarded (Beek 2004). Some read this as success of the agitation and the boycott as a strategy, while others see it as evidence that Buddhist and Muslims can accomplish things only when they come together. Razia, for instance, tells me that for UT or Hill Council, "all of us Buddhists and Muslims must work together. We are also residents of Leh. We have been born in Leh, and we have been raised in Leh. If something is good for Leh, if there will be development in Leh, it will be good for Muslims just as it will be good for Buddhists." Razia believes that Buddhists claim the boycott led to the Hill Council "to make themselves look good." This is, of course, distinct from how outside forces, such as the Kashmiri police, are described, as their role in shooting three Buddhist protestors in Gonpa Soma during a demonstration just a month after the fist-fight and the imposition of rules restricting gatherings of four or more had cemented how they would be perceived.

Ordinary folks tell this story quite differently from political leaders, layering ambiguity and their personal experiences of the events into a foggy narrative of bewilderment in relation to the breakdown of relationships between Buddhist and Muslim Ladakhis, complemented by an emphasis on stories that cast doubt on its efficacy:

> She had been staying in a Muslim household, and then she got a message, "you better empty your room." . . . but she didn't do it. One day when she was in the Main Bazaar, they said, you have to come in *Gonpa Soma* ["New Temple," the LBA headquarters in Main Bazaar] for a little bit, and then she went. She went in, and they asked her, "you are hanging around with [Sunni Muslims] and you are staying in a [Sunni Muslim] room, why are you doing that?" . . . So she told them, "where would I go, I'm poor, and where else would someone let me stay for free?" Then, they really slapped her, one of the boys, he slapped her, and she says that she still remembers the feeling of that slap, his name was ———, he just really slapped her, you know how someone might? And she just fainted. She had hair, what pretty hair she had. It was this long, fell to here. . . . They cut it all off, even worse than a boy's hair. Then she just went to her mother's house in Shey, and she stayed there for a while. Then her sister and so on, they came where she had been staying and took all her things, and they put her in a Christian's house, here in Leh. After a while, a Muslim came and then she just converted to Islam and married him. Because she said, "they did this to me, they cut off my hair, and how would I stay Buddhist?"

The account above was recounted to me by the woman's close friend, a Shia Muslim. In this signal event, a Buddhist woman who had not conformed to established boundaries between Buddhists and Muslims was punished through public, bodily humiliation by being slapped and having her hair, in this context a gendered sign of sexuality, chopped off. Many tell tales of interdependence in the boycott, but some political leaders describe the moment quite differently. Within the geographic frame of the district, Palden explains to me: "And then, the Buddhist community became the majority force after that. It got recognition of the majority after that. Otherwise before that I do not think the majority, it was not carrying cognizance, recognition of authority. After that, it became recognized as the majority." Buddhists faced violence during the agitation that is vivid in family memories. In 1989, three Buddhists were shot and killed in the Buddhist temple in Leh during a protest for autonomy, and many demonstrators were beaten. While the agitation was a time that created a minority feeling for the Muslims, some Buddhists describe it as a time when they came into their own and found strength in their minority revolt within the Muslim-majority state.

These political–religious blocs are not naturalized religious identities but were produced through historically contingent and strategic decisions made by political leaders based on their assessments of local and national political contexts (Aggarwal 2004; Beek 1996, 2001, 2004; Bertelsen 1996, 1997; Gutschow 2006; Srinivas 1998). The political climate of the 1980s and 1990s led Ladakhi political leaders to believe that a communalized strategy of religious representation was the most effective means to obtain greater autonomy (Beek 1996). This assessment is held by many in the Leh elite; more than one Muslim leader privately defended to me activist Buddhists' use of communal rhetoric, saying that Buddhist leaders must use communal language in the political sphere, even if they maintain close friendships with Muslims in private. The Buddhist agitation was a strategic decision made after other attempts to secure autonomy failed (not the result of long-standing animosity); many Buddhist leaders who participated in the agitation have close Muslim friends or relatives; some Buddhist leaders resisted the agitation; and the perception of territorial vulnerability and erasure is not unfounded. As long as Leh's fate was tied to that of J&K, its future remained uncertain, and its residents' voices often unheard in conversations over the future of the state.

At the end of the social boycott, representatives of the LBA and the Ladakh Muslim Association (an ad hoc coalition of Muslim groups) negotiated a ban on intermarriage. In my survey, every participant was aware of this unwritten agreement. Each side is responsible for the regulation of its own young people—if a Muslim girl runs away with a Buddhist boy, each side is expected to forcibly return "their" daughter or son to their family, which is then under considerable pressure to continue to keep the couple apart. In my 2008 survey, I found that 83 percent of women living in Leh Town and the vicinity had relatives across the Buddhist–Muslim divide. In 75 percent of these cases, these relatives were within one generation (a mother, father, aunt, or uncle). That 80 percent of the women also professed themselves to be against intermarriage suggests a significant shift in thinking in the space of one generation. Stories circulate about the enforcement of this agreement—some with apparently happy endings, some tragic. It has become impossible to legitimate desire for someone of the "wrong" religion through marriage, but anecdotes about broken hearts and secret affairs point to the difficulty of regulating desire itself (Smith 2011). The anti-intermarriage agreement rejects desire across religious identity and separates bodies of different religious identification: a means of conflict prevention and a means to prevent women from converting and producing babies of a different religion from the one of their mother's birth.

In the decades since the Hill Council was awarded, tensions have been rising and falling, simmering in the background. Despite attempts to unify religious and political leaders, as in the short-lived emergence of a noncommunal Ladakh Union Territory Front Party in 2004, incidents in 2000, 2006, and 2017 all led to fear of rioting and police-imposed curfews, and fears that tensions could increase to the 1989 levels. Disappointment with corruption and the slow pace of improvements in the district have led to a great deal of apathy and cynicism about politics, continuing the sentiments that emerged during the boycott years—that politicians were actively manipulating people's sentiments for their own votes regardless of the potential aftermath.

"Actually, I Want to Tell You": How Politics Happen

Hassan interrupted one of my banal questions to cut to the chase: "Actually, I want to tell you, it is politicians, who sometimes, for their own benefit, mix the religion with politics. And they make the people fight." This was a familiar refrain. After Nargis told me the story about her friend having her hair cut off, I asked her, "What was the point of the whole thing? Was it to get Hill Council or what?" She corrected me: "For each one's own seat. . . . There are also those among the Sunnis who did this or that, some Sunni young men who really did bad things." By "seat," she meant political position. Similarly, Nizam, a Sunni man in his mid-eighties, said that conflict is "all politics. For their own political position, that was the reason. Otherwise, there is no real reason." To Nizam, the use of religious rhetoric signaled that politicians were "not thinking about the whole country of Ladakh, but about politics," that they were thinking of their own political gain. He turned to me earnestly and asked, as though I was hopelessly naive, "One reason may be just to get more people in elections: have not you noticed how politicians go and lie everywhere just to get their votes?" When I asked Paljor about the boycott, he had told me it is "totally politics" and continued: "When you think about the 1989 riots, when you think about the tension between the two communities, the people who were very strong in shouting, who were in front of both communities, whether it was Muslim or Buddhist, the people who were in front of the demonstrations, who was the leader of the protest, they are now the head of the politics in Ladakh." When I asked him about this, it was shortly after the Ladakh Union Territory Front had been formed, and he saw this as another instance of their callowness, as these people who "were shouting for the disturbance" now have good political posts:

> And now they say, "We have to be one. We have to think about one. We are one. They are our brothers." . . . It's like this, Sara, yeah: if I want to go into politics, if I want my name to make it big, then for example, I want to have a good seat in the leadership, then I have to shout for Buddhists. . . . If a Muslim, if he wants a good seat in the politics, he has to shout for Muslims, then every Muslim will vote for him, and he will be the leader.

In the next chapter, this sense of agency on the part of political leaders will be complemented by people's sense that the ground beneath their feet itself is changing, that this is simply how democracy operates, that these operations by necessity leave their mark on the people who participate in them. Thus, Tsering, a Buddhist man in his seventies, told me:

> When democracy came into J&K, as a result of that, you see, the Muslims, being a majority in the state, the Muslims of Ladakh, and especially the Sunni Muslims were naturally having some, how shall I say, some good opinion of the Kashmir government. They think the Kashmir government is a Muslim government. Actually, they should think, the Kashmir government is a Muslim government, no doubt, because most of the ministers are Muslims, in the ministries they are Muslim, in that way it is a Muslim government. But it is a democratic government and in democracy, every citizen has got rights.

This concept of majority might falling upon religious difference instead of other forms of difference, such as economic class, landholder versus the landless, or regional differences, was felt to be inevitable and to have sparked changes that were irrecoverable. Akbar, a middle-aged Sunni Muslim, told me that the agitation had especially damaged Buddhism, so that Buddhists now "believe more in violence," "because their leadership resorted to violence." Even if individuals "may have their own reservations on this issue, but they started the first riot, you know. Now everywhere they think that violence is the best way." Echoing Beek's analysis of "peopleness," Paljor described the agitation as a time when "we made two communities. One for the Buddhists and one for the Muslims. . . . We have to decide, we have to show that we are one. So, we [Buddhists] have to be with LBA." This echoes the sense of many that this formation of oppositional communities is simply how democracy works. Tsering explained:

> One of the things you learn, you see, is that nonviolence is not as effective as violence. For example, say if we start a nonviolent agitation here. . . .

Nobody cares about it. Whether it may be the administration, whether it may be the government, whether it may be the radio people. . . . But, on the other hand, if you do violence, if you burn a house, and if you kill a man, all the newspapers . . . and they say . . . such and such man had been killed, this and this had been burned. So, you get an immediate reaction. On the other hand, in the nonviolent way, you are carrying on your agitation for two months, for three months, no one bothers.

War between Countries/War between People

When [the 1947–1948] war happened, that was like a war between two governments that were fighting and killing each other, but people were not fighting and killing each other. But now, or if something happens in the future, it is not only the governments fighting each other, but people killing each other. . . . There are two things: one thing is war between India and Pakistan. Another thing is conflict between Buddhists and Muslims here, and in Kashmir: communal tension. (Hajira)

Hajira, a seventy-year-old Sunni woman, differentiates between national war and interpersonal violence between Buddhist and Muslim Ladakhis to note the ways that people are being caught up in, or manage to live apart from, state violence. As for many of her generation, Partition is a key, though multivalent, point of reference, through which current events are refracted: "Pakistani troops came all the way to Nimoo. Our own people stood up to guard us, and who will do it these days? These days, whether it is Kache, Boto, or Christians, they will just run to save their own lives." Throughout our interview, Hajira reiterated and repeated these refrains in new words: "Muslims and *nangpa* [Buddhists, insiders], had trust in each other. . . . In 1947, there was a group of families from Shey, and when they heard that the Pakistanis were coming, they ran away into the mountains. . . . It was both Buddhists and Muslims that ran away. Not only did we run away together, but we ate together and helped each other. . . . No one would say, this is Muslim, this is Nangpa. If someone were to shoot a gun, no one would say, "this will hit a Nangpa, this will hit a Muslim . . . it could hit anyone." Hajira herself grew up the daughter of a Buddhist *amchi* (traditional doctor) but converted to Islam on marrying her Shia husband. Her use of the word *nangpa* for Buddhist is revealing, as even while she describes care and togetherness, and from her own position as a Muslim, *nangpa* means insider, emphasizing Buddhist belonging and Muslim otherness.[5] Day (2018) has written movingly about the ways that this togetherness comes in and out of focus when people reflect back on their lives and how the relationship has changed.

Sara Ahmed (2004) argues that emotions are social and cultural practices. Neither the inside-out model (emotions emerge from our interior selves) nor the outside-in model (emotions come from the crowd and move into us) are sufficient: "emotions are not 'in' either the individual or the social, but produce the very surfaces and boundaries that allow the individual and the social to be delineated as if they are objects." When we read that "the nation 'mourns,'" the nation is being generated, "*as if it were a mourning subject*" (S. Ahmed 2004, 13). It is in the experience of pain that we become aware of the surface of our bodies. The practice of emotions, then, matters for relations between bodies and directs our attention to the ways that emotional ties orient bodies. Hajira materializes this in her narration of history: the surfaces of bodies emerge over the second half of the twentieth century, when we reach a point at which perhaps a bullet can discriminate between these surfaces, and cups are no longer to be shared.

During the 1980s, Sonam Wangyal was in a position of political power and refused to comply with the social boycott in any form. His defiance was mentioned by many of the people with whom I spoke. Ali tells the story in detail:

> One man very openly defied them. That was Sonam Wangyal. He had to undergo a lot of hardships. . . . When his wife died, there was a problem about the cremation of his wife and the performance of the religious rites, and finally, for the sake of his children and his wife, he had to surrender, he had to beg the pardon. . . . The monks also did not attend the ceremony. According to the Buddhists, I was told that the performance of some rituals were very compulsory for the salvation of the deceased. So, that was the problem. Because I had some contact with Sonam Wangyal also. When his wife passed away, he sent a vehicle to me [to attend the ceremony]. So, only that one point, it was, there was one monk who came. Even at that point, the people came to know, so they came and they took that monk away. It was great hardships and great difficulty. Sonam Wangyal was telling me, for myself, I shall not bother, I do not bother, whether I am Buddhist, or whether I am cremated. But my children are very extremely worried for the mother, because she is not going to get salvation. That is why I am going to succumb to the pressure.

These stories sit uncomfortably alongside narrations of the boycott as an "explosion" of built-up resentment that increased political autonomy for Ladakh. These stories begin from intimacies of blood, death, and milk—intimacies born of marriage and neighborliness. Nizam, a Sunni grandfather, recalls that when his wife died, his Buddhist brother-in-law spoke of himself as someone who had shared a mother with his sister and thus would not be deterred from paying respect to her: "During that time, my wife died, and none of the relatives came, with the exception of one. This one relative came, and he said, no matter what happens, I will come. He said, 'I am a person who drank milk from the same mother as her, and I do not give a shit, whatever happens, I will come.'"

A multitude of intimacies proliferated from the marriages that once took place between Buddhists and Muslims. Kinship was made through marriage but also through celebration of *skidsdug*, or "happysad," a shorthand for the occasions of life that are celebrated and mourned: births, deaths, marriages. Recollections of the generation who experienced Partition speak to questions of what it means to be related (Nash 2005), as well as to Ahmed's call to attend to the ways bodies are oriented toward or away from one another. Relatedness and bodily intimacies continue to be invoked as an inoculation against violence, but this is tempered by the events of the social boycott. Perhaps, in the terms of Morrison, Johnston, and Longhurst (2013), this is "what love does," that is, it gives a familial sense of kinship that can refuse violence. Yet we know this is illusory—families and communities can also be sites of violence (Chatterji and Mehta 2007; V. Das 2007; Sharpe 2009; Singh 2011; P. Williams 2007).

Conclusion

Surya lives in a suburb of Leh but married into that family from her natal home in Sabu. She speaks about demonstrations and communal violence as things that might "break out," almost of their own accord, as though from the ground itself. At the same time, such incidents also are hazy with uncertainty: you might never get to the bottom of them. I asked her why conflict happens and then about rumors I had heard of a house set on fire in her neighborhood when the Shia occupants were at *matam*, a sacred day of mourning for Imam Hussain. Unlike political leaders who give clean answers, she emphasizes uncertainty:

SURYA: How that happens, we never find out. For example, if something happens today in Leh, what exactly happened, whether there was a fistfight, all we know is two kids started fighting in the Main Bazaar and next they're throwing rocks at the *masjid* (mosque), that's what we hear. All the rest, what happened and why, we hear nothing about that. That's all we hear. And "from that the demonstration started." Or, that's why it happened. That's all we hear.

AUTHOR: What about here, year before last, something happened. Why?

SURYA: Even about that, we don't know what happened. We were here and got this phone call, someone saying, "hey, they set a house on fire down the hill." Yeah, from then, that's how we found out. What happened, why it happened, we never find out. That understanding doesn't happen. Those people [who set the fire] didn't make it up here. It was down the hill that they set those houses on fire. Us, we have no idea. They didn't manage to get up here to set them on fire, so we don't even know why it happened.

AUTHOR: Who set those houses on fire? People from this neighborhood, or from outside?

SURYA: That's the thing we never find out. Who did it? All we know is after the fact someone calls up and says, "There's smoke from those houses. Someone must have set fire to them." Other than that, we don't even find out a thing. Who did it, we didn't learn anything.

As family histories both reflect and refute Buddhist–Muslim antagonism, so too the landscape is read in complex and contradictory ways. In Leh's bazaar (see figure 4), we find a Shia *imambara* (the Shia religious structure serving as mosque, mourning hall, and meeting place) and a Sunni mosque, the old palace of the Buddhist kings, and a Buddhist temple constructed beginning in 1957 on land provided by the government. The proximity of the buildings suggests the possibilities for coexistence, and the centrality of these religious markers points to their central role in the constitution of cultural identity as well. They can also be read as territorial claims to space. In the 1990s and early 2000s, the temple, imambara, and mosque in bazaar were each remodeled, taking on more globally recognizable architectural styles (Smith 2013), but in 2019 the new remodeling of the Sunni mosque has embraced traditional Ladakhi motifs. Structures of town only hint at the crossroads where traders from Afghanistan, Turkestann, and Mongolia met with Ladakhis, Tibetans, Kashmiris, and Punjabis. Leh's horizon has gradually shifted, as the trade routes toward Tibet and what is now Pakistan were blocked by militarized cease-fire lines.

The state–subject–territory formulation is vivid in South Asia, where the borders of the three largest states were drawn on and through bodies inscribed with religious identity. The independent states born through this colonial legacy are now challenged by these bodily calculations, as territories within territories reveal themselves as a set of never-ending Russian dolls: South Asia, divided into Pakistan and India in 1947, reveals J&K as India's sole Muslim state, within which Hindus and Buddhists find themselves minorities. In Leh District, members of the Shia Muslim minority declare themselves the most minority of all. These struggles and narratives hinge on the tallying of bodies and the assigning of territory to states that claim the loyalties of the largest number of those people that claim an affinity with other bodies of a certain religion, ethnicity, or other inscribed marker.

Colonial census categories comprised generative forms of knowledge production in tandem with the objectification of cultural identities (Cohn 1987). Building on this work and that of Said (1979), Appadurai (1996) emphasized the role of enumeration as a quintessential orientalist practice bringing together classificatory and exoticizing tendencies. In the colonial imagination, and later, in postcolonial political mobilizations, "number, by its nature, flattens idiosyncrasies and creates boundaries around these homogeneous bodies as it performatively limits their extent," such that "statistics are to bodies and social types what maps are to territories: they flatten and enclose" (Appadurai 1996, 133). Beek

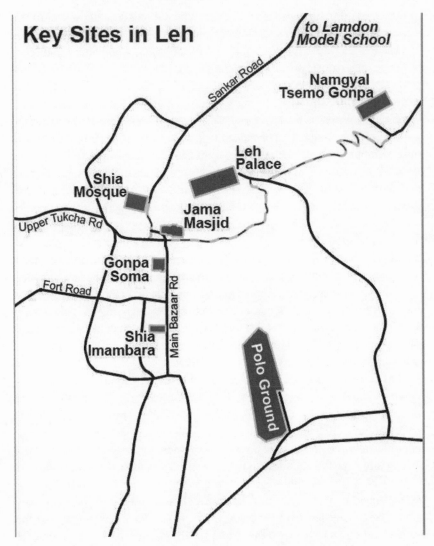

FIGURE 4 Map of Leh, with religious sites and important public spaces, created by Timothy Stallman.

(2000) describes one of the political outcomes of this reification as "identity fetishism," that is, the idea that if sovereignty is accorded to the right grouping of people, whether along religious, ethnic, or other lines, "peace and prosperity" will be enabled. Along with Cohn (1987) and Appadurai (1996), Beek (2000, 530) suggests that the definition of identity groups calls those groups into being, not because social difference does not exist, but because the meaning of social differences is "altered through objectification and institutionalization." The layering of identity fetishism, vote bank politics, and decadal censuses has produced a body of knowledge with particular political effects, particularly in the wake of Partition along religious lines and the attendant cartographic anxiety (Das 2007; Krishna 1994).

The concern over women's bodies in Ladakh conforms to colonial and nationalist narratives that conflate women's bodies, the nation, and religious identity (Bacchetta 2000; Butalia 2000; R. Das 2004; V. Das 1995; Gökariksel 2009; Menon and Bhasin 1998; Mody 2008; Nagar 1998; Nast 1998; Oza 2001; Puri 1999). The work of Beek to unravel historical trajectories demonstrates the strings and tangles behind this tapestry, revealing the ways that leaders and elite families were cognizant of shifting power dynamics at state and national levels and negotiated the creation of Ladakhi "peopleness" in various avatars to find one that fit what they understood to be the tasks at hand.

At the hearth, grandmothers and grandfathers focus not on the intricacies of political actors but on sweeps of history. They express cynicism about political machinations with throwaway quips that politicians just do things to get elected to a seat in council or parliament, but also with sincere gratitude for things like subsidized staple foods. This is captured by the familiar phrase "thanks to god and the government," but such gratitude is tempered with cynicism toward political actors whom they understand to be risking the pleasures and protections of everyday life for their own political gain. In the next chapter, I will turn attention to how these experiences transform relations between and within the home.

4

Intimacy on the Threshold

The arrival of a visitor at the gate sets in motion the making of tea with milk and sugar, searching for a package of cookies, or sending a child to pick some up from the nearest shop: Will plain glucose biscuits do? Are nicer ones nearby? Is the dish of almonds, cashews, and raisins full, or are there good walnuts and dried apricots in the house? The guest sits on a wool carpet, noting the quality and making small talk as the host chooses a nicer saucer and cup than the ones the family would use at breakfast—the most delicate china selected for a guest most distant or most respected. They might usher you into a room just for guests—but then you will not be able to chat while they fix your tea. These days a middle-class household will also have cold drinks on hand to follow the tea: Coca-Cola, "Dew," or Miranda and now packaged fruit juice (each summer a different flavor is in style). For long visits, a thermos of butter tea with salt is churned and poured into a Chinese thermos, and the host will refill that cup of salty tea with each sip—ensuring it never grows cold. If you only want one cup, you must drink it quickly, cover the cup insistently with your hand, or perhaps hide your cup under the low table in front of you. The crinkle of the biscuit wrappers, the sharing of food, the whooshing sound of butter tea being churned, steam from the cup, butter rising to the top as a golden liquid lid, small crucial practices build familiarity over time. "Attachment takes place through movement, through being moved by the proximity of others" (S. Ahmed 2004, 11). Bodies and objects are shaped by emotion and sensation. This movement is shaped by passing over the threshold of a house—whether permanently as a bride or groom or repeatedly over the years as a neighbor or family member. At what moments do these thresholds come to be proxies for other kinds of borders? When do they recede as unexceptional? How are the choices of the past re-interpreted in the future, and what does this mean for the threshold of the future, which will be the focus of chapter 5?

The treatment of guests on days of celebration will be much more elaborate. Eid, *Losar* (the Buddhist new year), a marriage, a retirement—these events will be marked with meals of eight or nine courses and hours of tea and conversation. Arriving back at home, you will be asked, "What did they feed you?" even as the one asking is themselves fixing you a just-arrived-home cup of tea. You might praise the tea and mention it was made with fresh cow's milk instead of condensed. You might relate that they offered you lunch but only one time so you doubted the sincerity of the offer and did not accept. These meals bind you to those who serve them, building a set of reciprocal attachments, relationships, connection, and interchange. As such meals make the body, becoming part of the very cells that constitute us, they also create home as a place of expectation and welcome. During my initial research in 2004, I was struck by the ways love, children, but also food emerged when I asked questions about politics: "When Buddhists used to come to our house, not only would we feed them, but we would send them home with plates of food." "In the past, no one would say, *lakma* [leftovers]," I was told, meaning: in the past we were family—people who could eat together from one plate.

This statement is meaningful because it is inappropriate to eat the leftovers of anyone but family: at a marriage, the bride and groom eat from the same plate to signal that a transformation has occurred. Guests call out "bride first!" or "groom first!" in a teasing way, implying that the one who takes the first bite will have the upper hand in the marriage. Descriptions of food evoke the familial and familiar. Some recall care taken by Buddhists not to offend Muslims with non-halal meat: Nilza, who you will remember from chapter 2, tells me that to provide a Muslim with non-halal meat or to use a pot with beer residue would be "a sin for us, because it is against their religion." One Muslim man pointed to shared meals in Kuksho (a village in western Ladakh) as a model for Buddhist–Muslim community: "They do Islamic slaughtering, then they boil the meat and tie a string, to distinguish which is halal. But they boil it in the same pot."[1] He went on to add, however, "This is not invoked very often these days, unfortunately. People have gone, and they are briefed, 'that is un-Islamic,' or, 'that is very un-Buddhist.'"

When I asked Nizam,[2] a prosperous Sunni trader now in his eighties, about relationships between Buddhists and Muslims, he told me: "Between Muslim and Buddhist, there would not be differences. People would not even say Buddhist and Muslim. We would play together, we would celebrate together, we would fight, we would beat each other, but by the end of the day, we would be friends again. And eat and drink together from one cup. . . . My relatives are in the thousands. My whole family is Buddhist. My grandma was Buddhist; most of our relatives are Buddhist."

Nizam describes a weaving together of people across religious difference through marriage and ordinary everyday intimacies, into a fabric that cannot be torn. But how do we read Nizam's lyricism of relatives in the thousands with the words of Nargis, a Shia woman also living in Leh? During her oral history, she told me of the time when Muslim homes were burned in nearby Thikse, and I asked her why that happened:

NARGIS: They were just thinking to put an end to the Muslims. They said to get out, for the Muslims to get out, that's what they were saying. . . . Where would we go? And in Kashmir, there are Kashmiris.[3] Where would we Ladakhis go? The older people would say, "What are they saying? People who were born right here, telling them to get out, how can they get out?" Land and fields and houses, we all have them. . . .

AUTHOR: Why would they do that?

NARGIS: There are some who say, "The Muslims are taking all of our girls." . . . That's one thing. Then, simply saying to get rid of the Muslims, some must have been thinking like that.

Both Nizam and Nargis begin from a fundamental premise: that there is a close and tight relationship between Ladakh as place, embodied life, and the people "who were born right here." When Nargis talks about the fragmented 1989 attempt to exile Muslims from their natal villages, women's bodies become territory. The burning of Muslim houses, including her husband's childhood home, slips into a possessive discussion of women's bodies—no explanation is deemed necessary: "The Muslims are taking all of our girls," as explanation for expulsion, for flames. Eighty-five-year-old Nizam's "relatives in the thousands" were formed through Leh's long history of intermarriage, through which affective, emotional, and practical ties were forged. Marriage is not between two people but between many—over time these marriages can create "relatives in the thousands." Nizam's familial relationships are common for a member of his generation. Neighborhoods, marriages, and daily life have bound people together in intimate ways. What does it mean to eat from one plate or drink from one cup?

Bodies not only are territory but also make territory: the body itself, with its vulnerability, its hunger, weariness, longing, and desire, plays a role in the claiming and bounding of space. Affective claims to belonging happen through marriage, through relationships that spiral across generations from a single marriage, from friendships, and from living together as neighbors. These affective relations claim and bound the space of the home in ways that enable or foreclose the bounding of identity-based national borders onto the body. But this bodily participation in the bounding processes is fragmentary. Boundary making is met with moments of refusal and of enthusiastic collusion, as well as acquiescence under duress. Among those in and around Leh Town, in 2008–2009, 83 percent had relatives across the Buddhist–Muslim line.[4] The most common relationship was within the last two generations—a mother, father, aunt, uncle, grandmother, or grandfather had been born in a family of a different religion. In 1992, at the end of the two-year social boycott of Muslim Ladakhis (described in more detail in chapter 3), such marriages were banned in an unwritten but widely known agreement made between the LBA and the Ladakh Muslim Association (LMA), an ad hoc collection of Muslim associations including both Shia and Sunni Ladakhis. In this chapter, I trace how current concerns about intermarriage reflect the territorialization of the body, as well as the complex ways spatial configurations and time become part of how people understand this territorialization. Love, care, and home are intertwined and political (Blunt and Dowling 2006; Morrison et al. 2013), as the politics of emotion reshape the surfaces of bodies to redefine who is and who is not related (S. Ahmed 2004; Nash 2005).

Yet the past in which "[we would] eat and drink together from one cup" continues to be celebrated, even by those who are complicit in its undoing. Forced to grapple with a past that is honored even as the future unfolds quite differently before our eyes, people make sense of this by describing a hardening of household and familial borders as the result of time itself, by re-narrating the past, or by embodying rapid change in relation to a new generation—even as their own telling reveals fissures in this narration. "Relatives in the thousands" were created through marriages that are impossible today, due to a change "in hearts" and in the temporal structure of life itself.

Territory is abstract space delimited on a map, but it is also the floor of a home and the arrangement of guests at a wedding party. Colonial practices of cartography, census taking, and categorization (Appadurai 1996; Edney 1997; Krishna 1994; Lowe 2015) culminated in a deadly territorialization of religion and sovereignty onto the body (Butalia 2000; R. Das 2004; V. Das 1995; Menon and Bhasin 1998). This violence is erased on the map that delineates the deceptively homogenous and distinct nation-states of newly founded India and Pakistan. Nationalism is embodied and instrumentalizes reproductive lives in mundane and spectacularly violent ways (Jayawardena and de Alwis 1996; Korac 1999, 2004; Mayer 2004; Morokvasic-Müller 2004; Nast 2000; Yuval-Davis 1989). Divisive bodily differentiation did not end with decolonization but continued or proliferated in new and insidious forms (Bacchetta 2000; Nagar 1998; Oza 2007; Sabhlok 2010). Following the fracture of the subcontinent in 1947, cracks and fissures made their way into the home itself, separating family members along lines of religion, changing guest lists for parties, giving new meaning to what people do with and wear upon their bodies. Territorialized and nationalized religious identity is enmeshed with the everyday violence of heteronormative and reprosexual expectations around desire, love, and reproduction (Friedman 2000; Nast 1998; Warner 1991), as young people will describe in the next two chapters.

Better than Distant Relatives

On icy winter mornings we gather around the water tanker to fill up jugs of drinking water. Neighbors help direct the hose from the tanker into each of the recycled cooking oil containers. We are gathered in the home clothes that only neighbors or family see—worn jeans no longer suitable for town, faded *salwar kameez* (loose-fitting tunic and trousers) in the styles from two or three years ago. Splashing water freezes to our hems, and we walk slowly back home not to slip on the ice. We help each other, recognize faces, and inquire after children studying in Jammu or Chandigarh. All these years after the boycott, such interactions between Buddhists and Muslims are again common enough to be unremarkable. The proximity of neighbors encourages additional dependencies and intimate interactions—sharing the line to collect water, picking up something from the neighborhood shop and paying later, asking if the truck delivering gas cylinders has come and gone already. When I asked Faeda, a Sunni woman in her fifties, about her relationship with her Buddhist neighbors, she gestured at the houses of her Buddhist neighbors and explained a saying to me: "'Better than distant relatives are our nearby neighbors.' If you look at my example, my own relatives are far away. If something happens to me, for instance if my house is on fire, if someone dies, if I die, if something happens to my children, if I am shouting, it is the neighbors who will run here first. How will my family come from Nubra? The ones right around here, they are the ones who will come."

How might we make sense of neighbors who might rescue us when neighbors may also be enemies?[5] And how to maintain romantic memories about eating from one plate in the past when intermarriage is no longer sanctioned? When houses were set on fire, surely it was not the neighbors who did so, but it must have been someone's neighbors. To reconcile the irreconcilable, each person marks her or his neighborhood as a sanctuary, humor is deployed, and time itself is evoked as an agent of change.

Perversely, then, in many neighborhoods, when I asked about the social boycott, I was told "nothing happened here." This event, which everyone witnessed, happened both everywhere and nowhere at all. As one of the young men in a 2008 participatory oral history group observed, this may be a way of dealing with the past that is more about maintaining present-day relations than about describing events as remembered. Now that the boycott has receded but left high-water marks reminding people of what is possible, descriptions of it hone in on secret nighttime visits to relatives and friends, feelings of shame, and moments of repudiation. Nazir and Namgyal, Muslim and Buddhist neighbors in their seventies (whom we met in chapter 3), described such moments:

NAZIR: Even when there was communal violence, we had very good relationships with our neighbors, all the Buddhist families. Especially one grandpa used to say, "Don't you guys worry. Let's just see how long they [the LBA] can keep this up." Our Buddhist relatives used to come to our house, secretly during the boycott. If we needed anything, the Buddhist neighbors would give us anything we needed.

NAMGYAL: Even during the agitation, I had good relations with my Muslim neighbors, but there were Buddhist community members who put pressure on me, for example, they chopped down my trees. I had some community pots that included both Buddhists and Muslim pots, and the Buddhists said, "We should divide the pots, we cannot be together." But I said, "Ultimately, look at us, we have to be together."

Nargis had just recited for me the story of her childhood Buddhist friend whose hair was chopped off for consorting with Muslims during the boycott and the story of her husband's home burning. But then, suddenly, she transitioned to a more animated style of recitation and giggled when telling me about her older brother. She relies on an often-referenced idea that slight differences in appearance or dress could indicate someone's religious identity:[6] "My brother's face is like that of a villager, he had this coloring . . . he looked like a Buddhist. And then at that time, you know, he went to a Muslim shop, and they weren't allowed to purchase things from Muslim shops. He bought something there and outside someone said to him, "Hey, you have to come with us for a bit in *gonpa soma*" ["new temple," the Buddhist temple in the middle of town]. Caught off guard by Nargis's sudden laughter I smirked nervously and said, "hey," a neutral explanation of surprise.

NARGIS: He said, "Why, why do I have to go?" It didn't occur to him that they thought he was a Buddhist, he thought there must be some business he had to attend to. So, he had heard about that, because at that time, if you bought something from a Muslim shop, they would take you in *gonpa soma* and beat you, the monks would beat you.

AUTHOR: Beating people in a *gonpa*, what?

NARGIS: On the way to the *gonpa,* he saw somebody he knew, and he did *salam,* you know, how we do, he said, "asalam aleikum," and then those people, who were taking him, they just ran away.

Nargis's story of mistaken identity, told through laughter, satirizes the boycott, a time of danger and isolation, as ridiculous, laughable. In relating boycott stories, those who experienced it question it and portray it as an error, even as they continue to live in its wake.

Ordinary Intermarriage

What do people talk about when they talk about intermarriage? They tell me it is impossible, dangerous, that it could destroy Ladakh. They tell me it is a thing of the past. They tell me of their own marriage thirty years ago, or they tell me of their grandma who converted. They tell the story of the Buddhist woman and Muslim man who live in Leh, both now in their seventies and eighties. Although the most common scenario, at least in and around Leh Town, is for the woman in an interfaith marriage to convert, in this case, the wife never converted. Two or three people independently told me the same story: that the (Muslim) husband reminds his wife to light the lamp at the Buddhist altar when she forgets. I have only heard this spoken of as a celebration of communal harmony, never as failure of religious identity. And yet, when I have asked acquaintances about whether I could possibly speak to the couple, I have been told that the wife is shy or that it would be too difficult to arrange. Though I had often seen the woman in bazaar, they remain a cypher. I trusted my friends that reaching out to talk to them might be inappropriate; instead I attended to the ways that their story served as a touchstone for descriptions of what was no longer possible: their marriage itself like an anachronistic artifact, a grandfather clause unavailable to those considering a relationship today. Past intermarriage is almost exclusively celebrated, but the possibility of intermarriage today is almost exclusively decried.

In reference to the past generation, intermarried couples are spoken of in terms of practical accommodations between families or within the household, but often these are refracted stories—tales of intimate accommodation that I received secondhand and with awareness that these narratives were framed for my consumption. Another Buddhist woman of that generation married a Muslim man and kept her Buddhist practice, insisting before the marriage that not only would she remain Buddhist, her children would also be Buddhist. One Muslim woman explained that her mother was Muslim at home but Buddhist when she returned to her natal family for holidays. The Muslim daughter used Buddhist terminology to explain that this was her mother's *lanchags*, her karmic burden. Others told of couples that worked this out in advance as a matter of fate—that boys would be raised in one religion, girls another. Toward the west, some villages are known for being full of complicated and contingent religious practices: Muslims visiting the Buddhist temple, children whose names reflect a hybridity: Tsering Ali, Dolkar Bano (this example, brought up by several in interviews, is also described in Shakspo 1995).

Sakina is a direct and self-confident woman born into a Buddhist family of limited means. As a child, she rarely went to school—just enough to learn the alphabet, which she tells me she has now forgotten. The education of her two children motivates Sakina's life. She requested a tubal ligation at twenty-five so she could focus all her attention on her son and daughter. She spends most of her time isolated in a large city she dislikes elsewhere in the state so they can attend a better school. Sakina fell in love with her husband, a Sunni man, in the middle of the social boycott and converted. Sakina married him in 1991 and had her first child at the age of nineteen. Frank and outgoing, she candidly described the challenges she had faced, from giving birth at home, about which she says, "I never felt enough pain to go to the hospital," to her family's rejection of her marriage: "My family was angry, they were so angry. For one year, I couldn't do anything. They wouldn't even talk to me." After this time, their anger faded, but neither family offered to help them establish themselves—instead Sakina sold handicrafts and her husband worked overtime as a driver to buy a small piece of land and build their modest four-room house. Sakina uses her own life as evidence to counter the promulgation of fearful narratives of what intermarriage might lead to. Sakina told me: "Love marriage is happier. Even if you're poor, you'll support each other. With someone your parents picked for you, then if you have problems, if you suffer . . . but if you choose yourself then even if you have hard times, you still have to make an effort and stay. It's better and happier since you chose yourself. Since you chose for yourself, even in suffering there is happiness. Isn't that how it is?"

Although Sakina's family reacted with anger to her marriage, this was a new development in the family's history. Sakina had heard that in the past, "if you liked a Muslim and married with them no one would say anything."

SAKINA: That's what I've heard. We have a grandma who married a Muslim, and an aunt who married a Muslim, and another aunt who brought a Muslim as *magpa* [groom who joins the home of his bride] and he became Buddhist. In the past, there wasn't this kind of thing [the intermarriage ban]. This thing has just come up in the last fifteen or twenty years. It never was before. Because we have so many Muslim relatives. My father who passed away, his aunt. You know Dolma? That grandma is from our house. Then we have an aunt, my father's sister. She is in Shey, and her husband is a Muslim who became Buddhist. Then we have another grandma who converted to Islam. We have so many relatives.

AUTHOR: And you have *del* [relations] with them?

SAKINA: We do. We do. We invite them to our *skidsdug* [happy and sad occasions—births, weddings, and funerals] and go to theirs.

Sakina celebrates a romantic ideal of marriage and an optimistic vision of heteronormative life (Berlant 2011; Morrison et al. 2013); it is simultaneously a reorientation and redefinition of marriage as companionship, as a break from kinship, and a decision to create a different form of future orientation that does not aspire to carry on a family name. Sakina was the youngest person in a successful intermarriage with whom I spoke. When I spoke with or heard about attempts to intermarry after this time, I heard almost exclusively stories that ended in the breakup of the couple and the return of the bride to her parents' home or of the couple leaving Ladakh to live elsewhere. The exception is discussed in detail in the conclusion. I talked to Sakina about such couples. While most people say intermarriage should be blocked, she disagreed and offered a critique of the gendered ways in which the breakup of intermarriage occurs:

> Since it's their fate, why bring them back [to their parents' home]? It just makes things worse for the girl. . . . People will gossip about her and no one will marry her and it will be terrible for her. . . . If there is a Buddhist who goes with a Muslim, and they bring her back then everyone will say, "she went." . . . Then if there's a Buddhist who goes and comes back, and has a child, then it's also *dikpa* [a sin, a pathetic object of pity] for the child. . . . From the time she goes, from that time, it is totally not necessary to bring her back. She's already gone. Before she goes, you can give all the advice that you want. . . . For the man, no problem. They'll just bring another woman to be his wife. But for the woman, from the time she comes back . . . then everyone will talk behind her back. "Oh, she's one who went with a Balti." "Oh, she's one that a Kache took." "Who needs her?" If somehow she does get married, it won't be to a nice house, it will go badly for her and they won't treat her well. They will give her trouble, saying, "you're one that a Balti didn't want," or "you're one that a Kache didn't want."

I asked if it was always the woman who ended up in this *dikpa* situation, and she replied that "It's always the girl" and that this can result in them being without kin in their old age. "Then they end up going as coolies. When they get old, who will look after them? Who will give them anything? It's so difficult for them. Women are so *dikpa*." Instead, Sakina told me that intermarriage should be prevented from the beginning or that, at the least, it was the parents' responsibility to care for a woman returned after an intermarriage: "If you do bring them back, then you better build them a nice house and get them a nice *magpa* [a husband]. Or send them as a bride but really do it nicely." In the context of this sentence, *magpa* refers not only to husband but to one who is brought into the home of the bride to become part of their family lineage (rather than the bride joining his family). Sakina's wishes for runaway brides in intermarriage reveal that a practice that once could result in "relatives in the thousands" could now result in complete isolation and a loss of kin that could lead to abject abandonment.

The stories that are told about Buddhist–Muslim couples today are stories that end badly. I heard the stories of two specific young women who ended up back at home and many others who were referred to more generally. One woman was described as "wasting away," never to get married. The other woman works in a distant town, and the child that resulted from the affair is being raised by her parents. Another Buddhist–Shia couple had left the district to be together, and the woman had been completely erased from her natal family. In an interview with her mother, she began by telling me that she had two daughters. One hour into the interview, the mother mentioned a third daughter—the one who had married into the Muslim family.

Exceptions to this rule were mentioned as unfinished business: a husband who left his wife to run away and leave Ladakh with a Buddhist woman, leaving his wife and children to seek support from the Anjuman (Muslim association). In another example, Hasina and I sat on a rug in a bare courtyard with a weeping Shia grandmother, whose son-in-law had converted to Buddhism and left to become the *magpa* of a Buddhist family. We glanced at each other nervously not sure whether it had been rude to bring up this delicate matter—but she seemed eager to recite the story and its multiple injustices. The desertion was described as a surprising turn, as the grandmother, in between cuddling and scolding her daughter's toddler, mentioned repeatedly that the Buddhist woman who had walked away with her son-in-law was ordinary-looking and plain, not the trendy fashion *chokan* (someone who "does fashion") you would expect. Her surprise and anguish revealed also the tropes of interreligious love—that one is lured away by flash or glamor (or sometimes by magic—a Hindi word, *jaddu*, deployed in a tone making it impossible to discern whether this is meant lightly or seriously). We tried to comfort the grandma, awkwardly, with Hasina reassuring her that community members would right this situation and make sure that her errant son-in-law would return to took care of her, her daughter, and his child.

How to Make or Break a Marriage

> We met in Leh. He had asked another girl [to] ask about me, and my friend snuck me away [to meet him]. . . . My friend told me all about him—"he's like this, and like this." . . . You have to check people out and find out if they are really good. My friend said to go [to his village] to marry him . . . but he has four brothers and so we decided to live in Leh. (Leila)

Love marriages are described as something new and something risky. And yet the relationships between Buddhists and Muslims were formed through love marriages in the past. How do marriages happen? And how are marriages made geopolitical? The ways that marriages are understood and how this is entangled with other concerns is fundamental to the management of the geopolitical potential of the body. Thus, marriages of the past are described as arranged and orderly, even when the teller's own story is quite convoluted and begins from an introduction by friends or the appearance of a handsome man from out of town in the market. Meanwhile, marriages between young people are described as new and unruly, even though they have been quite effectively managed, to such an extent that intermarriage has been almost eradicated.

The border between a "love" marriage that starts with a glance in the market and an "arranged" marriage that begins with aunts and uncles but continues with a chaste but flirtatious picnic is quite blurry. Older women described sincerely wishing to delay marriage and hiding in upstairs rooms when the family of the boy who they would marry came to call. In other cases, women had a secret boyfriend for years and then sought the agreement of their family. Both scenarios may be presented as arranged marriages to those beyond the immediate family. In between are layers of nuance (see Pande 2014 for an overview of arranged marriage as a complex and contested concept). Arranged marriage is, of course, distinct from forced marriage in that it includes veto power on behalf of either party. Rather, it is "a mode of matchmaking in which 'a cultural logic of desire' is administered and mediated by the self and the family and where the exercise of choice and agency may be conditioned by a number of socioeconomic factors" (Pande 2014, 76, citing Del Rosario 2005, 253).

Today, men and women counterpose their own marriage stories against stories of "grandma and grandpa's time," but then again, grandma and grandpa do quite the same thing. Grandparents also allude to premarital relationships, stolen brides, and extramarital affairs. In the early twentieth century, there was likely a greater range of possible forms of marriage in Ladakh. For Ladakhi Buddhists, polyandrous marriages (marriages with two or more husbands and one wife) were widely formed until the middle of the twentieth century. They were banned in the 1940s and phased out in the 1960s and 1970s, though many have endured—my first four months in Ladakh were spent living with such a family. There were also occasional polygynous marriages, especially when the first wife did not have children, which sometimes meant bringing in a second wife (sometimes the first wife's sister). There were arranged marriages, but oral histories also suggest a fair number of marriages formed through the choices of the couple. Some Buddhist men and women never married but instead became monks or nuns.[7] Conventional wisdom on polyandry suggests that it led to the potential for "imbalance." That is, I was told that assuming equal gender ratios, if some women married two or three men, "extra" or "leftover" women would not find spouses. I was told that this meant prosperous Ladakhi Sunni Muslims in Leh Town as well as Muslim traders from outside of Ladakh might have provided these women with "temptation," that is, might have been seen as a more attractive option than remaining in the parents' home as a nun.

Women who came of age in the 1980s and earlier often describe themselves as reluctant or nervous brides or contrast their "shyness" with a perceived forwardness of young people today. But describing yourself as shy or reticent to get married has social value—refusing offers is polite evidence of good character. Due to the custom of *dzangs* (insincere refusal), everyone knows even if you have skipped a meal and your stomach is growling, you ought to refuse a plate of food several times before accepting. Part of desiring something is pretending that you do not or offering it to others. As we drank tea and snacked on cookies under a bright winter day, and after she assured me that she knew exactly who I was, Leila, a Shia farmer and housewife, began with a dismissive tone critical of love marriage: "It's runaway love marriages . . . the majority. All the young people, they just run away without asking their parents. In the past, it was bringing tea, promising wealth, pleasing the parents—otherwise no one would go. Now, what, where they come from . . . no one even finds out! You just hear, 'he ran away' or 'she ran away.' There's such a change. It's all runaways."

And yet, when I asked Leila about her own marriage in the early 1980s, she described not one but two love marriages. She chose her first spouse, divorced him, and then chose a second husband, to whom she remained happily married. The thing that she identifies as a change (runaway love marriages) is closer to her own personal experience, but she locates it not in her own past but in the present. This playing with time will be elaborated on in the next chapter.

Arranged marriages are described as tradition, as providing stability, and evidence of a familial future-looking love of parents who desire their children to be cared for and happy. Parents' research to find an ideal partner is understood both as status-driven and as an act of affection. Both of these are reflected in the Leh saying that parents should marry a child into a family with "a house beneath the palace, and fields beneath the irrigation pond" (*kar-i yokne khangpa, dzing-i yokne zhing*). Arranged marriages provide women with a safety net—that is, if the marriage did not work out, parents were at fault and the bride could return home and demand they provide for her. Though this is the pervading logic, women do also return home to their parents from love marriages. I have been told it is more difficult for women to remarry, but I also know women from every generation who have remarried after a love marriage ended in divorce.

Atiya, a practical and energetic Shia woman who looked much younger than her forty-five years, explained the idealized version of a marriage in which the bride is *tiste*, and the couple is *thonte*, that is, the bride has been inquired about and formally requested in marriage (*tiste*), and both spouses have matured in the sense of being on a career path with relative independence (*thonte*). She said:

> It's better to go *tiste*. Where, if they just run away, if they don't go *thonte*, if they haven't finished their studies . . . he might abandon them. If it's done through the parents, it will turn out better. What do we know? If once she's there, if the family turns out to be good or bad? What will happen? What will not happen? If the mother and father are good? . . .

It's the rest of your life, it will be difficult if you don't look before you go. Then after having one or two children, if you get divorced, it will be difficult.

Today both parties are assumed to have veto power over prospective suitors, often after meeting in public places to get to know each other. In the case of Sunni and Shia marriages, in which marriages between cousins are possible, the prospective bride and groom often know each other already and say yes or no based on that knowledge. It is increasingly common for marriages to be what I would term "post-arranged." In these marriages, a couple has been going out clandestinely or discovers they like one another through a more fleeting set of interactions. They then seek the approval of their marriage. The families communicate directly or through intermediaries and agree that the marriage should go ahead. The agency in relation to choosing a partner, however, has a very clearly defined limit: marriage across the religious line (and also at times other lines of class, occupation, and caste). Marriage is about coming and going and is discussed in such terms. *Bakma khyongches* is to bring a bride, meaning to bring a bride into the home of the groom, at which point she becomes part of the groom's family. *Magpa khyongches*, bringing a groom, is also a possibility, in which case the groom becomes part of the bride's family.

The Intermarriage Ban

In January 2015, the LBA wrote a letter to India's (then) new prime minister, Narendra Modi, accusing local Muslims of waging "love jihad": a campaign of religious conversion through marriage, in the words of the LBA secretary Sonam Dawa, "luring Buddhist girls" and converting them to Islam (Ashiq 2015; Ul-Qamrain 2015). This was a public declaration of local political narratives that had been in force since the social boycott of the late 1980s into the national language of Hindu nationalism. The phrase "love jihad," deployed for the first time in the public record in Ladakh in 2015, has been used across India since at least 2009 to denote a supposed campaign of demographic aggression on the part of India's Muslims: conversion through interreligious love marriages accompanied by conversion to Islam (C. Gupta 2009; Mohan 2011).[8] Veena Das (2010) has written of how the love jihad trope is entangled in the gendered violence of partition and need to police women's sexuality, and this kind of trope is one form of the kind of demographic fever dream that animates right-wing politics globally (Gökariksel et al. 2019).

Twenty years after its inception, the ban on intermarriage is discussed as something that protects peace or disrupts it, as the result of education, or as the result of moral degradation. Mohammad, a seventy-seven-year-old father of six, described the shift:

MOHAMMAD: At that time, the relationship was really very nice. There was no reason to say *Boto* [Buddhist] and *Kache* [Sunni Muslim]. There were a few Boto girls who would marry Kaches, and so on. And then if it was written on their fate, some Boto girls would convert after marrying. That is fate. Like me, I had younger and older brothers. That fate was written on one brother's head, and he converted to Buddhism. He has three or four children now. Like what happens today, when they say, "Oh, he converted, she converted," and try to block it, then we didn't have that. At that time there was nothing, it was fine: if today a Boto girl was brought to a Kache house, tomorrow they would take tea to celebrate the marriage. There was nothing to say, don't drink, don't eat. We totally would not say that.

AUTHOR: That change, when did it happen?

MOHAMMAD: At the agitation. At that time, they said, our neighbors said, there is a boycott. They said they are going to boycott us. And then, our relatives, Buddhist relatives, if something happens to them, even if something happened, like a death, they wouldn't come since there was a boycott. . . .

AUTHOR: In your opinion, why did that conflict and boycott happen?

MOHAMMAD: Because of religion. Because of the Boto girls going with Kaches, they made a disturbance. At that time, they also set houses on fire.

When asked if it would be all right if a son or daughter married someone of another religion, the answer was almost unanimously no, even for those who had themselves done the same. Reasons for opposing intermarriage are far from uniform. For some, it is concern about religious practices itself: some Muslims object to or fear cremation; some Buddhists criticize sacrifice as a religious practice or make reference to Muslims killing animals as butchers (though most Buddhist families are not vegetarian and rely on Muslim butchers for the meat they purchase). Buddhist women might point to differences of ethical and religious belief that could not be accommodated within a Muslim household, saying that to be born into a Buddhist human life is a precious gift that must not be wasted. Others praised both religions, but it was emphasized that a Muslim or a Buddhist could not fully practice their religion without a family to support that faith or will not be able to develop their religious practice to the fullest extent because they will start from scratch on conversion. Referring to my marriage into a Buddhist family, one young Buddhist woman explained: "To marry Kache or Balti, it's better not to do it. It's better to stay in your own religion. And our Buddhists, if they become Muslim, they have to learn the religion from the very beginning. For that reason, it's like education. They have to be taught. For instance, just like you had to learn. For that reason, it is difficult."

These references to religious practice itself were scattered. More often, those I interviewed discussed the avoidance of interreligious marriages today in

reference to the possibility of interreligious violence and conflict and suggested that something as trivial as a love affair is not worth risking an end to
what is perceived as a fragile and contingent peace. Literacy and education
often come up in reference to the Buddhist–Muslim conflict, and this was
sometimes tied to intermarriage as well, with some, like Mehdi, saying, "Now
they don't allow those kinds of marriages. In the past they did. . . . Now that we
have more literate people and we understand our religion, we do not do that."
A young Nurbakshi woman, married to a Sunni Muslim, described herself as
having Buddhist relatives in her grandparents' generation and said that her
husband's relatives "are all Boto." I asked her whether intermarriage continued today:

RABIA: Today, there's nothing like that. Not at all. Maybe there might be one or
    two, who went way over the mountains and stayed there for years before
    coming back. Then when they come back, the word doesn't really get out.
    Otherwise they will just start a demonstration immediately.

AUTHOR: Why?

RABIA: They say that the Boto girls are going to run out. And the Kache girls. If
    the Botos convert to Kache and the Kache convert to Boto, then, that being
    the case, then that will be the end. That's what they say. This started with
    the *phasad* [disturbance], with the agitation.

AUTHOR: For instance, do you have any friends who have intermarried?

RABIA: No, I don't know anyone like that. In the past, there must be many like
    that, before the *phasad* there would have been many like that.

AUTHOR: Is it better to prevent or allow such marriages?

RABIA: It's better to prevent it. There will be a protest.

Hasina, a fifty-six-year-old Sunni woman, had a similar response: "If there
will be a demonstration, it's better to prevent such marriages. If there weren't to
be a demonstration, then just let them come, no problem." She added, "In the
other path [the afterlife], then we find out whose religion was what. Then we'll
understand. Now, immediately they do a demonstration, saying all kinds of
things." Atiya suggested that Buddhists would protest a marriage but that Muslims would be reluctant to do so because of their minority status: "No one says
anything. Us, we won't say anything, not at all, whatever happens, even if they
go. . . . We Muslims, we totally don't do protests. Among them, they always protest. If one girl goes, then they just sweep together everyone from the whole *yul*
[village] to do a protest."

Others add the idea of balance, thinking of religious identity as an equation. Jameela repeats the idea that intermarriage should be prevented to keep
demonstrations from breaking out but also adds, "Then our own community will

last, if we don't bring from outside. Then there's the danger of what will happen to our women. It's better to just stay in your own *choslugs* [sect]." Like Jameela, Nilza is in her fifties, a Buddhist, and speaks of balancing the population of marriageable women: "It's better for it to be blocked. Because if a Kache marries a Boto, then there will be a leftover Kache girl, who won't find a boy. And that's an obstacle. That's difficult. If each one stays in their own religion and marries in their own religion, there won't be arguments, there won't be *dikpa* [sin]."

Zainab's opinion about intermarriage was ambiguous. She said ideally people should stay in their own religion, especially if there was to be interference, but added:

> If they are going to please themselves, you can't stop it. If we block it, that doesn't come in religion. To make a *pasad* [disturbance] over a Muslim girl being taken or a Buddhist girl being brought, they do all kinds of things. From that, that's when the *pasad* happens. What? We are all from one country. If they go for themselves, if they decide, there's nothing that we can do. And it's not in Shariat either . . . if they've gone for themselves. If they're pleased themselves. If you bring them back, they'll go again. They will meet again. There are those who were meant to meet. If you bring a Buddhist here, they do all kinds of things. There are those who have come.

Class is an undercurrent in discussions about the regulation of intermarriage. Several people suggested that it is those who have the highest social standing who are the most carefully policed. They told me that the children of elite politicians and aristocrats would never be allowed to run away but that those of lower economic standing or those who are from Mon or Beda families might attract less attention. Beda and Mon are the small population of Buddhists in Ladakh who are deemed low caste and continue to face discrimination despite campaigns against caste by the Dalai Lama and others. Parallel is the judgment on those who do run away with someone of another religion as likely coming from supposedly less desirable families. Angmo, a Buddhist woman in her sixties, transitioned easily from talking about religion to class and moral values: "Isn't it better to stay in your own religion? Their Kache religion is good, our *Nangpai* [Buddhist, insider] religion is good. Each person's own religion is precious to them. To stay in your own place, that's good. Those who will go, will go. Those without, those who are poor, they will go. Those who are good will never go. It's those who have nothing, whom no one is taking as a bride, they are the ones who will go."

Nizam, though he has a wide network of Buddhist relatives, suggests both a critique of caste and provocation on the part of the Buddhists. Dha Hanu, referenced below, is a region in the west of Ladakh with distinct cultural practices:

> I think that law is mainly for rich families. For instance, that guy went with a woman from Dha Hanu, and nobody says anything about that. And

also if a Muslim takes a Beda or a Mon, nobody talks about it. It is only when someone takes the daughter of a rich family that there is a big clamor. So, I think that it is just that people want to create conflict. For example, within the Buddhists, there are so many Muslims. So, despite the fact that we have so many women, some of them just marry Buddhists. So, among Buddhists, despite the fact that there are so many women [for Buddhist men to marry], they just pick one of our women. I think some people, they do it just to create conflict. We have women in our own community, so what's the point of getting married to someone from the other community? In the past, we call it *skyongstotu, wagsumtotu*. That means that in the past, all the families in Leh were under the palace, all 120 of them. People were very nice, there were only Ladakhis in the past. Now we have people from all over the world. So, do not even think that things will get better and better. Things will get worse and worse I think.

Nizam's reflections here nuance the discussion of intermarriage regulation, by weaving it into a broader conversation about economic class and caste and then layering a broader set of concerns about dissolution: "there were only Ladakhis in the past. Now we have people from all over the world." In his rendering, even though he began by celebrating living together across difference, he ends by suggesting that ethnic difference will lead to conflict.

Roots Remain under the Surface

Looking at the past, [the agreement to prevent intermarriage] really does not look like a good thing, does it? People used to get married in different communities. That creates harmony. Saying "these people are bad" or "those people are bad," it's really bad. In the past, we did not have that kind of thing. . . . Everyone follows the same god whether it is Buddha or Jesus. Now there are fights saying "this is good," "that is good." In the past, there was none of this. But these days people say, "yours is not good, our religion is better."

Mary, quoted above, is a member of one of the few hundred Christian families in Leh, descendants of Ladakhis who were converted by Moravian missionaries in the nineteenth century. Christians comprise 0.5 percent of Leh District's population according to the 2011 census. They experienced some incidents of discrimination during the social boycott, including a bomb planted in a Christian household after the marriage and conversion of a Buddhist Ladakhi into the home (Devadas 1988).

Several people disagreed with the LBA–LMA agreement to prevent intermarriage. Still others agreed in principle but also insisted that desire is an unstoppable force. Spalzes, a Buddhist woman in her seventies, summed up many of these narratives when she said, "I think it's better to just let them go. If they want to go, just let them go. What can we do? There's no point in stopping their life." The trope of unstoppable love was a common one in the interviews, for instance, when Amina spoke about her daughter:

AMINA: That wouldn't feel right. As much as possible, I would tell her not to go. Then, if she insisted on going, there would be nothing I could do. There are no parents that would tell a girl to go—whether it's a Buddhist or a Muslim, they would never say yes, go [with the person of another religion]. No one would give their child like that. But if the child themselves insists they will go, then there is nothing that you can do about it.

AUTHOR: Right, there's those who are brought back and run away again.

AMINA: That's right, it's in the child's hands. Isn't it the case where a Buddhist goes with a Muslim and her family takes her back, but then later she just goes away again. There's nothing you can do.

Morrison et al. (2013) ask: "what does love do?" Being fated to fall in love is an escape from societal norms and political expediency. Fate was often referenced in discussions about the possibility of intermarriage, as in Atiya's and Bano's opinions, below:

ATIYA: If they are pleased themselves, just let them go. If their own hearts are happy, then there's nothing anyone can do, is there? If today you like someone, then can anyone stop you? It's their own *takdir*, it's their own fate. There are those who go, even from Muslims there are those who go. No one says anything, there's nothing anyone can say. Whatever is written on your forehead, that's yours. You're the owner of your own self and your own fate.

BANO: If they block it, that also looks good. If you think about the *pasad*, it's better to block it. What if it starts a *pasad*? Rather than that, isn't it better to prevent it? If you can. You know what they say, that this is written in the lines on our forehead [fate]. If it's written there, then there's nothing you can do to keep them from going. They'll run away. After marrying another, they'll abandon him and run away again. It happens like that. Otherwise, ideally if they pay attention to their own religion and stay in their own, that is better.

A Sunni grandfather in Chushot told me about his grandchild, "If I'm thinking that I am going to prevent this child from being a Buddhist, and I think I can tie him up and keep him, with his fate, he will escape from the window. That's how it is. It's our fate; it is what is written on our foreheads." In another interview, Hamida said, "if they fall in love, what can we do?" At that point, her sister interrupted her to point out that people would cause a disturbance in such a case, and Hamida said, "Even if they do, the couple will run away anyway, since they are in love." I asked what would happen if her young daughter, playing nearby, fell in love with a Buddhist—but this question only produced laughter and a muted "who knows?"

As we will return to in the next chapter, in discussions about marriage these days, there is the assumption that love marriage is on the rise and an attendant flurry of concerns around this practice. Women's descriptions of such concerns are gendered, often revealing an implicit critique of the ways that women's lives are hurt by their own impulsive behavior. Yet this can also be read as a folding of time in order to make it fit a coherent narrative.

The Threshold: Making Home and Homeland

The movement of bodies between Buddhist and Muslim families echoes the language of marriage in the Ladakhi context (bringing, going, coming, taking), and when a woman went into a new household, she usually, though not in all circumstances, took on the household religion. When people tell the story of the breakdown of close Buddhist–Muslim relationships, they resort to metaphors and examples that draw on family, food, and bodily imagery: "we were like brothers," "we ate from one plate," "we were like one person." As they do so, they evoke qualitative change over time in such a way that seems to evacuate individual responsibility. Economic change, salaried employment, women in the workforce, incorporation into a neoliberal economic sphere, and other events make it possible to tell the story in this manner. But what does it mean that the stories of eating from one plate continue to be told?

On the day that I first met Nizam, I visited his house with Tonyot. Nizam's son and daughter-in-law prepared endless small plates of food and cups of tea while Nizam told us stories about his youth and about close relations between Buddhists and Muslims. At the same time, if his grandchild was to send text messages or meet up clandestinely with the grandchild of one of those late-night Buddhist dinner guests, the families would be anxious and eager to prevent that flirtation from forming a new bond between both families. In this context, what does it mean to be related? What are the implications of marking the occasions of marriages, births, and deaths together with relatives and friends of a different religion? Does crossing the threshold of the home enact a particular set of political and geopolitical relationships? Affective, emotional, and material flows open and close homes and bodies to the possibility of connection. As political projects foreclose the capacity to be related but different, narratives of lineage, heritage, and connection continue to circulate and have become part of the conventional reading of Buddhist–Muslim history in Ladakh. This taken-for-granted past is read not in opposition to today's more agonistic relations but rather as a closed-off place, impossible to visit any longer. What is thought-provoking about these materializations of territory, which I argue are more than metaphorical, is the manner in which bodily invocations of the territorial are spoken of to celebrate a (perhaps exaggerated) past in which there was greater intimacy between Buddhist and Muslim Ladakhis, even as practices that unlink bodies are deemed necessary.

Like Nizam, Spalzes has Muslim relatives as well as friends. She tells me that before the social boycott, her house was "full of Muslims," visiting for Losar and other festivals, but now, "they only come for the most crucial things, like marriage, birth, and death ceremonies. In the past they used to come more often." In Sara Ahmed's (2004, 6) terms, "emotions operate to 'make' and 'shape' bodies as forms of action, which also involve orientations toward others." There is a geopolitical story to be told in Leh about affection for family members and the relative openness of a home as an indicator for the bounding of territory, but this story is woven into a fabric of other concerns with spatial and temporal dimensions. Bodies and homes are contingent assemblages of material objects, flows, and life. Territory is part of this story but does not determine it completely.

In Nizam's lifetime, India freed itself from British rule and upon obtaining that freedom, was fractured into India and Pakistan. Like many, Nizam has relatives whom he now cannot visit because they live across the Line of Control, in Pakistan. As the ground beneath his feet was soldered in new ways to the emergent state, political shifts began to echo these territorial transformations. The permeability of homes and bodies was reoriented. As the national border separating Nizam from his relatives who now lived in Pakistan became impenetrable, the thresholds of homes were likewise crossed less frequently by those of other religions. These changes were woven into, and in some cases obscured by, changes in the other threads in the fabric of society. As a young man with an eighth-grade education, Nizam was sought out by a government officer, who pleaded for him to become a teacher. Nizam declined the position as the remote village he would be sent to was inconvenient, and he wanted to stay in Leh. Today, hundreds of young men and women compete for such a position. Those of Nizam's generation are eager to point out other changes as well—that the pace of life has quickened. This changing sense of the temporal enables particular arguments to be made that evacuate responsibility for the politicization of religion and the breakdown of social ties, laying blame at the feet of time itself. So many things have changed in the course of a few lifetimes, and so much of it seems beyond the agency of any one individual. Why or how, then, could neighbors and relatives push against the swell of time that seemed to make intimacy across religion so difficult? Why push against a tide that is felt to be sweeping everyone into a time of work, television, and atomized lives, with less interaction between neighbors as only one among a catalogue of small and incremental changes that add to the dissolution of close and tight bonds?

Spalzes and her friends will also tell you that they have less time for socialization of all kinds, that neighbors drop by less frequently, and that nowadays people hardly have time to talk on the phone. Those I spoke with often said that these days the family and home is formed in a more haphazard fashion, as young people run away with one another and bring home a bride or groom of their own choosing, without considering how that person will meet the needs of the family. The process of creating a functioning family, a home, is also complicated by economic and social changes that include a shifting Buddhist–Muslim relationship as one crucial aspect. Many concerns about home and family emerge: love marriage, atomized family structures in which no one is home to care for children. For students who failed their tenth class exams, the crucial exam determining future education and job prospects, home is a place one ends up when other hopes have failed.

Time, like an earthquake, fissures the ground underfoot, creating the sense of an inevitable turn from leisure and community to fast-paced and individualistic life, a life in which you do not have time to have tea with your neighbors and the complications of building a relationship between the families of a Buddhist and Muslim appear insurmountable. Perversely, perfectly, the past is evoked as a simpler time and young people today are described as a source of conflict—but in the next chapter the voices of young people themselves complicate this telling.

Blunt and Dowling draw our attention to how the place and spatial imaginary of home is productive of identity, "whereby people's senses of themselves are related to and produced through lived and metaphorical experiences of home. These identities and homes are, in turn, produced and articulated through relations of power" (Blunt and Dowling 2006, 256; see also Blunt 2005). Home is multiscalar—existing as a place but also as an idea that travels, that is co-constitutive with the national idea. The making of home imaginaries can be part of both inclusion and exclusion, reification of difference and the creation of intimacy. As "an idea and an imaginary that is imbued with feelings" (Blunt and Dowling 2006, 2), home is more than a house or a structure. It can also be read as an "*orientation* to the fundamental values" (Bunkśe 2004, 101; Bachelard 1994). Making home in the house for the "other" may or may not signal making political space for that other at the level of the nation or jurisdiction.

Even as intimacy breaks down across the religious border, there is a continued celebration of Buddhist–Muslim relationships in the stories that people tell about the past and an insistence on the wild and ungovernable nature of youthful desire. While acknowledging the deterioration of relationships, many claim their own families or neighbors to be exceptions to this deterioration, like Abdul, a Sunni man in his eighties: "Even now, the relationship is good. With the people who are related to my family and me, it is still very good. Especially those who are Buddhist related to Muslims or Muslims related to Buddhists. I cannot speak for others, but those who are related, for us, we have good relationships. We take care of them and they take care of us . . . for us, the relationship is very good, even as it was in the past. But today there are some young people, and they are reckless."

The orientation of bodies and homes is described as being fundamentally altered by the political events of the 1980s but also by time itself, as though that time had acted on the space of homes and bodies—there is a tendency to invoke an irreversible temporal shift away from a time when the Ladakhi kings married across religious lines and toward one in which such alliances are dangerous.

Conclusion

The stories of Mary, of Nizam with Buddhist relatives in the thousands, and those to follow indicate tight links between body, home, and territory. Homes are made through negotiation. In Ladakh, most homes continue to be built around a marriage: the mother and father, *ama-le* and *aba-le*. This bond links two families, and relations ripple out from this bond in widening circles of care and responsibility. While a bond of marriage is often formed through happenstance—a young man seeing a young woman on the bus, a woman introduced to one of her cousin's friends—most Ladakhis describe an arranged or semi-arranged marriage as ideal. The collection of information before that bond is formed is assumed to increase the chances of a marriage's success because the couple will be suitable and the families will be of similar social standing and in agreement about the marriage.

As homes became bounded, so too did the borders of bodies. Since the end of the social boycott, the enforced restrictions on these interactions have been lifted, though they may linger as habit or as a shift in the orientation of bodies (turning away from a shop because of the religion of its owner or toward the shop of someone who shares your religious beliefs). These homemaking practices were and are fraught with political and class dimensions. Kitchens and formal occasions involve seating guests by rank, with the most respected and oldest guests given the most prestigious seats. China, rugs, the choice of biscuits all indicate financial status. Thus, they mark difference even as they bind and attach. Talking about change over time, women today both lament social changes that they see as divisive and celebrate ascension to a more middle-class lifestyle.

As these narratives of love and care, separation and tragedy indicate, romantic love, familial love, and the love between friends and neighbors contain counter-geopolitical intimacies (Marshall 2014), but these are not foolproof. During the social boycott, Buddhists lamented their failure to make bread as tasty as the *balti tagi*, but they walked past Muslim shops so that they could give their rupees to a Buddhist shopkeeper. Some of these feelings linger today:

AUTHOR: Nowadays, if you look at Balti, Boto, and Kache, what's the relationship like?

DOLKAR: Since the past, like the past, that kind of good relationship, we don't have it anymore. We're not close like in the past. In the past, we were really, really close. Now in everyone's heart, there's this thing, that's a Kache store, I won't go there, since it is Kache, I'll go to a Boto store. Now all the children and young people, they think like that. In the past, it was just like family members, that's what everyone says.

Dolkar echoes a widely held assumption that today's young people are more volatile and hold more divisive views of interreligious relationships; this perception is also part of a metanarrative that enables conflict and tension to be marked as part of time itself—to be held as an inescapable though regrettable component of modernity. Paradoxically, however, young people I work with today challenge this reading of history. They express regret for interreligious divisions, which they attribute to actions taken by their parents and grandparents, and paradoxically place their hopes in their own generation, even as their parents look to them with anxiety. It is to these young people that I now turn in the next chapter.

Some kinds of fabric, once cut, can be nearly impossible to mend. If part of the strength of these relationships was the ways that they had been strengthened through the enmeshment created by endless cups of tea and plates of rice and meat carried home late in the night after a long party, what happens when those Muslim grandmas or Buddhist grandpas grow old but no new marriages across that divide have been built?

5

Raising Children on the Threshold of the Future

It is the end of a hectic day, and a talkative group of children and young people, from eight to their early twenties, are crowded around a laptop. We are in the Ladakh Arts and Media Organization Center, at the historic Munshi house. The building is carefully restored, with fawn-colored mud-brick walls, carefully laid poplar beams and willow twig ceilings; this meticulous restoration feels forward-looking as a backdrop to paintings, ceramics, and other art installations by local young artists and international visitors.[1] The rooftop courtyard and balconies look down to Leh Town below and the Indus River and then the Stok Kangri mountain range beyond.

The young people have spent the day taking photographs in small groups. Now they are explaining the images while friends and neighbor kids interject with their own interpretations. Some of the photos are staged for effect and telegraph their meaning clearly: the littlest kids who wanted to tag along have been asked to pose, first as child laborers holding shovels and pretending to build a road, and then diligently studying while they sit on a stone wall, swinging their legs and smirking. The teenage director of the photographs explains that he wants a future in which all children go to school rather than laboring. In other photos, a smiling young woman poses by what they describe as an "old fashioned" woodstove with the hat and *bok* (satin cape) that is intended to signal "tradition," and then in a T-shirt while lighting a gas range. Most homes have both—a functional and decorative stove of clay and metal that burns wood and cow dung and a range that uses compressed natural gas canisters. Though nowadays people primarily use the gas stoves, depending on generation, season, occasion, and weather, both could be in play. The same group has had four of the younger girls pose in their mothers' hats and colorful satin *bok*: their message here is that Ladakhis should preserve their beautiful cultural traditions. In the light of these narratives—rapid change, decisions about the future—we arrive at the next pair of photographs.

Stanzin has posed with Leh Town in the background. He is smiling in a heather gray Calvin Klein knock-off sweatshirt and a red hat—the letters USA visible over an obscured logo. Behind him, we see the houses of old town nestled together and the roof of a Buddhist temple. In the next photo, we see a *meme-le*, or grandpa, wearing what everyone recognizes as *meme-le* clothes: the maroon *kos*, a handspun and handwoven wool robe that reaches the knees, a charcoal and white hat from local wool, and a thick coat (in summer). He is holding a walking stick and wearing faded blue sneakers. Everyone has a meme-le like this in their family—or several. This seems immediately interpretable, and Stanzin is soft-spoken, so other children begin calling out suggestions: Stanzin is the future, "our youth," "modern," and *meme-le* represents the past. Stanzin interrupts: "no, this is me in the present. But in the future, I will be like *meme-le*, that's the meaning."

The conversation continues, and it is only later, when I see the photos paired on the wall at the exhibition, that I begin to contemplate them more. Why did we—the students who called out, and me as well—see Stanzin's baseball cap and big smile and think "future" and immediately place *meme-le* in the past? After all, we were all right there in what was the present. Why do we play these tricks with time and space, and what do they accomplish? Why did none of us guess that when Stanzin saw *meme-le*, he saw his own future—that he was imagining a future of continuity, in which he became like his own parents and then grandparents? Instead, attention had almost exclusively focused on change—sometimes using the word *gyurja* (change, development), sometimes using English words like "modern." When a young man took a picture of two young women in skinny jeans and sweatshirts holding notebooks, he explained that this is what "modern girls" are like: stylish, studious. Here, his tone was clearly admiring. Yet this is also the team that posed younger girls in *bok*; the valuation of studious women in skinny jeans and the importance of local fashion is not in conflict but complementary. In this chapter, people young and old play with time to do political and cultural work, often by projecting people and events backward or forward in time.

Our preconceptions about Stanzin's image were cut from the same fabric as the daily conversations about "young people these days," around kitchen tables and in the meeting rooms of nongovernmental organizations, women's groups, and religious associations. Such organizations in Leh organize awareness camps on religion, on the environment, on entrepreneurship. These events are for and about young people, but they are also future talk. Who are young people becoming? What does that mean for Ladakh? I had heard rumors that young people educated outside Ladakh could no longer speak Ladakhi properly, while English and Hindi flowed fluently between them. Were they really studying out in Jammu or Chandigarh? Or were they just "doing fashion," doing drugs, and sleeping around? These concerns were expressed both in reference to parents' children and more broadly in relation to "our young people" as a category. When I started working more with young people in earnest, their narratives complicated the stories and interpretations that I had been accustomed to hearing from their parents and grandparents. While I had heard young people described as a source of volatility and conflict, they spoke at length about their hopes for a peaceful Ladakh and their organic friendships across religious (though not necessarily class) difference. I had heard about young people frittering away time and money; young people described, yes, having fun with friends but also struggling to manage household expenses, learning how to make their own dal and *tagi shramo* (chapatis), and coming to respect their parents from a distance. This chapter will work through the kinds of future talk that play out in the ways that young people are spoken of across generations and how young people become an object of concern. In the discussion that follows, attention will turn more directly toward these young people's own lived experience.

Young people are a lens through which both older generations and young people themselves read the future of the region. Adults place or displace past violent incidents onto the young people of today, figuring youth as chaotic and unruly in ways that make past ways of life impossible. The ways in which people envision the future also shapes how they understand the category of youth across time and space (Anagnost 2008; Ansell et al. 2017; Botterill et al. 2018; Cheng 2014; Fong 2011; Jeffrey 2010; Lukose 2009; Nayak 2003). Following the premises of intimate geopolitics, if territory is lived, experienced, and enacted through the body, if bodies are geopolitical, what does that mean for young people? Their bodies and lives are the bridge connecting the territorial configurations of today with those of the future. Bodies, as laid out in the introduction, both become a proxy site of struggle and experience and make geopolitical strategy through their daily lives. While they decide whether they want to be a graphic designer or a doctor or whether they scramble to obtain a living by piecing together handicrafts, running a shop, or turning to the tourist industry as a fallback, whether they fall in love on accident or intentionally ask their parents to find them a spouse, young people are inhabiting a contested geopolitical realm. Their lives are entangled with the afterlives of colonial categories that constructed and weaponized identity, historic flows of trade and life across Central Asia, the vagaries of neoliberal capitalism, and the secular aspirations and contentious nationalisms of independent India (Lowe 2015; Stoler 2013).

Conversations about young people reflected political tensions around religious identity. Everyone has heard of a college student who was secretly dating someone of the wrong religion in a faraway town with parents none the wiser. But this is only one among many anxieties swirling around young people: parents want to see themselves in their children, but not precisely. Jigmet, a schoolteacher like her mother, had told me that even though she had obtained what many view as a golden ticket—a stable government job with a pension—she felt she had let her mother down by taking up the same work as her mother, by not going further professionally. Parents work to provide for their children and do political and cultural work so that their children can build a world that is recognizable but not identical. Anxiety and nostalgia hover around both past and future, and when parents tell their children about the future, they tell them about themselves. How do we talk to children about the past? What signals do they receive?

In conversation about communal tensions of the 1980s and 1990s, parents of college-going youth told me that young people start fights, young people cause political divisions. Of course, I did not make the connection right away: the people telling me this story were young people during the height of Buddhist–Muslim conflict. But were they blaming their own young selves? That is not the way I heard them: in their stories, the possibility of violence lay with young people today. What does the category of young people allow for? Is youth a liminal space stretching the possibilities of moral codes? A scapegoat for societal ills? A vector into which to channel our future-oriented panic?

Time in this way is fluid and foldable, fashioned to support the story being told about a place that might have existed or might exist in the future. I have written elsewhere about what parents and community leaders say about young people and will revisit that briefly here. But this chapter not only considers what is said about young people but also begins to engage with what they hear and how they enact, refuse, or mess around with these messages. These refusals, evasions, compliances, and playful acts will be centered in the next chapter of this book. If the future of place and territory is lived and embodied, what futures do young people envision and embody in the present? What is their future talk about? Parents and community leaders try to manage the future by orienting young people to one another and to the world, but this guidance is entangled in the messiness of embodied life, economic pressures, and societal change.

Raising Territorial Youth

A few years before Stanzin told us that *meme-le* was his future, I was with another group of young people, sitting around in our upstairs guest room, drinking sweet tea and Fanta and eating potato chips and dried apricots. The young women wore everything from T-shirts and jeans to elegant *salwar kameez* with headscarf. They had one by one sat next to one another while the young men (each one in jeans and a T-shirt) filed in on the other side of the room. This becomes more apparent when I see the picture that Tonyot took and realize it is impossible to see that the group is mixed gender in one photograph. The inclination to sit apart does not affect their immediate willingness to talk across to one another, though a few of the boys are reticent relative to the girls. These young people have interviewed an older relative or family member and taken photographs as well. Now we have a conversation about what they have learned. It starts out a little stilted. Rahima, poised and clear spoken in a T-shirt and stylish jeans, began.

"We've interviewed old woman and an old man, about seventy-five and above. We've learned many things, about how they interact with people, about the relationship between Buddhists and Muslims." Rahima's friend continues, "I spoke to an aunt and an uncle, and learned things I didn't know."

While those of their parents' and grandparents' generation often launched into their life stories with alacrity at the first question, young people were often shy, unsure if their knowledge counted or not, unwilling to deem themselves experts, even on their own life experience. By the time we get around the circle to two young men who attend school together and did the project as a team, the second young man said only, "I went with Abdul and I think the same." I was getting nervous. Students take time to voice their opinions, usually waiting until one or two who are more outspoken begin. On this day, that was Ladol[2] and then Rahima, both of whom breached the subtext of the conversation, causing a third young woman to chime in and the conversation to take on a life of its own. I note the terms they use—*Boto* for Buddhist, rather than the also used *nangpa*. *Boto* is the term for Buddhist Ladakhis as a legal category in the state—one of the Scheduled Tribes. *Kache* is commonly used for Muslims broadly, but its use is complicated by its hint of place-based identity—Kashmiris are *Kachulpa* in Ladakhi.

Ladol begins: "The relationship between Buddhists and Muslims, it's like this. Myself, I went to Islamia [the best-regarded Sunni private school] since I was young. Since I was in their school, I didn't have this feeling, that I am *Boto*, and they are *Kache*. So, for me, I don't have this negative feeling, saying they are like this. That being the case, for me, I have a good relationship."

Rahima spoke immediately, reflecting on the experience of interviewing elders: "In school, they will give us just bookish knowledge. This kind of practical experience, we will remember it more."

LADOL: It's not that, it's that in this interview, we learned about Ladakh. We are always chatting about Indian history or world history. That's what it is. And Ladakhi history, they are not covering it. Ladakhi history, we never studied, and we never took it so seriously as we took it at this time, because it was really good for us.

As the discussion went on, students begin repeating the explanations they had heard for interreligious tensions.

LADOL: I mean, how do I know? I was born in 1989. And I hadn't really heard until now about the boycott, so I can't say that much, but I do think this is all because of politics. If people say that we have good relations, but I think that from one side, they might still be afraid. What I think is that what people tell us, it's not 100 percent true. Because they must be scared about what or whom we might tell. So we can't say this is 100 percent true.

As the conversation developed, students began to lament that they had not learned about the very local history of religious relations—with some students learning about the 1989–1992 social boycott only during these interviews. They mention the rumors: that everything spread from one fistfight. That conflict was all about politics, meaning the pursuit of individual political power, not for a larger goal. But they also expressed uncertainty: "I mean, how do I know?"

If they had not learned the past, they wondered, how were they to know how to live together in the future? But, of course, we all are learning the past; this education is just not always articulated to us as such. Who is at the dinner table? Who is on the television screen? Where is danger located in the gossip at home or on the street or in the fairy tale? If this place as territory was being lived and embodied by successive generations of young people growing up and acting on the knowledge passed down by their parents and grandparents, how were they taught to interact? Who were they intended to be in relation to their families and the shifting ideals of the rapidly changing town in which they were growing up? While parents were reluctant to talk about the religious conflict that they grew up enmeshed in, and schools focused on India and the world as the sites of real importance, young people were putting together their own sense of self and their embodied orientations toward multiplicitous Others (S. Ahmed 2004). They did this through fragmented conversations, through noticing the implications of the stories told around the stove at dinner. They did this in moments of correction or stories intended as a warning: "don't wear your scarf like that, you look like a Muslim"; "after her romance with the Muslim, she ended up back at her parents' home with the child—have you seen her now? So skinny, it's so sad."

Rahima and Ladol were vocal and animated talking about how things ought to be in present tense, even when acknowledging that this is not how things are. Rahima's mother was a Buddhist who had converted upon marriage to a Muslim, and Ladol had spent a great deal of time with her converted Muslim aunt in Chushot. Rahima reiterated a common storyline: "Now, if a Muslim boy, if a Buddhist girl, if she goes with him, then everyone beats up that boy. The girl's family, it's not just them, but everyone puts pressure on that family, saying you can't let her go, you have to bring her back. But whatever happens, however much they bring her back, in the end, she will end up going to be with that boy. Otherwise, unless she ends up going, things will never be okay. For that reason, it makes more sense if they just say it's okay from the beginning."

Here she describes Leh today: a space in which religious boundaries are carefully enforced through such separations. In talking us through these scenarios,

Rahima suddenly and easily flipped her own religious identity, with a spark in her eyes. She began, "Because it's my life, say I am a Buddhist, it's my personal life. If like this, if we are modern, religion doesn't matter today. But it's society, they will say that this person is doing this or that person is doing that. I think Lehpas [people from Leh], they are even more narrow-minded. Because if a boy and a girl go somewhere, *bas* [enough], they think something is going on. They don't think of friendship. In Leh, they think friendship is not possible between boys and girls; for that reason, they think these things. They need to be educated."

Rahima describes her parents' generation and Lehpas as narrow-minded gossips. Lehpas do gossip—it is a small town with a long winter and a central street perfect for people watching. More than one person has told me that gossip is Ladakh's national sport. When I interviewed one woman in her thirties, she blurted out: "you're the *chigyalma* [foreign woman] from ten years ago, who used to ride on the back of that tall man's scooter and then married him!" Beyond her characterization of Lehpas, Rahima flips generational roles, depicting her parents' generation as those who need to be educated by young people—even as the older people these students had spoken with had repeated the tropes that in the past everyone got along, and religious conflict was a modern problem. Ladol similarly calls for a different kind of present and future. She wants more education and turns to India's liberal democracy: "I know what my right is, I have got a right of freedom of religion. Now, I can have my rights. Because I've studied, I am educated, that's why."

In these moments, Rahima, Ladol, and those with whom they spoke are all talking about Ladakh as a fixed and identifiable place. They are evoking the lens of time: past Ladakh, present Ladakh, future Ladakh. But time is complex, messy, and folded up in their narratives: all at once we hear that in the past Ladakhis were as one and that they also feel the need for change, for education, to be "modern," but then also that change and modernity are drivers of conflict and that in the past they "ate off one plate." Time is unfolding, but what is to come? Young people's parents work to generate the future that they desire—but does that contain elements of the past? Which past? The one in which people could coexist? The one in which they failed to coexist? How to untangle these possible pasts and futures from the pace of change and from the almost unrecognizable futures that unfold for their children?

In the focus group, Palzes tells us:

Me, before, when I was staying in the quarters, we had Muslim neighbors, and we never fought with them. Then, I used to go over there, and they would do their prayers sometimes in front of me, and I used to copy them, spreading out the cloth in front of me, and putting my head on the cloth, I thought it was pretty, you know, how you would, seeing other people's customs, so I would just copy them. Then I would just copy them. But my

mother scolded me, saying don't do that. Our religion is our own religion.
Our own religion is precious.

Palzes and Rahima sense something. Their parents and the people gossip-
ing in Leh Bazaar have not sat them down and told them how to interpret the
past (though some may have). Instead, a series of small moments register as a
nudge, a push in a different direction—of course, this can escalate to the recap-
ture of young people who have gone too far astray and to the separation of young
people who have crossed the religious line in romance. The trajectory that this
group of young people envisioned (and they are, of course, the ones who agreed
to participate in a project about this topic) was largely one in which they figured themselves as those who would heal a temporary rupture in the past, not
by returning to that past, but through learning to be together in new and "modern" ways or through the intuitive and embodied feelings of friendship and the
aesthetics of prayer or shared food.

Young people's narratives intersect with, diverge from, and are entangled
within the ways that older generations speak of young people. When they diverge,
they still reference those narratives, indicating familiarity and pervasiveness.
When grandparents speak of young people, they speak of changed hearts, of education that makes you selfish, or even of the ways that young people's bodies are
changed through the consumption of new forms of food, such as rice and packaged noodles instead of the whole grain and water-milled roasted barley and
wheat that abi-le and meme-le ate as children. These "rice children" are said to
be less hardy and weaker than those that came before them, to have all kinds
of diseases that were unheard of—yet these same interviews include laments
of children lost as infants and praise for the ease of life today. Narratives about
the past are not singular across interviews or even within a single conversation.
The past is not only complex but shifts as a chimera depending on the story you
wish to explain about the present or future. Traveling through these tangled
narratives, one consistency is the displacement of danger onto other people,
other generations, as well as a complex folding and reconfiguring of time.

"Kids These Days," "They Never Walk on the Ground"

In the midst of a long interview, Alima, a Sunni woman in her seventies, a matri-
arch in a well-off family of traders and entrepreneurs, reflected on the changes
she saw in her life. I had been intimidated to visit her, but, eager to tell her story
and familiar with U.S. culture from her son's hotel, she had surprised me by
greeting me with a warm hug, followed by the more expected barrage of snack
food. Alima had converted from Buddhism to Islam as a young woman in order
to marry her husband. She had been witness to partition and to the social boycott, which she avoided discussing. Despite having lived through these moments

of crises, her conversation with me was woven with generational vertigo, a sense of being on the cusp of a strange and unknowable future, a generational change fraught with danger in its very uncertainties (Smith 2012b; see also Gergan 2014). She told these stories through anecdotes of kindness and food. Describing *langsde* between Buddhist and Muslim families, in which families would take turns plowing one another's fields, she recalled:

> Buddhists and Muslims would help each other and it was so nice. Then after we were done with the agriculture, there would be parties and they would visit each other's houses. And also sometimes they would go and stay, and in the summer time they would go and sit with each other under the trees, and in the winter they would all sit in the sun and do things together, and not only that, there would be festivals: Muslim festivals and Buddhists would go, Buddhist festivals and Muslims would go. So, during Eid, the Buddhists would come to the Muslim houses. So, when the Buddhists would celebrate Losar, then we would go and visit them. When there was Eid, Buddhists would go; when there was Losar, Muslims would go. When Buddhists fast in the first month of the Tibetan calendar, the Buddhists would get something that they would share with the Muslims. Similarly, when the Muslims were done with Ramadan, they would have the dish with raisins and rice, and they would share it with their Buddhist neighbors. For example, when there was New Year's Day and the Buddhists lit the lamps, and children say "Bulo, Bulo, Lama la Bulo," then Muslim kids would go to Buddhist families.

Elements of Alima's reminiscences may seem romantic, and indeed her account echoes through older people's stories like a refrain from an old song heard on the radio: sitting under the trees in summer, sitting in the sunshine in winter, these sunny moments carry us through other kinds of moments. Even as her words are both light and heavy with this refrain, joining a constellation of stories that many people have created together, her reading of the past is complex and nuanced. Alima describes her youth during the time when militants or soldiers from Pakistan came over the contested border, before J&K's king had signed the papers to join India. She recalls Buddhist and Muslim neighbors protecting one another and streams so clean that you could drink from them, as well as hard work, heavy burdens carried on her back, and fleeing into the mountains above the village when rumors of war spread. The idyllic scenes of parties and sitting together under trees were counterposed with a bundle of fears and worries about the future, in which even children's bodies are fraught with unknown dangers: "Compared to the past, now we have all kinds of food: tomatoes, rice, different vegetables, cauliflower, bananas, but now there is lots of disease, I don't know why. But in the past, when we, or even in my own times, I have seen *paba, thukpa,*[3] *pulau*, they used to make good *pulau*. But these days, there are

varieties of food, but there are all kinds of diseases, so many children die young."
In Alima's remembrance, "People were so nice, kind, innocent. *Chos* [religious
teachings] was in their way of life. Now these days, so many rinpoches come and
give such good teachings, but still people don't follow it. People's *semba* is not
tangpo, it is crooked. *Sem* and *chos* were the same in the past. But now there is
good *chos*, but the *sem* is opposite. Because the *sem* and the *chos* were the same."
"Youth" here comes to stand in for any number of complex things. The romantic
memories of the past are by now familiar, but consider how they are played
against embedded youth, who stand in for future uncertainty. In the preceding
passage, Alima recalls that in the past, *chos*—religious teachings—were not necessarily read or understood, but they were lived and embodied in the *sem* or
semba—the heart-mind. Today, people's *semba* are not straight or upright but
crooked. Today, though people can read religious texts for themselves, and gain
a more comprehensive understanding of their own religious identity, they do not
embody the values of those texts. In Alima's telling, today's children have all
kinds of food but also disease, all kinds of prayer but crooked hearts.

This generational vertigo is experienced in different ways across economic
class, generation, life experience, and political perspective. Alima is part of a very
wealthy Sunni family in Leh. Consider Amira, thirty years younger than Alima,
Amira is a Shia Muslim living in one of the Chushot villages along the banks of
the Indus River. Like Alima, she also refers to food as a marker of generational
change, by mentioning rations in passing—the government-subsidized inexpen-
sive grain allotted based on family size.

AUTHOR: How did you feel when you got married? Was that a happy time?

AMIRA: Ta, what, happy? At that time though I thought I was happy, but then
I had children and everything was hard. At that time, even if someone just
gave you something to wear, you were so happy. We didn't have all these
things. We didn't have rations or anything, we would just eat whatever we
had. We weren't *takpo* [impressive, successful] at all. We were poor.

That same winter, I spoke to Padma, a medical professional in her fifties, on a
break from work. She spoke to me earnestly, wearing glasses and a white lab coat.
From the same village as Amira, she remembered her own childhood in this way:

AUTHOR: If you think about your mother's and grandmother's life, what is the
difference?

PADMA: At that time, there was only farming, there was nothing else. Whatever
we had was from farming. Now, there are all kinds of food and vegetables
and flour. At that time, everything we had was from farming. No one studied. Now there is a lot of change.

AUTHOR: What do you think about the change?

PADMA: I think it is really nice. At that time, all we ate was *paba*, and we didn't have education, or school uniforms, or shoes. Now, whatever you want to wear you can wear, the changes are nice.

When I asked Padma what problems young women face today, she answered earnestly: "Nowadays, women don't have any problems. What problems do they have? They all have jobs and don't have to do farming. Nowadays, the young people, they never walk on the ground, they only go in cars. What a happy time." Yet, for Padma, this did not bode ill or signal a dystopian present with diseased children, though she left the future uncertain. She envisioned that women's lives "are happier and happier every year. In the future, then, who knows. I can't say anything about that." Alima, Padma, and Amira present us not with a clean and clear assessment of the past, nor with a linear trajectory from point A to point B. More carefully, they weave pleasant memories and present concerns with nuances of hunger and anxiety and hesitate to make predictions or general observations.

Saba, a grandmother in her seventies, also saw today as a happier time even though today no one has *duklong*—literally time to stay or time to hang around. Some stressed contemporary desire for material goods as a sign of a bad heart; others described today as *skitpo*, meaning, happy or comfortable.[4] The word *skitpo*, however, did not necessarily imply a moral judgment of good or bad. A happier time could also be a time in which people were less devout and had more moral failings.

SABA: In the past, things were nice, we used to have more time, and we would have picnics and hang around together. Nowadays, no one has time to do that [*duklong*]. The time today is happy, all kinds of clothes, all kinds of food and drink. For us we just had *paba* and *thukpa*. At that time, we would wear patches on our clothes. Now no one will wear patches. Children wear jeans and all kinds of things.

AUTHOR: Yes, even me, I am wearing jeans! Which time do you think is happier?

SABA: Today's time is happier, now they are wearing earrings and necklaces, silver and gold, and wearing all kinds of clothes, eating all kinds of things. At that time, even wearing those torn red things we used to be happy. We would hang around with the neighbors and celebrate Losar and Eid. Now we don't have that. Now everyone goes by themselves.

AUTHOR: Why did that happen?

SABA: It just happened with the time. We hadn't seen an airplane or a Jeep, now it has been many years since I have seen those things.

Saba and Alima describe rapid changes signaled by young people's lives through a diverse set of examples. However, narratives about generational change often focus around marriage in complicated and sometimes confusing or apparently contradictory ways. The next section follows these labyrinthine paths.

Mobile Phones and Jealous Hearts

The sense of generational vertigo is enmeshed in talk of moral values, sexuality, materialism, and marriage. It is simultaneously the changing relationships between the world and Ladakh, understood as a local place with its own language, food, architecture, and ways of being. Contra the romance of Ladakh as an isolated place (Norberg-Hodge 2000), Ladakh has always been a crossroads (Aggarwal 2004; M. Ahmed 2002; Beek and Pirie 2008; Fewkes 2009; Rizvi 1996). Shifting borders and new means of connection (airlines and automobiles, mobile phones and cable television) have reoriented those connections to different places, but it is not that Ladakh has only now been connected to the outside world. Nevertheless, across generations, people are caught in a sense of rapid change and conversations about what form these changes should take or about the inevitability of these changes (see also Aengst 2014; Ozer et al. 2017; Vasan 2017; Williams-Oerberg 2016). For those who have witnessed this transformation over the course of their life, alongside India's turn to right-wing nationalism, the escalation of conflict in Kashmir, and the economic change wrought by the transition away from a primarily agricultural economy, these changes are rightly understood to be nested and entangled in one another.

Discussions about change reveal a cluster of fears described in the embodiedness of youth. Older generations deploy the idea of change in order to make distinctions between their own actions and the actions of young people, even as this sometimes requires a temporal sleight of hand, in which tragedies of the past were blamed on young people of the present. Young people are described in terms of their ability or inability to plow using animals, their propensity to flirt using their mobile phones, with being in a hurry and reckless with money because they have never experienced hardship. To return to the themes that opened this book, young people are conceived of as embodying messy territorializing potential, and thus political and moral questions emerge in discussions of their movements, interactions, and bodies. Even so, something escapes or exceeds these logics, whether in those couples that do run away or in the expressions of compassion, sympathy, and consolation for young people who become swept up in problematic marriages.

Madhia's daughter was divorced, but her community had put the blame squarely on the shoulders of her husband, who had quickly remarried. Her daughter has now happily remarried as well, with a husband who accepted her child from the previous marriage. Madhia told me: "It's not good to go too young. But nowadays, thoughtlessly, they get married really young and have children and just get divorced. They haven't properly matured. And then you see him going around with a new wife. Poor thing. They haven't properly matured [literally: *semba ma-skey*, meaning their heart-minds have not developed]."

On an unseasonably warm day in winter, we interviewed Amira and Haadiya on the outskirts of a fallow barley field in Chushot. They were carrying *tsepo* (woven baskets) home from the fields, resting them on the brick wall in the fading sun. Though they seemed reluctant to sit down at first, once they began speaking, they egged one another on with slightly dirty jokes and gossip about neighbor girls. Hasina asked Amira if she had a love marriage: "No, not at all. . . . At that time, there was nothing like this thing that people have today of sneaking and writing letters. All those things: talking to each other, going places in cars. We didn't have anything like that. That's what they have today. Today they talk about all kinds of things on the phone. Really. Today's time is really bad. Today if *ama* and *aba* [mom and dad] say they're going to bring a bride . . . the boy won't want her. He'll want someone else."

Haadiya elaborated: "Nowadays there are more people with *sem thadok* [jealous hearts] or *sem-ngan* [ill-intentioned]. . . . Those people who think, 'I want to be better than him.'" Thus far, interwoven into discussions of marriage are multivalent readings of the *semba*, the heart-mind: as uncooked or undeveloped, as jealous or ill-intentioned. What kind of *semba* emerges in a time of social and political change?

When I ask about marriage, Zainab, in her late forties, chatting with me in the kitchen with her just-married daughter, tells me:

> Love marriage is more common. They don't know what they're doing. After a short time they end up divorced. These days, even those with arranged marriages, even some of them get divorced. Nowadays children don't know what they are doing.

AUTHOR: Why?

ZAINAB: They think that they will find someone else. Nowadays, they are not patient. Otherwise today is happy. What did we have in the past? Everything we had was dust. We didn't have a gas stove. We were stuck in dust and soot.

Jafar, a Shia man in his sixties who is a community leader, tells me that "It's the younger and educated people who disturbed the communal harmony here. Otherwise the old generation, they were living like brothers." As Jafar's comments indicate, education is another sticking point or lens through which people speak of the future: for some, it is a sign of modernity and a beacon for a peaceful future; for others, education has been sowing seeds of division—of course, many see it through both lenses. Jafar describes intermarriage as "the main problem" and goes on to tell me:

Now everybody, I, as a Muslim, always used to talk in conferences and in
meetings, that we should not marry with the ladies of other communities.
Because it is the main cause for communal disharmony.

AUTHOR: Why do you think that is?

JAFAR: Now, because of education, people are angrier. They think that our community's people should not marry with others. Like Buddhists, Muslims are
also angrier. Muslims think that our women should not marry with the
Buddhists.

For Jafar, the unruliness of youth is tied to their education and must be tempered and managed by adults instilling discipline in young people and teaching
them to uphold religious boundaries to preserve the peace.

In relation to age at marriage, others echoed similar sentiments: that
after education or one's mid-twenties is a good age to get married but that
"Nowadays they like each other and just get married young." But the discussions about young people and marriage become tangled and confusing. On
the one hand, I might hear that nowadays young people get married on a
whim. Nargis tells me that women should get married when "everything is
completed, if they are studying for them to have completed that studying,
and in their mind, if they are prepared, then they should get married. If they
just get married young, without being ready, then they don't stick around,
they just get in fights and soon the marriage is over. Isn't that how it is?" And
yet, in the same interview, she also tells me that in the past young people got
married too young, causing difficulty for women who would have children
before their bodies were really ready. This was echoed by many women, like
the Shia women's organization leader, who told me that education had led to
later marriages, contrasting that with a past in which young women would get
married: "At that time, they didn't understand, and their mother and father
would just say, 'get married,' and so they would get married. At that time, they
wouldn't understand, and the girl would get married young and have a child
and wouldn't understand, what is life? What isn't life? What is happy or what
is not. They didn't know anything. For some of them, they would just get married and have a lot of children and wouldn't understand anything about
enjoying life."

Sometimes older women depicted a past in which women married too young
and had children too young, while other times they told me about young girls
today who run away and marry young. Even though the descriptions were of the
same result—a young married woman with a child—they were drawing a distinc-
tion between their own lives and the lives of young women these days. The
conversation Hasina and I had with two middle-aged Sunni men in Chushot
covers many of these themes:

AUTHOR: Nowadays, do most people go arranged marriage or love marriage?

MOHAMMAD: Nowadays, people go in love marriage, hardly anyone does arranged marriage.

AUTHOR: Oh, I forgot to ask *aba-le*, what do you think about going in love marriage?

RASHAD: Love marriage is not okay. Not okay at all. Because nowadays lots are going in love marriage, but aren't there those kinds of young people, who get mad quickly, and don't listen to anyone? If you give them advice, they just get mad.

HASINA: They aren't patient.

RASHAD: Those who ask their parents' advice, it will turn out better. They will be happier and the children will also be happier. If girls go in arranged marriage, then they will be valued in the house.

Hasina interjected to ask about Rashad's marriage (arranged) and which was more common. Rashad replied referencing popular Hindi/Urdu soap operas on television, sometimes called *saas-bahu* dramas for their propensity to focus on conflicts between malicious mothers-in-law (*saas*) and their daughters-in-law (*bahu*). He told us, "Nowadays love marriage is more common. Nowadays, in the TV, there are all those serials and so on. Now everyone does things they've seen there," and Hasina nodded knowingly and repeated: "They copy the serials." I asked if Rashad or Mohammad had Buddhist relatives:

MOHAMMAD: I do. My *abi*, my *khas* [true] *abi*, my father's mother.[5]

AUTHOR: So in the past, were there many marriages like that?

MOHAMMAD: There were.

AUTHOR: What about now?

MOHAMMAD: Now, I don't know, they might. But it's not possible.

AUTHOR: What do you think about it? Should they be allowed or blocked?

MOHAMMAD: It's right to block them.

AUTHOR: Why?

MOHAMMAD: From that side, they'll go astray in their religion. We have to block it.

From a tangle of past and present, early marriages arranged by parents in a time of poverty, runaway marriages today in a time of plenty, parents and grandparents emphasize both the need to manage young people's development and personal growth and, at other times (as we saw in chapter 4), the impossibility of doing so. Like the future itself, young lives are unruly, and yet somehow you must prepare.

Conclusion: Future Talk

What are the geopolitics of territory, love, and babies for young people who find their bodies its crux? Young people forge their subjectivities at the intersection of geopolitical tensions and religious identities in formation. As the material embodiment of adults' hopes and fears for the future of this territory, youth are rendered a site of particular intensities of care and anxiety. As young people work out their own sense of self and desires, they must navigate a path made more difficult by expectations described as "modern," as well as fears projected onto their nascent sexuality and independence. Fears about young people's morals, values, and lack of supervision emerge in discussions about family life, and young people chafe against the restrictions that emerge. At the same time, they are caught between their own sense of belonging in Ladakh and the economic opportunities of urban India (Vasan 2017; Williams-Oerberg 2016).

Laila, a middle-aged mother of six, tells me, in regard to modesty and veiling, that "there's no 'modern' in Islam," using the English word with a derisive tone:

> In the past, it was better, now it is a little worse. Now they are a little bit more into fashion and being "modern." They say "modern," "modern." Isn't that what they say? There's no modern in [veiling]. There's no modern in Islam. You must have seen in Iran-*biran* [Iran and other such places].[6] Those women wear *niqab* and do everything, have jobs and all such things. They have it in Iran. They have all kinds of things. Here, they're a little big lazy, a little bit weak. That's why here they take off the veil and walk around and do all kinds of things, they're not capable of obeying.

Laila dismisses the idea of being "modern," though she also implies praise for women wearing *niqab* and "do[ing] everything, hav[ing] jobs and all kinds of things," so she does not imply a need for women to return to work in the home. In other interviews, some Buddhists and Muslims suggested that Muslims were better at educating young people into proper behavior. Akbar, a well-respected Sunni leader with a daughter attending graduate school, told me in regard to managing young people's morals and propensity for runaway intermarriages: "You should have a policy, of course, but you cannot go after every individual, but [the Buddhists] are going [after intermarried couples]. It is very unfortunate. But we [Muslims] are very small. We never bothered. We give our directions, we give sermons on Friday: control your girls, control your boys. Do not encourage your boys to take liquor or intoxicants, make your family system more strong, more Islamic, or if you have your own religion. We do that." This was part of Akbar's larger interpretation of gender relations and generational change in

Ladakh. He felt that policing intermarriage was one of the LBA's main projects, but that they were ineffective. He told me that to be effective, they would need to begin through work at home: "They don't have a code of conduct; they don't look at what the Buddhist girls are wearing, what society they are keeping and in what activities they are involved. This is the main thing, to control the girls right from the house to the school and the college. And if they can deny a girl to marry a Muslim, and if they can threaten, or have an agitation on this point, why can't they make a code of conduct? A dress code?"

Echoing Kong's (2010) and Gökariksel and Secor's (2012) understandings of religion as an embodied, performative, and intersectionally understood component of subjectivity, Akbar suggests that the work of religious border maintenance rests on the family and community. It is family and community members who must engender a desire and self-discipline in young women (and, in other places in the conversation, men as well). This performance is understood to be tied to the ontological security of both family and "community" (Botterill et al. 2018). Thus, Karima, a Muslim woman in her thirties, explained to me that intermarriage has been banned because "They say that the Buddhist girls are going to run out. And the Muslim girls. If the Buddhists convert to Islam and Muslims covert to Buddhism . . . then that will be the end. That's what they say. This started with the disturbance, with the agitation."

Paradoxically echoing Akbar's comments, Dorje, a Buddhist, references Muslim youth's discipline as emerging from the social boycott itself: "I think that Muslims had gone for a little more ambition after that . . . more hardworking. That was the Muslim feeling. At that time, there used to be a lot of Muslim boys idling in the market. Today you will find none. They used to be very, very uninterested in school."

When older generations talk about the present and future, they often hone in on competition, on impulsivity in marriage or politics, and sometimes on religion as well. Young people might be described as unruly and undisciplined, but ironically, young people socially police one another in the cities that Ladakhis migrate to for education—commenting on women's clothes, on late-night parties, on parents' hard-earned money squandered (Aengst 2014; Smith 2017; Smith and Gergan 2015; Williams-Oerberg 2016). Particularly in the city of Jammu, which has the largest population of Ladakhi youth studying outside Ladakh, young women tell me they feel they cannot have friends who are men or wear specific kinds of clothes like shorts in hot weather as this will quickly mark them as trouble or get back to their parents.

Adult representations of violence and unruliness as the work of young people is used to discipline boundaries of religious identity, not to suggest a return to the nostalgic past that was described in chapter 4. By displacing potential for violence and chaos onto young people's unruly bodies, the case is made that the past is a distant land that can no longer be reached, an impossible utopia. Meanwhile, young people use future talk to characterize themselves quite differently. In their future talk, young people guide me through the ways that they navigate questions of love, loyalty, and independence. What do young people owe their parents? When do their values overwhelm those debts?

Namgyal Angmo has deep and abiding respect for her mother and father. When she participated in a photography project, her mother featured prominently in photos from back home and in her discussion of her life. When I asked what her parents do, rather than saying her mother was "just a housewife," as I had heard young people do from time to time, she launched into a more nuanced discussion: "My mother is a housewife and a farmer, as well as a tailor, and also she is multitalented, because sometimes she also makes bricks, because when she has no work she makes bricks. And sometimes she goes to the mountain to fetch grass for use for the roofing, and then she sells that."

Namgyal's father similarly does farming, carpentry and masonry and weaves at home. While she speaks of them with admiration, she struggles to reconcile what she feels to be her authentic self with their expectations and worldviews. Perhaps because of her love and respect for her parents, she does not wish to or feels she cannot fake it at home—but rather finds herself enmeshed in attempts to explain herself. She has always felt more at ease with her father and one day asked him questions about her period instead of her mother, and for days her mother would say, "What have you asked? It's blasphemous." Namgyal's response was, "I don't know, I find my father quite more friendly than you, so I don't know . . . that's why I asked him."

Kunzes, an aspiring modern artist, aligns with Namgyal's strong sense of self. Talking about social policing in Jammu, she said she would just ignore gossip and do her own thing. Kunzes does not know if she wants to get married—only if she meets someone who is like her. If she only meets "possessive people," then "I just want to stay alone. But, of course, marriage is important, so if I meet someone like me . . . then I'll think about it."

In young people's future talk, which we will turn to in the next chapter, young people like Namgyal and Kunzes, Rahima and Ladol use time and place to talk about their lives and the collective and territorial life of Ladakh. What kind of person do you need to be for Ladakh to survive in a manner that is recognizable to you and your grandparents? And is that the Ladakh that you desire? Ladakh's territorial future is being lived and embodied by young people who act according to what they learn about their past, but they themselves express doubt about what is and is not being passed down. Future talk is also a prefigurative politics (Dyson and Jeffrey 2018; Gergan and Curley in preparation; Gergan forthcoming), in which young people use storytelling to enact in the present the future that they desire. Stanzin's explanation of the photos he showed us of himself and *meme-le* caught my attention perhaps in part because this is what he was asking us to consider: who will we be in the future?

6

Generation Vertigo and the Future of Territory

Kunzes was irrepressible, switching seamlessly between exuberance and seriousness.[1] It was a bright sunny day, and we sat, rapt, in the cool dim room at the Ladakh Arts and Media Organization (LAMO), arranging ourselves to adjust to the contrast from the blue sky vibrant through the windows of the small balcony. Kunzes was telling us about her experience as a college student at Delhi University. Confident hand gestures underscored her assertions. "You guys have to understand, I am a feminist, okay?" Kunzes's college, Miranda House, at Delhi University, is known for its feminist orientation: its Web site proclaims, "Miranda House is more than a college, it is . . . a community of practice," and "Mirandians are bold, brilliant and inspiring. They change the world and the way we think about it."[2] Kunzes has embraced this vision. Projected on the screen behind her, we see her smiling face framed with stylish glasses and hair bleached in a trendy copper ombré style. She has taken a group selfie. Half of her face fills a good part of the frame, but she has taken care that her friends' faces are visible and radiant in the background, their all-black ensembles making the photo more striking. It is the kind of photo that you unintentionally smile back at, even though it is now only a collection of pixels lighting up a screen. "This is me, we're doing a feminist flash mob in the Delhi metro! Claiming space for women!" She goes to the next photo. "And here I am, doing the bamboo dance with my Mizo friends, can you believe it? Do I look like a northeastern girl?" Kunzes is referring to friends from Mizoram, a small state in India's northeast, between Bangladesh and Burma.

Kunzes is laughing and charismatic. She has told us she had to struggle, that she has been through moments of self-doubt, has been called racist slurs, and has wondered if she could ever succeed outside Ladakh. Somehow it was hard to reconcile this self-doubt with her confidence, despite knowing so many other young people whose hardships have made them strong. Kunzes was using her favorite photographs to tell a room of other charismatic college students about her life in Delhi, while my collaborators, Mabel Gergan, Rinchen Dolma, and I watched from the sidelines.[3] Religion, Ladakhi identity, gender, all these things were wrapped up in how Kunzes describes herself, but there was so much else going on as well that is about her own idiosyncratic view of the world and her own life's trajectory. She is fashioning a life and a sense of self that fits the person she feels herself to be, and she is able to do this through her ability to move between family home, Leh Bazaar, and college campus, picking up new ways of being in the world. She takes small tokens from home with her: a family photo, a book by the Dalai Lama, given by a close friend. She reads the book each day, trying to make small changes in her life and remember who she is. She wants to travel, to go abroad, and see the world, but in the end, she wants to return to Ladakh—what would it all be for, she wonders aloud, if she did not come back to work for her own people?

Youth hold a particular space in the geopolitical imagination and in geopolitics.[4] In chapter 5, we encountered parents who work to intervene in the future, through love and care, through management and policing. In this chapter, young people describe their own geopolitical lives and futures. Parents' love-as-management, care-as-policing implicates the body and bodies as territory imbued with ethnic, religious, or national identity. The body is also an intimate site through which we shape and are shaped by the world. Think of the child who wished to move her body in prayer but was told not to or the young woman who tied her scarf around her head to protect from dust and was told to refold it so she did not look Muslim, as well as the woman who checks her scarf to be proper on return to her own village from the anonymity of a larger town. Parents, grandparents, and community members work to protect and care for the young, as well as to instill in them a sense of who they are to carry that identity into the future. This could be in encouraging marrying among your own (however defined) or upholding values through other means: speaking the mother tongue that is not taught in school and carries its own logic and intention, preparing a food for which your village is known. It could also be conforming to what you believe the future holds for your child. In preparation for an unknown future, we sometimes ask young people to participate in the "promise of happiness," the idea that if you wish for the right things, your wishes will come true— but if you wish for the wrong things, the wrong people, or the wrong kind of life, you will languish and flail in an unfair world (S. Ahmed 2010). Young people occupy a particular geopolitical position as the object of concern for older generations and as political actors in their own right (S. Ahmed 2010; Benwell and Hopkins 2017; Gergan 2014; Gergan and Curley in preparation; Hörschelmann and Refaie 2014; Huijsmans 2016; Lam-Knott 2018; Smith and Gergan 2017). They also occupy a precarious status as a site of aspirations that are often unmet, sometimes leading to desperation and distress (Chua 2014). Understood as a vector into the future, young people become a way to manage the unknowable time to come, but they also chafe against the constraints engendered by this position.

In this chapter, we also return to the idea that geopolitical bodies have a physics—the sticking-together fun of a flash mob that makes your feminism flesh, the sudden feeling of the city-as-hostile space when a racial slur arrives unexpectedly and your body becomes a wish for home (S. Ahmed 2004; Bayat 2009; Saldanha 2008). But unruly bodies are also disciplined and managed in the aggregate: told individually at home to take care with those of the other religion. In the morning, a wave of parents dutifully shepherd their children into the white shirts, slacks, black ties, and black shoes of the British-inflected school uniform to learn to be on time, to memorize, and to take exams in English and then to compete across the mountains in the colleges and universities of urban India. They are preparing for a future through an education system that itself cannot be disentangled from the imperial intimacies (Lowe 2015) of the past, imperial intimacies that plied notions of modernity and development even as they worked to foreclose the meanings of these words for colonized places. Simultaneously, in the lives of young people, striving, thriving, but also sometimes stumbling, there is the messy lively life of the unbounded territory that they desire.

This chapter asks what inhabiting a geopolitically charged body feels like for young people. Since 2011, in collaboration with Mabel Gergan, I have been working with young Ladakhis who attend university outside Ladakh (Smith 2017; Smith and Gergan 2015, 2017). Ladakhi parents increasingly send their children to major urban centers, especially Jammu, Chandigarh, and Delhi, or, rarely, abroad (the three students studying abroad whom I have met do so through fellowships) (also see Ozer et al. 2017; Vasan 2017; Williams-Oerberg 2016). The ability to send your children away to study is, as you might expect, connected to socioeconomic status, but it is also surprisingly common even for those who are economically struggling but able to pool money from relatives and entrepreneurial activities. This practice adds layers to the geopolitical logics that we have seen people grapple with up until this point. In Jammu or Delhi, young people socialize or even date across religious lines and also cultivate intentionally cosmopolitan subjectivities (Smith 2017; in other contexts, see Cheng 2018; Fong 2011; in relation to Northeasterners, see McDuie-Ra 2012). Students also experience racialized discrimination: local residents, peers, or teachers call them Nepali, Chinese, or racial slurs; and point to their eyes or sartorial style as evidence that they are not properly Indian (for more on "looking Indian," see Wouters and Subba 2013). All these experiences are layered on a tangle of precarity emerging from ecological, economic, and political change (Gergan 2014). This finds young Ladakhis developing a sense of Ladakhiness in opposition to the world "outside" but also policing one another's embodied performance of Ladakhi or religious identity (Aengst 2014; Aggarwal 2004). Parents see education in distant urban centers as a necessary means to a desired "modernity" but also as a site of danger where unruly love, lack of supervision, and immorality might compromise students' Ladakhi or religious identity.

The Lively and Irrepressible Future of Territory

Places are formed through their interconnections with other places, not through inherent characteristics tied to that locale (Massey 1991). In the stories that parents and children have told me, place as a cultural phenomenon, as a sense of cultural practices in relation to where they play out, is tangled in an overlay of territory as an intensifying political determinant of the future. If, as I have argued here, territory has not only a demarcated and legal existence but is also a lively and lived experience, what role will these young people play? How does this territorial overlay, contained partly in their own bodies, intersect with their sense of place, of home, and of the world? In the opening chapters, men and women became part of the life of territory by falling in love across religious lines, by being encouraged to bear children who would not only extend family lines but also secure a future for Buddhism and maintain an electoral majority in Leh District. Through these embodied means, women and men become part of the life of territory: their embodied life decisions understood to either maintain the configuration of territorial sovereignty as it is or to be part of its dissolution. Looking toward the future, parents, but also children, can feel a sense of generational vertigo at the precipitous changes looming (Smith 2013). This vertigo manifests in an overwhelming dizziness when contemplating an unknown future to come; in this embodied reaction, fears for one's own children, one's own family, and the geopolitical future of one's own place mingle. A sense of ontological insecurity infuses family life (Botterill et al. 2018).

Leh's status as part of India's contested J&K state means that (local) political questions, and, in this case, intimate questions about birth control, marriage, and the raising of children, are geopolitical, that is, they are tied to control of territory and the lingering question of J&K's future. This is the case wherever you live, whether that is in Ladakh or in North Carolina, where I spend most my of days. The fractures and geopolitical spark lines may traverse difference differently, and the intensity may not always be evident, but we participate in the future of territory nonetheless. In the context of Ladakh, young people are understood to be the material rendering of Ladakh's future, holding the questions of politicized religious identity, but much more as well. What are the links between the temporal and the territorial, and how is territory imagined beyond the lifespan of those who strategize its trajectory? How do our small plans for our future and the future of our loved ones add up to something larger? This chapter delves into the ways that the young become the focus of concern through how that they represent the future and touches on young people's aspirations and the potential for counter-geopolitical spaces that resist politicized religion.

Mobility ricochets these young students across the mountains and down into urban centers in the plains, where their faces, names, clothing, and ways of being in the world are illegible or wrongly categorized by many of those they encounter. The feeling of jostling against new people, some of whom do not see you as you understand yourself, some of whom embrace you as an exotic other, some of whom slowly come to know you, this feeling also affects the body and leaves geopolitical traces. Are you Indian, as you had once understood yourself to be? Will you become Indian, which you never felt yourself to be? Leaving Ladakh, even if it is not bounded on a map, has a particular feeling to it. You must either traverse two days of mountains on a crowded bus or shared taxi (sometimes getting stuck by snow on top of a pass if you travel too late or too early in the season), or you buy an expensive plane ticket that transports you over impossibly endless mountains, as even locals become tourists snapping photos out the windows of glacier after glacier. From November to May, the plane is your only option, as the mountains have become impassable. This movement over mountains transforms you.

If our bodies do geopolitical work, what kinds of spaces do young people engender? What kind of future do they prefigure in the present (Dyson and Jeffrey 2018; A. Vasudevan 2015), as they move between India's metropolises and Ladakh? Like their parents, young people also feel a rush of generational vertigo as they contemplate the future: a dizzying storm of a feeling that they are looking over a precipice and cannot know what is to come but know that they must prepare.

Generation Vertigo: Intergenerational Inheritances of Family and Place

Parents have invested love and devotion in these young people and perhaps do not realize how much this is on their children's minds. Struggling with how to encourage students to be more confident in describing their experiences, Mabel and I experimented by asking students to write letters to their parents, and they took to it with a greater earnestness and pleasure than we had anticipated. They wrote of their abiding love and respect, that they did see their parents' sacrifices for them. When Rigzin Angmo finished her letter to her parents, she instantly took a photo on her phone to show them later: she had wanted to tell them these things for a long time. Another student wrote: "I can feel your pain, it's just that I don't show it much. Though we don't agree on most points, but I respect you both, and love you dearly. Thanks for being an inspiration." Though students grapple with how to honor their families, they also feel pitched forward, into the future, and work to develop their own sense of self through the mobile trajectory on which their parents have sent them.

Reading students' letters to their parents brought to mind the conversations I had with Zainab, two years before. Zainab, like Kunzes, is charismatic and energetic, wearing a bright smile and big sunglasses as she waves at me from across the street the first time we meet to chat. She is comfortable talking about her own life's narrative even in the sunny open-air coffee shop where we meet. Zainab is bubbly, confident, and expressive even though it is our first meeting.

Zainab keeps telling me about her parents. She tells me how they had encouraged her and her brother to read from an early age and to read widely; how her dad had been sending her and her brother books to read for pleasure and how that had developed her intellect and made her close to her brother through little things like their exchange of Harry Potter books; how her parents had a deep faith that she would grow into Shia religious traditions in her own time and on her own terms. Parts of this story she tells through her own embodied comportment and relationship to clothing (Gökariksel 2012; Gökariksel and Secor 2014). She wants to talk about hijab. Her parents had never asked her to perform her Muslim identity through her clothing, though her mother had asked her to cover her head when they visited relatives back home in her village, just to show respect to them and not to raise questions. But Zainab asked for guidance more directly: was it okay for her to uncover her head and be wearing jeans and a T-shirt in Delhi, as she had been used to doing? Wasn't it important for her to wear some iteration of hijab, however she defined it? And shouldn't this be consistent, not varying based on whether she was studying in the city, hanging out at home in Leh, or visiting her mother's "stricter" relatives?

Like the other young people in this book, Zainab is finding her way to live in a body charged with geopolitical potential, rooted in parental love, and moving through and guided by community expectations. Mobility is part of how she cultivates and locates herself. But this mobility also has limits, and seventy years after the partition of British India into new states delimited by religion, some of these curtailed horizons parallel those logics of staking territory across embodied life. In response to her earnest queries about her religion, her clothes, and her faith, her parents laughed and told her she would figure it out. She remembers her dad telling her, "There will come a time in your life when you will know what you want to wear and what kind of person you want to be in your life." And yet, she also suspects there are limits to this openness and that if she was to go bare-headed in Leh she would be asked to put the scarf back on. On the other hand, she feels free to choose her line of work or education. Talking to me that summer, after health issues had led her to return from her studies and stay in Leh, she had talked all these things over with friend and family, read up on religion on the Internet, and felt that she had finally reached the point that her father had predicted. She was confident, open-minded, and serious about her faith but sure she could interpret it for herself. She did not feel the need to correct her friends who made different choices—rather, she felt that others (Buddhist or Muslim) could define terms like modesty for themselves. She summed up:

ZAINAB: So these are the things. And my parents always trusted me. They never put their opinion about what modesty is and what you should do. The freedom that they gave me in this area also . . . I think that is how I have developed myself as an open-minded person regarding religion in every aspect. Not only prayer, but in the way you dress up, in your speech. And everything. That is the reason about religion and why I am open-minded.

AUTHOR: It's nice, it sounds like in so many ways your parents have put a lot of faith in you.

ZAINAB: Yes, it's like they have actually given me the freedom to think about things myself instead of telling me, you know this is the thing you should do and everything. And I think this is important. Because I think when you grow up, it is true that you get very influenced by people. Yeah, what their opinions are . . . of course you need your parents' guidance, and they do provide me with that. They do provide me with that guidance whenever I need it. But when I have to think about things like what I want to do and what I want to wear, and how should I go about things . . . they give me that freedom and space to think about it and ultimately to make my own decision. I think they understand that it's really important for a person to develop their minds themselves and thoughts themselves instead of getting influenced by somebody else's opinion.

Zainab's unfolding journey is only her own, but it is also revealing of how young people come to find a sense of self and the ways they wrap this up in the story of their movement and encounters across time and place. Zainab describes her parents as both "traditional" and open-minded—perhaps not surprising as young people described "open-mindedness" as a characteristic of Ladakhis as a group (though they also described Ladakhis as close-minded and prone to gossip). Conversations with Muslim young people in particular were more likely to reveal them grappling with a perceived expectation that Muslims would be "conservative," though this was not always clearly defined. Zainab, for instance, speaks of her experience in relation to her "community" when she tells me that few young girls from her community of Shia Muslims travel for boarding school, though it is common nowadays for young women of all religions to travel outside the region for college.

In other conversations, young people related anecdotes that they felt reinforced an idea of difference between Buddhist and Muslim young people. For young people, these kinds of Muslim difference were often signaled in a shorthand that always felt layered and disorienting: a young Muslim woman in jeans told me that Muslim women do not wear jeans. Another young Muslim woman painting her nails casually specified restrictions on Muslim women's social life but with very narrow or specific examples: "Buddhists can go in any field and participate. Muslims have some restrictions. For instance, in the [Ladakh] festival. You've seen that there aren't Muslim women [dancing] in the festival." In her telling, Muslim women had "a little bit less freedom, when compared to Buddhists," but in other fields, like teaching or medicine, there were no problems, it was easy, "*aram se*," she repeated, using the Urdu phrase to underscore her point.

When Zainab tells this story of developing her sense of self, places themselves emerge as specific characters: Delhi; the unnamed village where her mother grew up; home, where she returns and figures herself out; and the Internet, which she used to research hijab, as a transnational space of Muslim communication and community. Drawing on the foundation laid by her parents, Zainab uses the places and knowledge at her disposal to forge her own sense of self, always in relation to her understanding of her community. Her trajectory, like Kunzes's, is at once her own and geopolitical in its own right, remaking the world through movement between Leh's mountain landscapes and Delhi as urban center. Delhi is the place where she felt at home for a while wearing a T-shirt and jeans, but it is also the place where she and her father were told to their faces that a landlord does not rent to Muslims. Leh is the place where for a time she felt most comfortable in suit (*salwar kameez*) and headscarf but where today her sense of style and sense of self has shifted and she opts to wear jeans and headscarf. On one occasion, a stranger policed the way her hair was visible under her scarf, but she resisted making any changes and wears her scarf in the way that feels right to her. These experiences—what they open up and what they foreclose—foster how Zainab moves through space as a body both caught up in geopolitical narratives and forging her own path through these waters.

The cartographic legacies of colonial territoriality, which we read on the map through the alternating thick and then dashed or tentative border lines, borders that require footnotes, borders that require legal disclaimers—on the map separating India and Pakistan—sparked when Zainab and her father appeared before the door of a potential landlord in Delhi who rejected them for their faith. Alongside these territorial charges, community expectations of religion and class hum alongside the conversation when we talk about marriage and about the difficulty that some young women find in marrying. Once they have a master of arts or a doctorate, they tell me, it is hard to find someone with the same level of education who also has economic stability, is Ladakhi, and belongs to the same religious community. Zainab tells me of her Shia cousin who trained as a doctor. Her family could not find her a groom, and she eventually chose to marry a Sunni Muslim from outside Ladakh. I have spoken with many young women who are delaying marriage or secretly seeing an "unsuitable" boy. A polished woman with a doctorate tells me she will never find a Buddhist Ladakhi to marry. Young women tell me they meet appealing but unsuitable partners at college or at work, and then their encouraged free movement and exploration suddenly reaches a carefully defined limit: marriage across the religious border.

But even aside from religious identity, what does it even mean to be Ladakhi? In a group conversation at LAMO in 2016, one student began: "One thing is for sure that as a Ladakhi, nowadays we students won't be having much to tell our grandchildren because we are now modernizing, Westernizing. We would have nothing to tell [about] Ladakhi culture." This voiced aloud a common concern that had not been broached yet in the conversation—that Ladakhi youth are "losing" their culture by spending time outside Ladakh. The student went on, referencing the places that students were studying: "we think that you are still Ladakhi, physically you are Ladakhi, but mentally . . . you are not. You are, you are from America. I'm from Delhi, she's from Jammu, and I'm from America." This generated a wave of conversation and then another student interjected: "There's a difference between having an idea about our own culture and Googling from some encyclopedia." The students were drawing distinctions between lived daily experience of a place and an abstract "book knowledge" of Ladakhi traditions. They grappled with what lived experience of Ladakh might mean and how that might be inaccessible to them because of their need to spend years outside for education or even possibly after education to find positions that matched their qualifications. Young people thus also experience a kind of generational vertigo of their own, in which they question the futures that they are actively working toward, even while sometimes feeling that their own trajectories may be a little out of their hands.

Kunzes and others had first met for this project in 2016, when we began with this group conversation, and a barrage of opinions around being Ladakhi spiraled out of comments about movement between places and how this changes you as a person. Kunzes started us out:

> When I go outside, I feel like, yeah, I am a Ladakhi. I represent Ladakh. Yeah, I'm living in India, but then . . . Ladakh is kind of a bit separated from the other parts of India, I guess. And then when I went outside [Ladakh] it was a whole new world for me. It's not like the same classroom, the students are like very competitive. . . . Before the teacher asked they raise up their hands and they answer. I was like, Oh, how will I manage with them? . . .
>
> And then those people are like, oh, you are from the Northeast because they . . . from the eyes. "No, I'm a Ladakhi!" and they, some people are like so lame, [sic] they ask, "Where is Ladakh?" They're like, "Is it in Pakistan?" They ask all these lame questions and I'm like oh god. It's . . . I

show them on the map. First of all, I think of myself as a Ladakhi because
I live in Ladakh. If I go over there, I won't be settling, I won't go over there
and settle. I'll come back and serve people over here, my people here.

This sense of being Ladakhi in relation to one's own trajectory through space
is both personal and geopolitical—formed in relation to the embodied reactions
of those one meets as well as the discursive enmeshment in how the nation is
made. Tsewang Chuskit and Stanzin Angmo had traveled to the United States
via Delhi, receiving sponsorship to study abroad. As they traveled across borders, their own sense of geopolitical and national identity changed as their faces
were read by different people in specific locations:

TSEWANG CHUSKIT: When Stanzin Angmo and I went to Delhi for two months
    before we went to the United States and there when people asked, we say
    we are Ladakhi, and it is in J&K, but when we went to the United States,
    um . . . nobody knows Ladakh . . . you say, "I'm an Indian." "Oh, India" . . . so
    when you go kind of outside the country, you feel more like Indian, I think.
    And when you are inside India, you feel more, oh, I'm from Ladakh.

STANZIN ANGMO: So yeah, I'll say the same . . . but like yeah, when I went to
    United States I feel more Indian, you know, first because they ask questions
    about like Modi or Gandhi, or curry and everything. . . . Whenever you say,
    "I'm from India," and they're like, "Oh, you don't look Indian."

TSEWANG CHUSKIT: When we were coming back from United States in the air-
    port and there was this Indian section and for foreigners you have to go dif-
    ferent, and even the Indian line with our passports and the person said,
    "Oh ma'am, you should go to that side. This is for Indians."

They concluded their anecdote laughing together, "We are Indians!" and
a third student who had traveled abroad nodded, "Yup, mmmhmmm." The
movement across these borders had told them who they were to the rest of
the world. It had also shifted their sense of self as Ladakhis, but these movements and shiftings are not uniform. Later in the same conversation, the
students' descriptions of their experiences of discrimination take a turn. I was
asking them if they ever felt that they were treated differently, if they had the
feeling of being a minority when they were across the mountains elsewhere
in India. Kunzes jumped in right away:

KUNZES: We were in the minority. In my class, I was the only Ladakhi. And they
    were like, like . . . some people call us [racial slur omitted], like they call us
    that name. It's like, we don't feel good when someone calls us by a different
    name. We have our own personal name. There were a few people who are
    not so good. Good people, very educated people, they won't call us like that.
    But then there are few people who were like that, who just separated us on

the basis of our physical features, um . . . or the way we speak or because we can't speak Hindi like them, on the basis of language and . . . these were the reasons, yeah. They were separating us, like isolating . . .

TASHI NAMGYAL [INTERRUPTING]: There's that same thing here too, you know, I think you know you go anywhere, majority try to rule over the minority, you know, it's the same thing. For instance, you see here, everyone, even we might have called Bihari or Nepali to those guys, you know? It's the same thing, I guess. But the thing is, you know, it's all about opening up, you know, to everyone. Then you will get to know about who's good, who's bad. And the same thing we do here too in Ladakh too, you know. You won't be getting, you know like, meeting with lots of good friends all the time, you know? There are shitty people here too.

In a previous interview, Tashi had told me that traveling across India had caused him to interrogate just these issues: how he had understood ethnic difference and the economic migrants to Ladakh who are often referred to as Nepali or Bihari. There is actually a range of more complex stories about these migrants—it is true that some who settle or who take up paid labor harvesting in late summer are from Nepal or Bihar. Many, however, are also from Jharkhand and elsewhere, and their labor in rebuilding the mountain roads each year is both caught up in nationalist projects and a form of precarity that enables Ladakhis to buy Indian goods when the roads open each summer (Sabhlok 2017). Tashi and one other student, on returning to Ladakh after time elsewhere in India, found themselves questioning their reactions to being called "Nepali" in Indian cities and how they themselves had used that term back home.

Of course, this experience of being "Ladakhi" was further complicated and nuanced by one's village background, gender, and economic status.[5] Students lay out this geography for me in caricatures, depicting students from Leh and the surrounding villages as being economically privileged and academically lazy, while those from the more rural areas of Sham (western Ladakh) and Changthang (eastern Ladakh) were depicted as striving and struggling, more likely to be a "topper" (a top scorer in an exam). Tsewang Chuskit left her family in Muth, Changthang, as a child, to study in a foreign-funded Siddhartha private school in wealthier Stok village, just across the Indus River from Leh. "For me, it's different because I'm studying there, so they expect a lot because you are from Siddhartha graduate and you know, we are from, I'm from Changtang and you're . . . we're going first time for high school from Ladakh, so they feel like, my parents think or like her parents maybe thinks that [laughs] we'll come back and serve Ladakh, okay." Her movement from Muth to Stok and then to the United States had, she tells me, made her self-confident: "when you are at a place, there's no Ladakhi, you become more strong and you're more responsible," meaning that she would need to make friends with others who were not Ladakhi, making her more "bold," in her own words. At the same time, these travels led her to reflect on her sense of self in relation to Ladakh in ways that were entangled in experiences like being read as a foreigner rather than a citizen upon arrival in Delhi, but also in ways that complicate return:

TSEWANG CHUSKIT: Well, if someone tells me to wear like *sulma* or *phu-met*[6] instead of jeans, I would be like [Chuskit laughed and made a gesture of saying "what?"]. But I feel like it will stay, otherwise it will change, that would be our culture, so culture will be always there. So the only thing is the old people or like elders who say to preserve culture . . . I don't think it will go away. There are a lot of ways to preserve culture even though you're not wearing it . . .

AUTHOR: Right, that makes sense. Why do you think there is so much concern about that? [clarification omitted]

TSEWANG CHUSKIT: Because like the kind of childhood we had, the young generation had, the old parents they didn't have, so they expect the same, yeah, you know. That the young generation should have the same childhood [clothes] as they wore in their childhood and if they see like us like nineteen years old wearing jeans and they kind of think: "When I was nineteen, I wasn't doing this," you know? Now, culture is evolving, you know?

In a later conversation on this topic, Chuskit clarified her comments, adding that she empathized with older generations in Ladakh and their desires to preserve Ladakh, and she did not want to be disrespectful to prior generations. Rather, her understanding is that culture is evolving and changing and that this evolution is itself culture, rather than something fixed and static.

What Is the Future That We Desire for Ourselves and Our Place?

The idea of Ladakh and Ladakhiness emerges across conversations with young people, complicating and tangling with the territorial stories told by their parents and the encouragement to grow up to be a certain kind of person. The vertigo feeling, of uncertainty and rapid change, is felt both in relation to their own lives and in relation to the place itself. Young people narrate their own lives in relation to the idea of "Ladakhiness" and the future: what will it mean to be Ladakhi?

Namgyal Angmo is familiar with concepts of orientalism and othering and understands these to be the basis of colonial violence—when her teacher in Jammu stereotypes Ladakhis as a group, she is understandably furious, lampooning the teacher as a credulous dolt believing some nonsense from the National Geographic Channel. At the same time, Namgyal tells me she is not "fit to be Ladakhi," because Ladakhis by nature are "quite shy," while she is "very boyish, not that quiet girl." When she returns to Ladakh from urban India, she finds herself faltering, unable to play the role she imagines she should or to "become the furniture" (S. Ahmed 2010), fading into the background to play a supporting role in the life of the family: "Once the changes have come inside, you can't go back. I can't play the role of daughter, I can't play the role of sister sometime . . . there's not a fixed role for me anywhere. . . . They are thinking you are beyond normal. Heteronormative roles are very tough for me. That's why I can understand the problems of gays and homosexuals."

Namgyal just has one Ladakhi friend with whom her "personality match[es]": "I mean, hanging out or roaming around until 3 A.M. or something like that, I mean we don't care." She also hung around only with girls just to avoid the trouble and surveillance that comes from associating with boys, but for her this had her feeling that "I have only been to girls' school, girls' college, only girls, girls, girls, so maybe I am the boy among them . . . trying to be the boy among them."

Across interviews, "Ladakhiness" as a place-based identity, emerges, tangled as it is with sense of self, in not always comfortable ways. Even Namgyal, with her sense of not fitting in, idealizes Ladakhiness. When faced with stereotypes at school, she "had that strong Ladakhi feeling in me . . . and I'm happy that there are still people who understand the Ladakhi way. . . . People perceive Ladakhis as very gentle, very honest, very straightforward people. And I'm happy that Ladakhis are still trying to maintain that identity." Arriving in Jammu, she was shocked by open drains and pollution and missed Ladakh's cleanliness but also observed that "in Ladakh if you are hungry, you can just go to anybody's house, and you can have at least a cup of tea and some barley flour." Namgyal went on to describe Ladakhis as frank and non-xenophobic. She wants to define herself on her own terms: "I know what Ladakhiness is within me. Clothes don't define you . . . culture can change. And we need to understand the ethical nature of culture. The ethics of change. So we should, we should be, I think, very secular."

That sense of identity, like so many others, is folded within a shadow puppet figure of the other. This relationship is dialectical, building between interactions and fleeting moments of alienation. When I asked Namgyal if there was a relationship between Ladakhi youth's fashion sense and their experiences of discrimination, Namgyal was emphatic:

Yeah, of course, of course. The hate crime against Nido Tania, you know, that's the best example of that . . . once you go to Delhi, you realize that northeastern people or the Himalayan belt people are quite classy in their looks. Even though they don't wear quite Gucci or Prada and all that . . . they look classy: they know how to dress, very clean, and well-ironed, and what to wear and in what season. In that way I think, that still distinguishes you from the non-Ladakhis. . . . I would call it the binary of self and other. . . . I don't think people can easily digest when you are so classy or better than them. In terms of looks. Especially girls.

Kunzes, also independent and a self-described "free spirit," found the atmosphere of her Hindu boarding school in lowland India boring and frustrating, feeling that she was not able to engage with her Buddhist beliefs. Like Namgyal, she also cultivates her independence: she wears "whatever" and "[doesn't] care if people talk shit" about her. But part of Kunzes's discomfort stemmed from the sudden disappearance of Buddhism's daily rituals and landscape from her life when she was ensconced in boarding school. Buddhism is part of her sense of self, in how she reimagines the ways that she can carry forward her father's traditional form of *thanka* painting—in which pigments are ground by hand to create images of Buddhas and bodhisattvas that are educational and meditation devices—into her love of modern and transgressive art. Her father died when she was a teenager, and she dreams of opening Ladakh's first modern art gallery and naming it for him.

For others, what it meant to be Ladakhi came into focus only upon arrival in a distant place:

STANZIN ANGMO: I feel like I understood the beauty of Ladakh more, like how different it is, how unique it is, because when you come here and you take pictures and show them to your friends there, they're like, "oh my god! Where is it?" You know and you kind of feel proud because you're a Ladakhi. So and the culture, I feel like, "oh my god, our culture is so different and unique." But in certain way you're like oh, this is not true, you know, like certain, like, cultures in Ladakh are, like, not right. So, no, I can't follow this, so . . .

AUTHOR: What did you feel like that about?

STANZIN ANGMO: It's not really a culture, but it's just like how people think here. Like, you know, like teenagers shouldn't have sex before their marriage or, like, um . . .

AUTHOR: Like the gossipy . . .

STANZIN ANGMO: Yeah, gossipy and, like, many things, you know, they just criticize, they just know how to talk, they don't act. So I feel like they judge people more than . . . so yeah.

AUTHOR: Does that come up in your family or, like, with your friends when you're here? Do you feel like, oh, now I see them differently and then they don't kind of understand why I don't see things the same way? Do you have that kind of feeling, or do you just try to avoid those kind of topics?

STANZIN ANGMO: Like, some topics are really delicate that I can't talk. If I talk about that, then they would be like oh no, you went to U.S. and you learned this. But some, I would say, like I sent my mom and my aunt into cervical checking today. But they were so shy, they were like no, I don't need this. I was like, no, you have to go, you know? So . . . you know, some stuff they understand.

Other young people, like those we encountered in chapter 5, discuss the future more explicitly in relation to the same fracture points that their parents fret over: that of religion and its links to politics. Dorje is a devout Buddhist, who has reformed his life after a somewhat chaotic and belligerent first few years at college. Along with a few others, he has worked carefully to try to create student associations that incorporate Buddhists and Muslims: "So now, present generation has . . . the chance to do that. People like me alone, I cannot do that. So I'm studying. . . . I cannot come to Ladakh and Delhi, but many students, they can do it. Those who are in the Buddhist Association or Muslim Association, they can come together. They can solve things. If you are dividing in terms of religion, in future it is going to be worse. Don't you think so?" I told Dorje that many people had spoken to me of being close, "like brothers and sisters," and then said that everything fell apart in the 1980s, and I noted that young people often spoke in optimistic terms about their close relations with their classmates across religious boundaries. Older folks had told me the same stories but then also commented that they would never let their children marry across those religious boundaries. This made me feel unclear about the future, which Dorje spoke of confidently: "You can see, it is so clear. Those who grew up during the agitations, they had that mind-set, the Muslim and Buddhist one. We didn't see the agitation going on, so I have many Muslim friends. I treat them like brothers, so they come, uh, they come with me to monasteries and they know many things about Buddhism. So it is, it is the thing. Now, still right now, when they grow up and now I can see their . . . thinking changing, you know?"

Conclusion: Mobility and Mountains

When parents tell their children not to mix or mingle across religious lines, they are embedding that territoriality into comportment, into the body's orientation toward others. Parents wish that their children will not desire the other but also ask their children not to resemble the other—to distinguish themselves through consumption or nonconsumption of meat or alcohol, through eating or not eating the food prepared by others, whether because of the boycott, changing guest lists, or restriction on consumption of food by people of another religion. The physical boundaries on the landscape of this district are both militarized (the borders with Pakistan and China), ordinary and unmarked (where Leh becomes Kargil District and villages fall on one side or the other). At the same time, the borders of this place to the south are only (in)visible from the sky or mountain road, falling in glaciers and isolated mountain passes.

Bayat (2009) asks us not to underestimate the "encroachment of the ordinary," the ways that life is changed by one woman pushing a societal or political boundary, which is witnessed by another who decides to test the same limit, or by folks getting by—selling goods on the street, pursuing education to change their circumstances. What he calls "nonmovements," or incremental social change, could be about women gradually, with or without family support, managing, through a hundred small moments, to enact a little more autonomy than they had before. They could consist of young people in search of fun and frivolity. They could be about the small political moments that occur on the street, waiting at the post office, witnessing someone being hassled by police, and then the conversations that emerge from that moment, that begin to cohere into a "political street"—a term Bayat uses to refer to a shared sense of the political situation—that can turn into political action, whether spectacular or more slowly through encroachment. In Sara Ahmed's (2004) language of emotional politics, these small moments become part of not the feelings that go from outside to in, or from inside to the outer world, but rather the fabric that connects us or repels us.

In working to change their own lives, and with the support of their parents, students are participating in a nonmovements of sorts—just in trying to get by, they make small incremental changes that are adding up to something. But what are they adding up to? Who is in the street, and whom are they talking to? If spaces are closed down for those conversations or segregated by religious identity, if a Muslim boy and a Buddhist girl talking could become an incident, in the ways that Rahima and Palzes speculate, then those prefigurative politics (Dyson and Jeffrey, 2018)—modes of living in the present as one desires to live in the future—are limited in scope.

The maintenance of Leh District as a territory with its own autonomous government is not about defending the borders of a political entity but rather about instilling a sense of territorial awareness within each young person. But babies are not born carrying this knowledge, and young people are known to be unruly, both loving and defying their parents. What then ensures that territory will be born anew in each generation in the same way? Palzes, who copied her friends' parents to pray at home like a Muslim, may or may not take the message that her mother intends. Students like Kunzes and Rigzin Angmo, flying across mountains, across linguistic barriers, and creating their own new identities as they do so, may create new territorializations as they move into the future. This is not to valorize these new futures, which might bear hallmarks of neoliberal future fantasies, replicate difference in insidious ways, pick up different forms of ethnic and racial othering, or exacerbate class differences in the guise of social capital or fetishization of education.

The intimate geopolitics of young people emerges in their narratives here as fundamentally one of in-betweenness, one of movement. In chapter 5, parents sought to fix a territorial future, to ground their children's lives in a firm knowledge of who they are in relation to family and place and religion. Through this grounding, they sought to ensure the future that they desired. But these young women and men suggest that they see themselves already and primarily in flight, in motion, in relation to the world beyond the mountains in ways that also shift their relations to one another. Mobility adds to and complicates what is required for the defense of territory through intimate geopolitics. Influences multiply and movement itself disperses groundedness and reveals new horizons both opening and foreclosing.

The relationship between parents and extended family and children is intimate, ordinary, and political. It is a vector for transmission of the embodied identities of the present out into the future unknown. When Jigmet raises her children to succeed but also hopes they will lead joyful lives of unconditional love, when Palzes's mother tells her not to pray like a Muslim, when Namgyal insists on challenging her mother with her unconventional gendered views, these moments are cumulative and building, shaping the conversations that they have in the street and later in their own households. As these young people make their decisions about how to love and how to live, they will be creating territory in their wake.[7]

Conclusion

In September of 2017, an op-ed in the *Indian Express* was titled: "I Am Saldon, I Am Shifah." It begins:

> My name is Stanzin Saldon. I also call myself Shifah. I was born in a Buddhist family in 1987 in Leh. I had joined Government Medical College, Jammu, but decided to change my field after four years of training because I was interested in social work. Subsequently, I did my Bachelors in Social Work and have been working for four years now. My personal decision to marry a Muslim man is being used to fuel communal tension across Ladakh. The Ladakh Buddhist Association (LBA) wrongly claimed that the love of my life and my husband, Syed Murtaza Agah, has "lured" me to accept Islam. The LBA also gave an ultimatum to the entire Muslim community in Ladakh to "return" me or "leave" the region. In fact, the LBA issued this threat in a letter addressed to J&K Chief Minister Mehbooba Mufti on September 7. (Saldon 2017)

Shifah's public comments were made after she had responded with her own letter to the chief minister, countering LBA claims that she had been abducted and writing: "Ladakh Buddhist Association is trying to objectify me and demanding my return as if I'm a property, which I'm not and cannot allow anyone to perceive me as such." The LBA had alleged that Shifah had been kidnapped and forcibly converted, but she described her marriage quite differently. In an interview after the letters and protests, she told a journalist that she had been the one to propose: "I was pinned down in a car crash in Delhi in 2015 and the only person I wanted to see was Murtaza" (Varagur 2018b). In July 2016, the couple married, but word got out in Leh only in August of 2017, immediately leading to protests in the Bazaar and the letter to Mufti. The escalation led Shifah and Murtaza to leave Ladakh and travel without their phones through Kashmir, returning to Ladakh to Murtaza's family in Dras (in the Kargil District) for a family wedding ceremony only after protests had died down in the wake of her public declaration. In her editorial, she writes:

> I was aghast to see my decision to marry a Muslim man from Kargil (which, in fact, is part of Ladakh) being shown as a "theft of a girl" and a reason for the "dying culture of Ladakh." Our culture and ethos (in fact, all cultures on earth) in Ladakh haven't dropped down from the sky, where love and individual choices have no scope. That's the worst possible way for us to look at ourselves. The portrayal of a woman as a mere baby-making machine to save the community was another despicable reason given to question my life choices. . . . It is shameful to demand that I should be returned because nobody has taken or stolen me. . . . I am Saldon and also Shifah. I choose to be both and will always be a daughter of my family and Ladakh. (Saldon 2017)

Now the couple live in Jammu, where Shifah describes occasional stares and being asked to take selfies with those who recognize her (Gagné 2019; Varagur 2018b). Reporting on the aftermath within its larger context of demographic competition, Varagur (2018a) describes hearing from a Buddhist woman about an event at Gonpa Soma (New Temple, in Main Bazaar) in which "They were loudly broadcasting a sermon by a monk who was totally against contraception for Buddhist women and encouraging women to have five or six children" and comments that it is hard for Buddhist women to obtain abortions.

When Paljor and Fatima, the couple described in the opening to this book, first revealed their secret marriage to their families, I had believed that their relationship would endure the inevitable political challenges. I abandoned this naive hope—perhaps more revealing of my own life's trajectory and liberal cultural milieu idealizing individualized romantic love—as political leaders and family members soon conspired to drive the couple apart. Heartbreak followed, with the termination of Fatima's pregnancy and subsequent arranged marriages that reabsorbed each firmly within their own religious circles. Over years of subsequent research, my mind kept circling back to that summer and to Paljor dancing at my own wedding reception—a party of over a thousand guests held two years after our initial smaller ceremony. I had thought of myself as the true outsider: a white foreigner not born into Buddhism, speaking Ladakhi as a second language. Though I had not been what my in-laws wanted for their son, they came to terms with me. Within a little more than a year of the beginning of our relationship, they accepted me completely and made me feel as though I was meant to be a part of their family.

Our neighbors, distant relatives, and community members all accepted and even celebrated our marriage, each placing the *khatag* [white scarf] over my head, one after another, with my bridesmaid carefully removing a stack when the layers became unwieldy. In 2004, while Fatima's marriage unraveled, I was carefully following instructions on dance, dress, and behavior from my mother-in-law, sister-in-law, and aunts-in-law. Not wanting to embarrass anyone, I was relieved to be told I danced like a little doll; that the *sulma* and *perak*, the satin pleated dress and turquoise headdress snaking over my head and down my back, suited me; that I looked exactly like a Ladakhi bride. We laughed to see tourists sneaking into our wedding to get a glimpse of authentic Ladakh.

The forms of difference that I represented were complicated. As in so many formerly colonized places, even as colonialism is condemned, whiteness and fairness are considered desirable and to be deferred to broadly across India, as they are associated with wealth and modernity—though this association feels somehow different in Ladakh, which was over the Himalayas, part of a princely state, and somewhat insulated from direct interaction with the British. In Ladakh, this privileging of whiteness does flit in and out of focus, but white foreigners also come with connotations of immorality, unreliability, and jokes at the expense of "ragged" backpackers (informally called *chadpo*, in reference to patched and fraying clothes). Before accepting our marriage, my in-laws had recalled other cases of white foreigners who had blithely married Ladakhis only to later divorce them when the marriage became inconvenient. Ironically, and yet inevitably, given the ways that colonial difference is imbricated into these mountains, my foreignness was not as charged with geopolitical currents—it became suddenly a series of small inconveniences that could be compensated for through my in-laws' generosity and patience.

For Fatima, remaining part of a Buddhist family became impossible—the geopolitical forces became too much to surmount. Shifah has articulated the story of her own life as one of her own choice and refused to be conscripted into territorial struggles as "mere baby-making machine" or "property" (for excellent treatises on the politics of refusal, see Simpson 2007, 2014). Shifah's story unfolds alongside India's ongoing and deepening Hindu nationalist turn in which marriages across caste and religious lines, as well as other everyday events, are met with communal violence (Jaffrelot 2017; Sarkar 2018; Siddiqui 2017; R. Varma 2017). It unfolds alongside increased incidents of caste lynching and public discourse around Muslim women in need of protection from Muslim men, figured as threats (P. Gupta, Gökariksel, and Smith under review). Simultaneously, these logics unfurl in regionally specific ways, such as bans on women marrying outside their tribe (Correspondent 2018) and proposed amendments to provide citizenship only to migrants from non-Muslim groups (Ameen 2019). As I was revising this book, heightened tensions between India and Pakistan had ordinary people fearing for potential escalation or war.

Geopolitical Life

The ways that Shifah speaks about her own life and body, and her refusal to be instrumentalized in a struggle for demographic territory, resonate with countless conversations playing out not only in Ladakh and India but in the place where I wrote most of this book, the U.S. South. If a book is a time capsule, imagine this conclusion marking the political issues unfolding close to home as I write. Migrants from Central America, many of them women and children from Honduras, are traversing Mexico to seek legal asylum at the U.S. border, while the U.S. president deploys troops to counter the "security threat" they supposedly pose. Embodying refusal, women across the United States used their bodies and voices to try to prevent the confirmation of Brett Kavanaugh to the Supreme Court following accusations of sexual assault. Kavanaugh, nominated in part because he is expected to uphold the further restriction of abortion, is enthusiastically supported by the U.S. president, also accused of assault by multiple women. Eleven Jewish people, mostly elderly, were killed on Sabbath in the Tree of Life Synagogue for their religious identity and for welcoming refugees; a few days earlier, another white man shot two Black people dead in a grocery store when he was unable to enter a Black church with the intention of killing worshippers. Earlier in this same eventful week, Democratic leaders across the country received pipe bombs in the mail.

These events follow the family separation crisis, still unfolding, in which thousands of children were separated from their parents and caregivers at the border, as a deterrent to migrants and asylum seekers. News continues to deepen the tragedy of the U.S. migrant family separation policy, revealing more details about children separated, the difficulty of reunification, and the lasting effects of this policy. In this policy, a nation-state of white fictive kinship and family (Collins 1998) was centered as in need of protection while mostly Brown and Black children were denied access to their kin. This is, of course, a haunting echo of the conditions of Black parents and children under slavery, which was not a side effect but central to the maintenance of the logic of anti-Black violence (Hartman 1997; Perry 2018; Sharpe 2016; Spillers 1987; Weheliye 2014). These and other forms of eugenics persist in sublimated forms or sometimes in the explicit targeting of racialized and minoritized others for early death (see, among many others, Bridges 2011; Gilmore 2002; Roberts 2014; P. Vasudevan in press). It also recalls the theft of children from their Native parents that continued until the late twentieth century and continues today in other forms (Brown and Estes 2018; Child 1998; Dunbar-Ortiz 2014; Pilkington 2002). The family separation policy is an early twenty-first-century iteration of a number of policies and events that reveal the ways that kinship and family, and the right to have kin and have family, to pass ancestry, cultural knowledge, belonging, and place-based roots, down to your children and your children's children have been at the heart of sovereignty and its denial in the context of European imperial expansion (Smith et al. 2019). Empire and colonialism have, with crucial contextual specificity, meant that colonial and imperial officers, soldiers, bureaucrats, and academics rendered and gendered people into territory across the colonized world, working to hollow out their ancestral content, break their kinship practices, and to consolidate white European supremacy and extract value.[1]

The politics of the right in the United States have come to revolve around white demographic fever dreams, in which the white majority in the country is represented as at risk (Gökariksel et al. 2019; Gökariksel and Smith 2016; Smith and Vasudevan 2017). This often unfolds through gendered visions of white women threatened by Brown or Black men, as in Donald Trump's campaign announcement that promised to protect the country from "Mexican rapists" and his promises of a ban on Muslim immigration and visas and of the construction of a "border wall." In other contexts, the logic is often similar, but the fractures and topographies and contour lines shift (Katz 2001). The violence that these logics engender point to intergenerational relations as geopolitical practice: as the maintenance of political logics between past and future. In the case of the United States, racial geopolitics have involved the manipulation of or destruction of ties between parents and their children as a means of protecting white supremacy, parallel to a celebration of childhood innocence for white people. Reiterated across scales, the practices that transmit racial geopolitics are enmeshed in local manipulations of school districting (Anderson 2016; McRae 2018; Nguyen et al. 2017), in the racial politics that play out on my own campus at the University of North Carolina at Chapel Hill (Dimpfl and Smith in press), and even closer to home, in the everyday experiences that Tonyot and I have raising our daughter in a predominantly white neighborhood and school district.

When Shifah tells us that her life is her own, not property, she is living out and refusing a colonial territorialization that emerges not from the context of Ladakh itself but from broader territorial processes. Young people are taught that interreligious romance is dangerous. Upon marriage, they hear conflicting points of view on whether and what kind of contraception is ethically acceptable—from a religious point of view but also from the point of view of loyalty to the religious community-in-formation. Shifah's story is also grounded in the management of religious and moral boundaries through the disciplining of desire. New reproductive technologies, the medicalization of the body, and the emergence of a biopolitical state—focused on the maintenance of a population, not only the defense of territory—enable new forms of bodily management, and they also provide a new language for women to frame their reproductive history in terms of evidence and risk. Others have noted the pressure on women to embody national cultural identity through their sexuality and on the role the state plays in this process. Women are called to marry, dress, and comport themselves in ways that reflect well on the state and bode well for the upbringing of loyal and proper citizens: their bodies are thus inseparable from and contiguous with the nation as cultural idea and the state as manager of citizens, as they are likewise called to exist in relation to first the natal and then the marital family (Chowdhry 2007; C. Gupta 2009; Mody 2008; Puri 1999; Rajan 2003). This process through which bodies are called into relation to the state and nation is, of course, not particular or peculiar to South Asia. It is a pattern that replicates and proliferates across the globe, particularly in the wake of empire and its racial formations.[2]

Young people are forging a future for themselves and for Ladakh through their movement between the region and India's (or the world's) urban spaces and through their embodied interactions with border guards, classmates, and landlords. Their assertions about the persons they want to become, about whom (or whether) they will marry, about what they owe to their parents and their place of birth, are also geopolitical statements that reflect their orientation to these other bodies and other places. They create spaces for art; they embrace their Buddhist identity while learning more about Muslim poetry. Tsewang Chuskit and Stanzin Angmo, who reflected in chapter 6 on how their own movements had shaped their sense of self, have created the New Ladakhi Girls organization, seeking to make space for young people to learn about women's health and for intergenerational communication on such issues. Ladakh is a territory that is enacted on a daily basis when young people make their choices—whether to disperse to the far-flung corners of the earth or to return, remain, marry within the community.

Intimacy is an imprecise and tricky word—we might think of it as proximity and closeness, but intimacies of proximity can also be monstrous (Sharpe 2009; P. Vasudevan in press). Abusive, dangerous, and degrading relationships can also be founded in intimacies both small and subtle, spectacular and global, or mundane and unnoticed (Pain 2015; Pain and Staeheli 2014). Even when intimacy is imbued with love, care, and concern for well-being, that love and care can sustain structures of violence premised on difference. In some contexts, parents choosing a "good school district," in doing so, are furthering segregation and upholding white supremacy (Hagerman 2018; Hannah-Jones 2012, 2014; Pinsker 2018;). In others, concerns that an interreligious marriage or marriage between people who have been differently racialized will be stressful reiterate and strengthen the conditions that will cause it to be stressful. In all these ways, geopolitics are made intimate.

Since 2004, I have been working through accounts of love affairs, contraception, youth aspirations, and severed social ties in an attempt to understand the complex relationship between individual bodies and the territorial strategy deployed by political actors and organizations and built into the structure of the political system itself. Young people's lives are a geopolitical terrain for the orchestration of demographic futures, maintenance of existing racial structures, and simultaneous management of the present. This starts before children are born, as women and men manage their children's births alongside complicated political and ethical commitments. The landscape into which children are born is shaped by prior visions and versions of sovereignty and the imposition of colonialism, and women making decisions about contraception navigate the capacities of their own body, their expectations of joy and labor, a changing economic context, as well as the political narratives in which they are immersed. These ethical questions are entangled in the technologies themselves, and in the stakes of life choices, but also emerge in relation to the history of this place and to the mapping and categorization that the British Empire and subsequent sovereign states demanded. As these forms of political organization spread and became part of intimate life, they reorganized not only forms of formal political organization, from kings and courtiers to elected officials, but also the ways that people crossed or did not cross thresholds, were or were not invited to dinner parties, were or were not candidates for marriage. Here, I have sought to give life to territory by telling stories about people who are surviving or thriving in a territorialized existence, sometimes through heartbreak, and other times with joy and determination, and perhaps most often with a little of all these emotions.

While political forces seek to marshal bodies as symbols or deploy them as territorial instruments, our bodies have their own physics and affective relations to one another, and we inhabit these complex sites while carrying our ancestors' aspirations as well as our own. In subtle and explicit ways, people's lives become territorial—their friendships, reproductive decisions, and romantic decisions entangled with concerns about holding or ceding political ground and the looming uncertain future.

In this book, I have argued that all of us, young and old, are participating in the lively life of territory. What kind of place are we calling into being? How will our small choices—about love, about loss, about children—shape the world? Will we recognize this world we are making? When I speak to young college students in Ladakh today, the future is an open horizon, both expansive and precarious. Their parents worry and fret and also marvel at the generational differences they witness in their children. They recall times of conflict, and that young people were at the forefront of that conflict, and project this onto young people and the future. When young people talk about themselves, however, they present a different understanding of both past and future. In ways both large and small, through the interactions we are thrown into but do not desire, and those that we yearn for, we are creating a territorial world.

ACKNOWLEDGMENTS

Every word of this book was made possible by the humbling generosity of women and men in Ladakh who opened their homes to me and trusted me with their stories, even while they also fed and cared for me. This is a gift I will never forget, a gift that can never be repaid, and one that has changed my life. Every manner of support and kindness was provided during the initial research particularly by my mother-in-law, Dolma Tsering (Kagapa), and my research assistant Hasina Bano (Maski). In the early years of this research, I was helped immensely by Dr. Lhadol, Abdul Ghani Sheikh, Tsewang Lden, Fatima Bano, Becky Norman (and her dictionary!), as well as Moulvi Omar, Ashraf Ali Barcha, Nazir Ahmad Khan, Mohammad Ayup, Abi Padma, Spalzes Angmo, Thinle Angmo, Y. Angmo, and Ama Putit. Thanks also to the high school students who did an oral history project with me and who were a joy to talk to: Fatima Batul, Sumera Bano, Wahida Khursid, Nawaz Ahmed Khan, Bashir Ali, Tsering Dolma, Padma Tsering, and Sonam Yangdol.

As this work expanded, the Ladakh Arts and Media Organization became a home away from home for me. In particular, Monisha Ahmed, Tashi Morup, Rinchen Dolma, Mabel Diskit, and Rigzin Chodon have provided all manner of advice, suggestions, and assistance. Mabel Gergan has been more than a colleague but a co-conspirator and inspiration through every phase of our collaborative work with young people. The young people I have spoken with in Ladakh in recent years have taught me more than I ever expected or deserved: in particular, Namgyal Angmo, Fatima Ashraf, Tashi Namgyal, Kunzes Zangmo, Tundup Churpon, Tsewang Chuskit, Stanzin Angmo, Chozin Palmo, Tsewang Norboo, Rigzin Angmo, Stanzin Jidey, and others have been generous and insightful in all the experiences they have shared with me. In my first visit to Ladakh, in 1999, the Siksa family in upper Phyang was unfailingly kind to me, especially ama-le, and Amber Field and Naoko Tano were my supportive, funny, and charming companions.

Young artists in Ladakh have transformed how I see the world and made me hopeful. I do not deserve the generosity of Chemat Dorje Serthi, who created the cover image, "Mountains Are the True Ancestors," and kindly agreed to let me use it for this book. His description of it as Ladakh back when it was under the sea has evoked for me a longer timeline for this place that I love.

I would not have completed this book without the camaraderie, hilarity, and generous spirit of our dangerous playground writing group, not to mention their intellectual gifts: Lilly Nguyen, Andrew Curley, Maya Berry, and Banu Gökariksel. They have provided support I did not know that I needed, taken chapters apart and put them back together, and patiently endured the way that writing a book took a toll on my personality. Erika Wise, Jocelyn Chua, Jean Dennison, Jenny Tone-Pah-Hote, Banu Gökariksel, Jennifer Ho, Jecca Namakkal and Danielle Purifoy, Anu Sabhlok, and Anindita Datta all provided key advice at specific moments, talked me out of giving up, or generally encouraged the project when it was needed. Erika has been a loyal friend through every stage of this project since 2002, even as my capacity to be a good friend was compromised by writing this book. Jocelyn never says no to eating a giant greasy slice of pizza with me and that has meant more than she knows. Banu patiently talks through every personal and intellectual crisis that I create for myself. My current and former graduate students inspire me, tolerated my distraction and encouraged me to keep going. I could never have written this book without their kindness and support: Mabel Gergan, Pavithra Vasudevan, Mike Dimpfl, Chris Neubert, Pallavi Gupta, and Carlos Serrano. As my first two students, taken on far too early, Mabel Gergan and Pavithra Vasudevan have fundamentally shaped who I am as a scholar. In our geography department, Barbara Taylor, Dan Warfield, and Nell Phillips make everything we do as faculty possible. The students who made coffee for me at Meantime while I wrote this book also make my day. I'm also grateful for the countless staff who maintain the buildings that we work in on our campus and for the student activists who are the real innovators on our campus.

So many people read and provided comments on pieces of this in one form or another and went beyond that reading to calm me down, make suggestions, and let me know when I was repeating myself. This partial list spans years and includes Monisha Ahmed, Tsetan Dolkar, Mike Dimpfl, Pallavi Gupta, Carlos Serrano, Chris Neubert, Mike Hawkins, Lara Lookabaugh, Michelle Padley, Tsewang Chuskit, Fatima Ashraf, Jenny Tone-Pah-Hote, Namgyal Angmo, Jacqueline Fewkes, Nasir Khan, Rebecca Norman, and Jonathan Cobb. Two anonymous reviewers provided lovely comments that helped me develop my ideas further. Mabel Gergan and Andrew Curley deserve a special shout out because they read almost the entire manuscript and provided more helpful advice and encouragement than I deserve.

Sallie Marston was a source of unending support and the best advisor a student could have back when I originally started to think about these ideas long ago. Paul Robbins likewise asked all the right questions at the right time. J. P. Jones, Richard Eaton, Marvin Waterstone, Mark Nichter, Ana Alonso, and Yaseen

Noorani all contributed to the development of these ideas while I was at the University of Arizona..

This book would never have been written had Péter Berta not reached out and asked me to return to a then-abandoned book idea. Kimberly Guinta, Jasper Chang, and Kristen Bettcher at Rutgers were exceedingly patient with me, and the anonymous reviewers at the proposal and manuscript stage helped me a great deal. I am particularly thankful for Jasper Chang's help navigating the cover process. I am also grateful for all the feedback I received on an earlier version of this book idea through the Social Science Research Council Book Fellowship in 2012, which also included productive editorial feedback from Jonathan Cobb, which I returned to years later to complete the manuscript.

The first phase of this research was supported by the Fulbright-Hays Doctoral Dissertation Research Abroad Program, the Society of Women Geographers, the International Dissertation Research Fellowship Program of the Social Science Research Council with funds provided by the Andrew W. Mellon Foundation, the University of Arizona Social and Behavioral Sciences Research Institute, the Association of American Geographers Political Geography Specialty Group, and the Association of American Geographers Qualitative Research Specialty Group. Later phases were supported by a National Science Foundation Geography and Spatial Science Program Grant (BCS-1561072), "Impacts of Education-Driven Urban Migration on Youth Aspirations and Identity"; and by a University of North Carolina Asia Center Faculty Travel Award with funding from the Jimmy and Judy Cox Asia Initiative. Writing was supported by an Institute for the Arts and Humanities Fellowship and enriched by the guidance of Michele Berger during my time at the institute.

How can I thank my family? Teresa Swingle, Kiki Atkinson, Peter Smith, Dana Smith, and other family members in the United States have been patient with my long absences and years spent far away and have always supported my work. Kiki Atkinson and Peter Smith have tolerated and encouraged my wayward nature, rather than stifling it, and Teresa is the sister that everyone wishes they had. In Ladakh, Dolma Tsering, Tsewang Norbu, Stanzin Legdon, Tashi Dolma have been our home away from home and cared for Tonyot, Sasha, and I through every kind of circumstance. Dolma Tsering and Tsewang Norbu accepted me as an inappropriate, unruly, and usually pretty useless daughter-in-law, and I can never repay their kindness. Stanzin Angmo has made me feel like a sister, and some of my happiest memories in recent years are of us hanging out at her home making unnecessarily elaborate meals. Morup, Ane Eshay Ane Tsewang, Namkha, Jigmet, Nilza Angmo, Phuntsog Angmo, Dolkar, Yangdol, Stanzin Legsmon, Abi Tsomo, Ane Angmo and so many others lifted my spirits, cared for me when I was sick, danced with me at picnics, fed me, corrected my grammar, made me laugh, and taught me everything I know. I am so grateful to be part of the family. All the little cousins who play with Sasha each summer have filled all of us with delight: Adol, Namgyal, Chopel, Dangsal, Jigmet, Dargyal, and "Acho" Lotus are all part of this book.

Stanzin Tonyot has put trust in me and stayed beside me despite his deep skepticism about academic endeavors. His intellectual companionship has shaped the ideas in this book; his insistence on vacations, travel, beaches, and apple-picking has kept me human, and at key moments and deadlines, I could focus on this work knowing that he and Sasha were happily hanging out by the stream together, reading books at the library, or drawing. Our life together has taught me more than I ever expected, and I am endlessly grateful for this time. Our daughter, Sasha Kunzes, is our love and light and life, and this book could only be dedicated to her. She asks me about its progress and what is in it every day, and I hope when she is old enough to read it she will know how much that meant to me.

NOTES

CHAPTER 1 INTRODUCTION

1. Most of those with whom I spoke have been given pseudonyms, and in cases where details might identify the speaker, they have been slightly altered. A few of the young people interviewed for chapters 4 and 5 have requested to keep their names.

2. I am grateful to Jacqueline Fewkes for drawing my attention to this.

3. At the time the discussion of numbers heated up—between 1981 and 2001 (census data were not collected in J&K in 1991 due to the political disturbances)—the ratio of Buddhist to Muslims in Leh District remained fairly steady, though the ratio of Hindus increased. Kargil District's population, however, increased relative to Leh District, and this was a matter of concern and discussion and was sometimes used to back up the theory that Muslim fertility was outstripping that of Buddhists. This matters for local elections but also for Buddhist Ladakhis' sense of territorial security. In the most recent census (2011), the ratio of Buddhists to other religions did decline, mainly due to the increase in the percentage of Hindus and also perhaps in part due to Muslim migration from Kargil and from Kashmir as the political situation there continues to limit economic opportunity.

4. Nawang Tsering Shakspo tells similar stories about Kuksho (Shakspo 1995).

5. I have written more about my own positionality elsewhere (Smith 2016) and turn to this discussion in the book only when it seemed necessary.

CHAPTER 2 BIRTH AND THE TERRITORIAL BODY

1. *Dzos*, the male offspring of yak and cow, are valuable for plowing, stronger and more docile than bulls, while *dzomos* (the females) produce more milk than regular cows.

2. At the time of my research on family planning (2008), the most common forms of contraception were the use of the IUD to space (or limit) births and the use of tubal ligation to limit births. In speaking with 198 women, only one was using contraceptive pills, and one was using condoms. Gynecologists view the IUD as the most reliable form of managing contraception if the woman and her partner wanted to have more children. Gynecologists rarely prescribe the pill because of concerns women will not take it every day at the same time.

3. I do not claim that these figures can be generalized: due to the sensitive nature of the topic and my determination not to compromise my rapport and opportunities for future research and collaboration in Ladakh, I relied on opportunistic rather than random sampling. To complete the survey, my research assistant, Hasina Bano, and I began in each neighborhood with one person that we knew and proceeded to ask

each neighbor or woman that we encountered in the neighborhood or village to speak to us. In Leh, we tried to work across the neighborhoods, including Horzey, the Housing Colony, Skampari, Shenam, Old Town, Chubi, and so forth. Near Leh we visited the neighboring villages of Chushot, Choglamsar, Thikse, Shey, and Phyang.

4. *Konjok* refers to the Buddhist triple gem—Buddha, dharma (his teachings), and sangha (community of the Buddha's followers).

5. Yangdol here used the term *Balti* to refer to Shia Muslims. In Ladakh, the terms *Balti* and *Kache* are frequently used to distinguish between Shia and Sunni Muslims. These terms, however, are somewhat misleading as they are geographic markers—Balti means a person from Baltistan, and Kache means Kashmiri. These terms are regularly applied to Ladakhis to denote their religious identity, but in my interviews I have found it is more common for Buddhists to deploy these words and that Muslims more often differentiate using the terms "Shia" and "Sunni." In later interviews, I have translated "Balti" and "Kache" as "Shia" and "Sunni"; however, I have bracketed the term to indicate this substitution. A *rinpoche* is a high monk, generally the reincarnated spiritual leader of a particular monastery. Chushot is a Shia-majority village that meanders along the Indus River, just southeast of Leh.

6. My gratitude to Jocelyn Chua for the observation that not knowing is a form of knowledge production.

7. Literally her expression *mun-la* means, "in darkness"; here I am translating this as unconscious, as one who has fainted or passed out and cannot take action.

CHAPTER 3   THE QUEEN AND THE FISTFIGHT

1. The official flag of J&K has three lines—including one that stands for Ladakh.

2. These quotations are from Lonely Planet (Lonely Planet 2018, https://www.lonelyplanet .com/india/jammu-and-kashmir/ladakh) and the Incredible India video (available on YouTube at https://www.youtube.com/watch?v=ySrQ2h92mUg), which is a promotional campaign by the Indian Ministry of Tourism (Pianeta Gaia n.d.). Fewkes discusses this form of representation in more detail (J. H. Fewkes 2009).

3. "Nakshran ma chakna, shranril bo chak."

4. For insightful accounts of the politicization of religion, see Aggarwal (2004), Beek (1996), Bertelsen (1996), Gutschow (2004) Pinault (2001), and Srinivas (1998).

5. I am grateful to Jacqueline Fewkes for this observation.

CHAPTER 4   INTIMACY ON THE THRESHOLD

1. Several scholars mention Kuksho—in particular, see local historians Sheikh (2007) and Shakspo (1995), but also see Bray (2007) on how this research has been received by residents of Kuksho.

2. In other publications, I have given Nizam the pseudonym Ahmed. Here, I have changed this to avoid confusion when I reference author Sara Ahmed.

3. I am translating from *Kachul* and *Kachulpa*, the Ladakhi words for Kashmir and Kashmiri.

4. This percentage is based on a 2008 survey in which I asked seventy-three women (twenty-four Buddhists, twenty-four Sunni Muslims, and twenty-five Shia Muslims) if Buddhists and Muslims should be allowed to marry. Of those, fifty-four believed it

should be prevented, eleven believed it should be allowed, and eight did not feel able to answer the question. These numbers become more striking keeping in mind that most these women had relatives across the religious line—indicating intermarriage in their own families, most often in the previous two generations.

5. My thinking on neighbors is influenced by conversations with Banu Gökariksel, who has written on neighbors with Anna Secor (Gökariksel and Secor forthcoming).

6. This is far from foolproof. Several times during fieldwork Hasina would sometimes turn to me after a quick survey interview to tell me "I thought she was going to be Muslim!"

7. Gutschow suggests women might not have found this option very appealing, since nuns had a low status and often a difficult life (Gutschow 2004). The landscape for nuns is quite different today, with well-funded nunneries, travel, and higher status.

8. This rhetorical flourish appears in the wake of decadal releases of the Indian census, which mark a small shift in religious composition; the percent Hindu fell from 80.5 percent to 78.4 percent between 2001 and 2011, while the percent Muslim increased from 13.4 percent to 14.2 percent (Ghosh and Singh 2015; Jain 2015). The rate of growth for Muslim Indians was 24 percent, down from 29 percent, but higher than the national average of 18 percent (Ghosh and Singh 2015; Jain 2015). These differences are most likely the result of economic disparity and complex social factors, and the bigger piece of news is that birth rates for all have fallen drastically in the past two decades, but these slight differences according to religious identity are often pulled into nationalist political discourses (Dharmalingam and Morgan 2004; Iyer 2002; P. Jeffery and Jeffery 2002; R. Jeffery and Jeffery 2005).

CHAPTER 5   RAISING CHILDREN ON THE THRESHOLD OF THE FUTURE

1. The restoration of the LAMO center is documented on their website, available at lamo .org.in.

2. Ladol has appeared in other writing as "Kunzes," but I have changed her pseudonym here so as not to confuse her with Kunzes, introduced later in the chapter, who opted to keep her name.

3. *Paba* by itself or *paba-thukpa* are frequently referenced to signal "traditional" food and set it apart from today's diet. Paba is made by boiling seven flours together, including not only wheat and barley but also flours made from dried peas and beans. It is molded into a mountain shape with a wooden paddle, and you can break off pieces and eat them with any kind of dish or with buttermilk mixed with herbs or greens. Paba is notoriously heavy and signifies a sturdy solid food that might be preferred by *meme-le* and *abi-le* but not eaten by young people in the house. In this way, families often have multiple dinners, with old and young eating different food. Thukpa is a noodle soup with *churphe* (dried cheese) and *shranma* (dried peas).

4. I am grateful to Rebecca Norman for correcting my understanding of this word as meaning both happy and comfortable.

5. Mohammad is clarifying that this is his father's mother, not one of the many relatives who could be called his *abi*.

6. In Ladakh, you can double a word and start it with a "b" to imply "and all such things/ places/people"—for instance, *tagi-bagi* to mean bread and other such food, or *kharji-bharji*, all kinds of food. This usage is imported from Hindi.

CHAPTER 6   GENERATION VERTIGO AND
THE FUTURE OF TERRITORY

1. Some young people have chosen to keep their names, some to use pseudonyms. All of the college students were given a draft of this book upon submission for review to confirm their choices before publication.

2. This text is from the University of Delhi Miranda House website, available at http://www.mirandahouse.ac.in/.

3. This is part of an ongoing project on the lives of Himalayan youth studying in urban India. I have been collaborating on this project with Mabel Gergan (my former doctoral student and postdoc, now at Florida State). This project has included sixty-five interviews with Himalayan youth, a survey of sending families, three photo-voice projects, exhibitions, and a small zine. Rinchen Dolma works at LAMO and has been an invaluable collaborator as well as participant in the photo-voice project.

4. See, among others, Benwell and Hopkins 2017; Hopkins 2007; Hörschelmann and Refaie 2014; Huijsmans 2016; Smith and Gergan 2017.

5. These questions are explored in other writing, including Ozer et al. 2017; Smith 2017; Smith and Gergan 2015, 2017; Williams-Oerberg 2016.

6. *Sulma* is the pleated dress considered "traditional," especially for married women (but often worn by unmarried women at weddings, for dancing, and other special occasions). *Phu-met* (literally, no sleeves) is the Tibetan dress that was popular for unmarried women in the late twentieth century. I have been told that previously young unmarried women used to wear *kos* or *pho-gos*, the same dress as men.

7. I am grateful to Christina Sharpe (2016) for transforming the meaning of this phrase.

CONCLUSION

1. The entire breadth of the literature making these arguments cannot be cited here, but for starting places, please see Fanon 2008; Lugones 2010; Mohanty 2003; Perry 2018; Said 1979; Sharpe 2016; Simpson 2014; Tuhiwai Smith 1999; Weheliye 2014.

2. Fluri describes "corporeal modernity" as the way that women's dress and comportment in Afghanistan become targets for development, imperialism, and national identity. In the United States, the protection of white women is irrevocably tied to the violence used to maintain racial hierarchy.

REFERENCES

Abraham, Bobins. 2019. "Ladakh Breaks into Celebrations after its Long-standing Demand of Union Territory Status Gets Fulfilled." *India Times*. August 6. https://www.indiatimes.com/news/india/ladakh-breaks-into-celebrations-after-its-long-standing-demand-of-union-territory-status-gets-fulfilled-372937.html.

Adams, Vincanne. 2005. "Moral Orgasm and Productive Sex: Tantrism Faces Fertility Control in Lhasa, Tibet (China)." In *Sex in Development: Science, Sexuality, and Morality in Global Perspective*, edited by Stacy Leigh Pigg and Vincanne Adams, 207–40. Durham, NC: Duke University Press.

Aengst, Jennifer. 2008. "Representation and Perception: Why Reproduction Matters in Ladakh." *Ladakh Studies* 23: 4–11.

———. 2012. "The Politics of Fertility: Population and Pronatalism in Ladakh." *Himalaya, the Journal of the Association for Nepal and Himalayan Studies*, 32 (1–2): 23–34.

———. 2014. "Adolescent Movements: Dating, Elopements, and Youth Policing in Ladakh, India." *Ethnos* 79 (5): 630–49.

Aggarwal, Ravina. 2004. *Beyond Lines of Control: Performance and Politics on the Disputed Borders of Ladakh, India*. Durham, NC: Duke University Press.

Aggarwal, Ravina, and Mona Bhan. 2009. "'Disarming Violence': Development, Democracy, and Security on the Borders of India." *Journal of Asian Studies* 68: 519–42.

Ahmed, Monisha. 2002. *Living Fabric: Weaving among the Nomads of Ladakh Himalaya*. Bangkok: Orchid Press.

Ahmed, Sara. 2004. *The Cultural Politics of Emotion*. New York: Routledge.

———. 2010. *The Promise of Happiness*. Durham, NC: Duke University Press.

Ameen, Furquan. 2019. "Why the Northeast Is Protesting against the Citizenship Act Amendment." *Telegraph*, February 12, 2019. https://www.telegraphindia.com/india/why-the-northeast-is-protesting-against-the-citizenship-act-amendment/cid/1684432.

Anagnost, Ann. 2008. "Imagining Global Futures in China: The Child as a Sign of Value." In *Figuring the Future: Globalization and the Temporalities of Children and Youth*, edited by Jennifer Cole and Deborah Durham, 49–72. Santa Fe, NM: School for Advanced Research Press.

Anand, Nikhil. 2017. *Hydraulic City: Water and the Infrastructures of Citizenship in Mumbai*. Durham: Duke University Press.

Anderson, Carol. 2016. *White Rage: The Unspoken Truth of Our Racial Divide*. New York: Bloomsbury Publishing.

Ansell, Nicola, Flora Hajdu, Lorraine van Blerk, and Elsbeth Robson. 2017. "Fears for the Future: The Incommensurability of Securitisation and in/Securities among Southern African Youth." *Social & Cultural Geography*, 20 (4): 1–27.

Anthias, Floya, and Nira Yuval-Davis. 1992. *Racialized Boundaries: Race, Nation, Gender, Colour and Class and the Anti-Racist Struggle*. London: Routledge.

Appadurai, Arun. 1996. "Number in the Colonial Imagination." In *Modernity at Large: Cultural Dimensions of Globalization*, 114–39. Minneapolis: University of Minnesota Press.

Ashiq, Peerzada. 2015. "Now, Buddhist Group Seeks Modi's Intervention to Stop 'Love Jehad' in Ladakh." *Hindustan Times*, January 18, 2015. http://www.hindustantimes.com/jandk /now-buddhist-group-seeks-modi-s-intervention-to-stop-love-jehad-in-ladakh /article1-1307914.aspx.

Bacchetta, Paola. 2000. "Sacred Space in Conflict in India: The Babri Masjid Affair." *Growth and Change* 31: 255–84.

Bachelard, Gaston. 1994. *The Poetics of Space*. Translated by Maria Jolas. Boston: Beacon Press.

Bayat, Asef. 2009. *Life as Politics: How Ordinary People Change the Middle East*. Stanford, CA: Stanford University Press.

Beek, Martijn van. 1996. *Identity Fetishism and the Art of Representation*. Ithaca, NY: Cornell University Press.

———. 1998. "True Patriots: Justifying Autonomy for Ladakh." *Himalayan Bulletin* 18 (1): 35–46.

———. 1999. "Hill Councils, Development, and Democracy: Assumptions and Experiences from Ladakh." *Alternatives: Global, Local, Political* 24 (4): 435–59.

———. 2000. "Beyond Identity Fetishism: 'Communal' Conflict in Ladakh and the Limits of Autonomy." *Cultural Anthropology* 15: 525–69.

———. 2001. "Public Secrets, Conscious Amnesia, and the Celebration of Autonomy for Ladakh." In *States of Imagination: Ethnographic Explorations of the Postcolonial State*, edited by Thomas Blom Hansen and Finn Stepputat, 365–90. Durham, NC: Duke University Press.

———. 2003. "The Art of Representation: Domesticating Ladakhi Identity." In *Ethnic Revival and Religious Turmoil*, edited by Marie Lecomte-Tilouine and Pascale Dollfus, 283–301. Oxford: Oxford University Press.

———. 2004. "Dangerous Liaisons: Hindu Nationalism and Buddhist Radicalism in Ladakh." In *Religious Radicalism and Security in South Asia*, edited by Satu P. Limaya, Robert G. Wirsing, and Mohan Malik, 193–218. Honolulu, HI: Asia-Pacific Center for Security Studies.

Beek, Martijn van, and Fernanda Pirie. 2008. *Modern Ladakh: Anthropological Perspectives on Continuity and Change*. Leiden: Brill.

Behera, N.C. 2000. *State, Identity and Violence: Jammu, Kashmir and Ladakh*. New Delhi: Manohar Publishers and Distributors.

Benwell, Matt, and Peter E. Hopkins, eds. 2017. *Children, Young People and Critical Geopolitics*. Burlington, VT: Ashgate.

Berlant, Lauren. 2011. *Cruel Optimism*. Durham, NC: Duke University Press.

Bertelsen, Kristoffer Brix. 1996. *Our Communalized Future: Sustainable Development, Social Identification, and the Politics of Representation in Ladakh*. Aarhus, Denmark: Aarhus University.

———. 1997. "Early Modern Buddhism in Ladakh: On the Construction of Buddhist Ladakhi Identity, and Its Consequences." In *Recent Research on Ladakh 7: Proceedings of the 7th Colloquium of the International Association for Ladakh Studies*, edited by Thierry Dodin and Heinz Räther, 67–88. Bonn: Universitat Bonn.

Bhan, Mona. 2013. *Counterinsurgency, Democracy, and the Politics of Identity in India: From Warfare to Welfare?* London: Routledge.

Bhan, Mona, Haley Duschinski, and Goldie Osuri. 2019. "The international community must intervene on Kashmir." *Open Democracy*. https://www.opendemocracy.net/en/international-community-must-intervene-kashmir/.

Bialasiewicz, Luiza. 2006. "'The Death of the West': Samuel Huntington, Oriana Fallaci and a New 'Moral' Geopolitics of Births and Bodies." *Geopolitics* 11: 701–24.

Blunt, Alison. 2003. "Collective Memory and Productive Nostalgia: Anglo-Indian Home-making at McCluskieganj." *Environment and Planning D: Society and Space* 21: 717–38.

———. 2005. *Domicile and Diaspora*. Malden, MA: Blackwell.

Blunt, Alison, and Robyn Dowling. 2006. *Home*. New York: Routledge.

Bose, Sumantra. 2009. *Kashmir: Roots of Conflict, Paths to Peace*. Cambridge, MA: Harvard University Press.

Botterill, Kate, Peter Hopkins, and Gurchathen Sanghera. 2018. "Familial Geopolitics and Ontological Security: Intergenerational Relations, Migration and Minority Youth (in) securities in Scotland." *Geopolitics*, 1–26.

Bray, John. 2007. "Old Religions, New Identities and Conflicting Values in Ladakh." In *International Conference on Religion, Conflict and Development, University of Passau, Germany*. Retrieved from http://www.Phil.Uni-Passau.de/Fileadmin/Dokumente/Lehrstuehle/Korff/Pdf/Conferences/Paper_j._bray.Pdf. Citeseer.

———. 2013. "Readings on Islam in Ladakh: Local, Regional, and International Perspectives." *Himalaya, the Journal of the Association for Nepal and Himalayan Studies* 32 (1): 9.

Bridges, Khiara M. 2011. *Reproducing Race: An Ethnography of Pregnancy as a Site of Racialization*. Berkeley: University of California Press.

Briggs, Laura. 2003. *Reproducing Empire: Race, Sex, Science, and U.S. Imperialism in Puerto Rico*. Berkeley: University of California Press.

Brown, Alleen, and Nick Estes. 2018. "An Untold Number of Indigenous Children Disappeared at U.S. Boarding Schools. Tribal Nations Are Raising the Stakes in Search of Answers." *Intercept* (blog). September 25, 2018. https://theintercept.com/2018/09/25/carlisle-indian-industrial-school-indigenous-children-disappeared/.

Brown, Wendy. 1995. *States of Injury: Power and Freedom in Late Modernity*. Princeton, NJ: Princeton University Press.

Bunkśe, Edmunds Valdemārs. 2004. *Geography and the Art of Life*. Baltimore: Johns Hopkins University Press.

Butalia, Urvashi. 2000. *The Other Side of Silence: Voices from the Partition of India*. Durham, NC: Duke University Press.

Chandhoke, Neera. 2019. "State-breaking Is Not Nation Making." *The Hindu*. August 22. https://www.thehindu.com/opinion/lead/state-breaking-is-not-nation-making/article29214610.ece.

Chatterjee, Nilanjana, and Nancy Riley. 2001. "Planning an Indian Modernity: The Gendered Politics of Fertility Control." *Signs* 26 (3): 811–45.

Chatterji, Roma, and Deepak Mehta. 2007. *Living with Violence: An Anthropology of Events and Everyday Life*. Delhi: Routledge India.

Chaturvedi, Sanjay. 2002. "Process of Othering in the Case of India and Pakistan." *Tijdschrift Voor Economische En Social Geografie* 93 (2): 149–59.

Cheng, Yi'En. 2014. "Time Protagonists: Student Migrants, Practices of Time and Cultural Construction of the Singapore-Educated Person." *Social & Cultural Geography* 15 (4): 385–405.

———. 2018. "Educated Non-Elites' Pathways to Cosmopolitanism: The Case of Private Degree Students in Singapore." *Social & Cultural Geography* 19 (2): 151–70.

Child, Brenda J. 1998. *Boarding School Seasons: American Indian Families, 1900–1940*. Omaha: University of Nebraska Press.

Chowdhry, Prem. 2007. *Contentious Marriages, Eloping Couples: Gender, Caste and Patriarchy in Northern India*. Oxford: Oxford University Press.

Chua, Jocelyn Lim. 2014. *In Pursuit of the Good Life: Aspiration and Suicide in Globalizing South India*. Berkeley: University of California Press.

Cohn, Bernard S. 1987. "The Census, Social Structure and Objectification in South Asia." In *An Anthropologist among the Historians and Other Essays*, edited by Bernard S. Cohn, 224–54. Oxford: Oxford University Press.

Collins, Patricia Hill. 1998. "It's All in the Family: Intersections of Gender, Race, and Nation." *Hypatia* 13 (3): 62–82.

———. 1999. "Producing the Mothers of the Nation: Race, Class and Contemporary U.S. Population Policies." In *Women, Citizenship and Difference*, edited by Nira Yuval-Davis, 118–29. London: Zed Books.

———. 2004. *Black Sexual Politics: African Americans, Gender, and the New Racism*. New York: Routledge.

Correspondent. 2018. "Global Appeal Floated on Khasi Marriage Bill." *Telegraph*, August 8, 2018. https://www.telegraphindia.com/states/north-east/global-appeal-floated-on-khasi-marriage-bill/cid/1655040.

Cowen, Deborah, and Emily Gilbert. 2008. "The Politics of War, Citizenship, Territory." In *War, Citizenship, Territory*, 1–30. New York: Routledge.

Craig, Sienna R., Geoff Childs, and Cynthia M. Beall. 2016. "Closing the Womb Door: Contraception Use and Fertility Transition among Culturally Tibetan Women in Highland Nepal." *Maternal and Child Health Journal* 20 (12): 2437–50.

Crenshaw, Kimberlé. 1991. "Mapping the Margins: Intersectionality, Identity Politics, and Violence against Women of Color." *Stanford Law Review* 43 (6): 1241–99.

Das, Runa. 2004. "Encountering (Cultural) Nationalism, Islam and Gender in the Body Politic of India." *Social Identities* 10: 369–98.

Das, Veena. 1995. *Critical Events: An Anthropological Perspective on Contemporary India*. New Delhi: Oxford University Press.

———. 2007. *Life and Words: Violence and the Descent into the Ordinary*. Berkeley: University of California Press.

———. 2010. "Engaging the Life of the Other: Love and Everyday Life." In *Ordinary Ethics: Anthropology, Language, and Action*, edited by Michael Lambek, 376–99. Bronx, NY: Fordham University Press.

Davis, Mike. 2002. *Late Victorian Holocausts: El Niño Famines and the Making of the Third World*. London: Verso.

Day, Sophie. 2018. "An Experiment in Story-Telling: Reassembling the House in Ladakh." *Social Anthropology* 26: 88–102.

Del Rosario, Teresita C. 2005. "Bridal Diaspora: Migration and Marriage among Filipino Women." *Indian Journal of Gender Studies* 12 (2–3): 253–73.

Delaney, David. 2005. *Territory: A Short Introduction*. London: Wiley-Blackwell.

Dennison, Jean. 2012. *Colonial Entanglement: Constituting a Twenty-First-Century Osage Nation*. Chapel Hill: University of North Carolina Press.

Devadas, David. 1988. "Buddhists Flare up at Missionaries and Administration in Ladakh." *India Today—Indiascope*, July 15, 1988. http://indiatoday.intoday.in/story/buddhists-flare-up-at-missionaries-and-administration-in-ladakh/1/329549.html.

Dharmalingam, A., and S. P. Morgan. 2004. "Pervasive Muslim–Hindu Fertility Differences in India." *Demography* 41: 529–45.

Dimpfl, Mike, and Sara Smith. In press. "Cosmopolitan Sidestep: University Life, Intimate Geopolitics and the Hidden Costs of 'Global' Citizenship." *Area*.

Dixon, Deborah P. 2015. *Feminist Geopolitics: Material States*. New York: Routledge.

Dixon, Deborah P., and Sallie A. Marston. 2011. "Introduction: Feminist Engagements with Geopolitics." *Gender, Place and Culture* 18 (4): 445–53.

Dollfus, Pascale. 1995. "The History of Muslims in Central Ladakh." *Tibet Journal* 20 (3): 35–58.

Dowler, Lorraine, and Joanne P. Sharp. 2001. "A Feminist Geopolitics?" *Space & Polity* 5: 165–76.

Dunbar-Ortiz, Roxanne. 2014. *An Indigenous Peoples' History of the United States*. Boston, MA: Beacon Press.

Duschinski, Haley, Mona Bhan, Ather Zia, and Cynthia Mahmood, eds. 2018. *Resisting Occupation in Kashmir*. Philadelphia: University of Pennsylvania Press.

Dyson, Jane, and Craig Jeffrey. 2018. "Everyday Prefiguration: Youth Social Action in North India." *Transactions of the Institute of British Geographers* 43 (4): 573–85.

Edney, Matthew H. 1997. *Mapping an Empire: The Geographical Construction of British India, 1765–1843*. Chicago: University of Chicago Press.

Edney, Matthew H. 2007. "Mapping Empires, Mapping Bodies: Reflections on the Use and Abuse of Cartography." *Treballs de La Societat Catalana de Geografia* 63: 83–104.

Elden, Stuart. 2009. *Terror and Territory: The Spatial Extent of Sovereignty*. Minneapolis: University of Minnesota Press.

———. 2010. "Land, Terrain, Territory." *Progress in Human Geography* 34: 799–817.

———. 2013. *The Birth of Territory*. Chicago: University of Chicago Press.

Fanon, Frantz. 2008. *Black Skin, White Masks*. New York: Grove Press.

Fewkes, Jacqueline. 2009. *Trade and Contemporary Society along the Silk Road: An Ethno-History of Ladakh*. New York: Routledge.

———. 2018. "Perspectives from the Field: Interviews with the Alima of Ladakh." *Himalaya, the Journal of the Association for Nepal and Himalayan Studies* 38 (2): 12.

Fluri, Jennifer. 2011. "Armored Peacocks and Proxy Bodies: Gender Geopolitics in Aid/Development Spaces of Afghanistan." *Gender, Place & Culture* 18 (4): 519–36.

———. 2014. "States of (in) security: corporeal geographies and the elsewhere war." *Environment and Planning D: Society and Space* 32 (5): 795–814.

Fong, Vanessa L. 2011. *Paradise Redefined: Transnational Chinese Students and the Quest for Flexible Citizenship in the Developed World*. Stanford, CA: Stanford University Press.

Foucault, Michel. 1978. *Discipline and Punish: The Birth of the Prison*. New York: Vintage.

———. 1991. "Governmentality." In *The Foucault Effect: Studies in Governmentality*, edited by Graham Burchell, Colin Gordon, and Peter Miller, 87–104. Chicago: University of Chicago.

———. 2003. *Madness and Civilization*. New York: Routledge.

Friedman, Sara L. 2000. "Spoken Pleasures and Dangerous Desires: Sexuality, Marriage, and the State in Rural Southeastern China." *East Asia* 18 (4): 13–39.

Gagné, Karine. 2019. "Deadly Predators and Virtuous Buddhists: Dog Population Control and the Politics of Ethics in Ladakh." *Himalaya* 39 (1): 9–25.

Gamble, Ruth and Alexander Davis. 2019. "Geopolitical Moves in Jammu and Kashmir Have a Local Cost, Too." *The interpreter*. August 12. https://www.lowyinstitute.org/the-interpreter/geopolitical-moves-jammu-and-kashmir-local-cost.

Gergan, Mabel. Forthcoming. "Disastrous Hydropower, Differential Vulnerability, and Decolonization in India's Eastern Himalayan Borderlands." *Political Geography*.

———. 2014. "Precarity and Possibility: On Being Young and Indigenous in Sikkim, India." *Himalaya* 34 (2): 67–80.

——. 2017. Living with earthquakes and angry deities at the Himalayan borderlands. *Annals of the American Association of Geographers* 107 (2): 490–98.

Gergan, Mabel, and Andrew Curley. "Indigenous Youth, Environmentalism, and Decolonial Futures: From the Navajo Nation to the Lepchas of the Eastern Himalayas." Unpublished manuscript, last modified 2019.

Ghosh, Abantika, and Vijaita Singh. 2015. "Census: Hindu Share Dips below 80%, Muslim Share Grows but Slower." *Indian Express*, January 24, 2015.

Gilmartin, Mary, and Emily Kofman. 2004. "Critically Feminist Geopolitics." In *Mapping Women, Making Politics*, edited by Lynn Staeheli, Eleonore Kofman and Linda Peake. 113–26. New York: Routledge.

Gilmore, Ruth Wilson. 2002. "Fatal Couplings of Power and Difference: Notes on Racism and Geography." *Professional Geographer* 54 (1): 15–24.

Ginsburg, Faye D. and Rayna Rapp. 1995. *Conceiving the New World Order: The Global Politics of Reproduction*. Berkeley, CA: University of California Press.

Gökariksel, Banu. 2009. "Beyond the Officially Sacred: Religion, Secularism, and the Body in the Production of Subjectivity." *Social & Cultural Geography* 10 (6): 657–74.

——. 2012. "The Intimate Politics of Secularism and the Headscarf: The Mall, the Neighborhood, and the Public Square in Istanbul." *Gender, Place & Culture* 19 (1): 1–20.

Gökariksel, Banu, Christopher Neubert, and Sara Smith. 2019. "Demographic Fever Dreams: Fragile Masculinity and Population Politics in the Rise of the Global Right." *Signs: Journal of Women in Culture and Society* 44 (3): 561–87.

Gökariksel, Banu, and Anna Secor. 2012. "'Even I Was Tempted': The Moral Ambivalence and Ethical Practice of Veiling-Fashion in Turkey." *Annals of the Association of American Geographers* 102 (4): 847–62.

——. 2014. "The Veil, Desire, and the Gaze: Turning the inside Out." *Signs: Journal of Women in Culture and Society* 40 (1): 177–200.

Gökariksel, Banu, and Anna J. Secor. Forthcoming. "Affective geopolitics: Anxiety, pain, and ethics in the encounter with Syrian refugees in Turkey." *Environment and Planning C: Politics and Space*.

Gökariksel, Banu, and Sara Smith. 2016. "'Making America Great Again'? The Fascist Body Politics of Donald Trump." *Political Geography* 54: 79–81.

Government of India. 2001. "Census of India." http://www.censusindia.gov.in/2011-common /census_data_2001.html.

——. 2011. "Census of India." http://censusindia.gov.in/2011-Common/CensusData2011.html.

Grosz, Elizabeth. 1994. *Volatile Bodies: Toward a Corporeal Feminism*. Bloomington: Indiana University Press.

Gupta, A. 1995. "Blurred Boundaries: the Discourse of Corruption, the Culture of Politics, and the Imagined State." *American Ethnologist*, 22 (2): 375–402.

Gupta, Charu. 2009. "Hindu Women, Muslim Men: Love Jihad and Conversions." *Economic and Political Weekly* 44 (51): 13–15.

Gupta, Pallavi, Banu Gökariksel, and Sara Smith. "Politics of Saving Muslim Women in India: Gendered Geolegality, Security, and Territorialization of the Hindu Nationalist State." Unpublished manuscript, last modified 2019.

Gupta, Radhika. 2011. *Piety, Politics, and Patriotism in Kargil, India*. Oxford: Oxford University Press.

Gutschow, Kim. 2004. *Being a Buddhist Nun: The Struggle for Enlightenment in the Himalayas*. Cambridge, MA: Harvard University Press.

——. 2006. "The Politics of Being Buddhist in Zangskar: Partition and Today." *India Review* 5: 470–98.

Hacking, Ian. 1990. *The Taming of Chance*. New York: Cambridge University Press.

Hagerman, Margaret A. 2018. *White Kids: Growing up with Privilege in a Racially Divided America*. New York: New York University Press.

Halkias, Georgios T. 2011. "The Muslim Queens of the Himalayas: Princess Exchanges in Baltistan and Ladakh." In *Islam and Tibet: Interactions along the Musk Routes*, edited by Anna Akasoy, Charles S. F. Burnett, and Ronit Yoeli-Tlalim, 231–52. London: Ashgate.

Hannah-Jones, Nikole. 2012. "Living Apart: How the Government Betrayed a Landmark Civil Rights Law. *ProPublica*. https://www.propublica.org/article/living-apart-how -the-government-betrayed-a-landmark-civil-rights-law.

———. 2014. "Segregation Now." *Atlantic* 313 (4): 58–69.

Hansen, Thomas Blom. 1999. *The Saffron Wave: Democracy and Hindu Nationalism in Modern India*. Princeton, NJ: Princeton University Press.

Hartman, Saidiya V. 1997. *Scenes of Subjection: Terror, Slavery, and Self-Making in Nineteenth-Century America*. Oxford: Oxford University Press.

Hartmann, Betsy. 1995. *Reproductive Rights and Wrongs: The Global Politics of Population Control*. Boston: South End Press.

Heber, A. Reeve, and Kathleen M. Heber. 1926. *In Himalayan Tibet*. London: Seeley Service & Company.

Hodes, Martha. 1993. "The Sexualization of Reconstruction Politics: White Women and Black Men in the South after the Civil War." *Journal of the History of Sexuality* 3 (3): 402–17.

Hopkins, Peter E. 2007. "Young Muslim Men's Experiences of Local Landscapes after 11 September 2001." In *Geographies of Muslim Identities: Diaspora, Gender and Belonging*, edited by Cara Aitchison, Peter Hopkins, and Mei-Po Kwan, 189–200. Aldershot, United Kingdom: Ashgate.

Hörschelmann, Kathrin, and Elisabeth El Refaie. 2014. "Transnational Citizenship, Dissent and the Political Geographies of Youth." *Transactions of the Institute of British Geographers* 39 (3): 444–56.

Huijsmans, Roy. 2016. "Critical Geopolitics of Child and Youth Migration in (Post) Socialist Laos." *Children, Young People and Critical Geopolitics*, edited by Matthew C. Benwell and Peter Hopkins, 139–54. London: Routledge.

Hyndman, Jennifer. 2001. "Towards a Feminist Geopolitics." *Canadian Geographer* 45: 210–22.

———. 2007. "Feminist Geopolitics Revisited: Body Counts in Iraq." *Professional Geographer* 59: 35–66.

Hyndman, Jennifer, and W. Giles, eds. 2004. *Sites of Violence: Gender and Conflict Zones*. Berkeley: University of California.

Iqbal, Naveed. 2017. "An Inter-Religion Marriage Triggers Communal Divide in Leh, and Exodus." *Indian Express*, September 15, 2017.

Iyer, S. 2002. *Demography and Religion in India*. New York: Oxford University Press.

Jaffrelot, Christophe. 2017. "India's Democracy at 70: Toward a Hindu State?" *Journal of Democracy* 28 (3): 52–63. https://doi.org/10.1353/jod.2017.0044.

Jain, Bharti. 2015. "Muslim Population Grows 24%, Slower than Previous Decade." *Times of India*, January 22, 2015. http://timesofindia.indiatimes.com/india/Muslim-population -grows-24-slower-than-previous-decade/articleshow/45972687.cms.

Jalal, Ayesha. 2002. *Self and Sovereignty: Individual and Community in South Asian Islam since 1850*. London: Routledge.

Jayawardena, Kumari, and Malathi de Alwis. 1996. *Embodied Violence: Communalising Women's Sexuality in South Asia*. New Delhi: Kali for Women.

Jeffery, Patricia, and Roger Jeffery. 2002. "A Population out of Control? Myths about Muslim Fertility in Contemporary India." *World Development* 30: 1805–22.

Jeffery, Roger, and Patricia Jeffery. 2005. "Saffron Demography, Common Wisdom, Aspirations and Uneven Governmentalities." *Economic and Political Weekly.* 40 (5): 447–53.

Jeffrey, Craig. 2010. *Timepass: Youth, Class, and the Politics of Waiting in India.* Stanford, CA: Stanford University Press.

Johnson, Corey, and Reece Jones. 2011. "Rethinking 'the Border' in Border Studies." *Political Geography* 30: 61–62.

Johnson-Hanks, Jennifer. 2006. "On the Politics and Practice of Muslim Fertility." *Medical Anthropology Quarterly* 20 (1): 12–30.

Kabir, Ananya Jahanara. 2009. *Territory of Desire: Representing the Valley of Kashmir.* Minneapolis: University of Minnesota Press.

Katz, Cindi. 2001. "Vagabond Capitalism and the Necessity of Social Reproduction." *Antipode* 33: 709–28.

———. 2004. *Growing up Global: Economic Restructuring and Children's Everyday Lives.* Minneapolis: University of Minnesota Press.

Kong, Lily. 2010. "Global Shifts, Theoretical Shifts: Changing Geographies of Religion." *Progress in Human Geography* 34 (6): 755–76.

Korac, M. 1999. "Refugee Women in Serbia: Their Experiences with War, Nationalism and State Building." In *Women, Citizenship and Difference,* edited by Pnina Werbner and Nira Yuval Davis, 192–200. London: Zed Books.

———. 2004. "War, Flight and Exile: Gendered Violence among Refugee Women from Post-Yugoslav States." In *Sites of Violence: Gender and Conflict Zones,* edited by Wenona Giles and Jennifer Hyndman, 249–72. Berkeley: University of California Press.

Krishna, Sankaran. 1994. "Cartographic Anxiety: Mapping the Body Politic in India." *Alternatives: Social Transformation and Humane Governance* 19: 507–21.

Lakoff, Andrew, and Stephen J. Collier. 2004. "Ethics and the anthropology of modern reason." *Anthropological Theory* 4 (4): 419–34.

Lam-Knott, Sonia. 2018. "Defining Politics in an 'Apolitical City': An Ethnographic Study of Hong Kong." *Anthropology Matters* 18 (1): 24–50.

Legg, Stephen. 2004. "Review Essay: Memory and Nostalgia." *Cultural Geographies* 11: 99–107.

———. 2005. "Foucault's Population Geographies: Classifications, Biopolitics and Governmental Spaces." *Population, Space and Place* 11: 137–56.

———. 2007. "Reviewing Geographies of Memory/Forgetting." *Environment and Planning A* 39 (2): 456–66.

———. 2014. *Prostitution and the Ends of Empire: Scale, Governmentalities, and Interwar India.* Durham: Duke University Press.

Longhurst, Robyn. 2001. *Bodies: Exploring Fluid Boundaries.* London: Routledge.

Lowe, Lisa. 2015. *The Intimacies of Four Continents.* Durham, NC: Duke University Press.

Ludden, David. 1996. *Contesting the Nation: Religion, Community, and the Politics of Democracy in India.* Philadelphia: University of Pennsylvania Press.

Lugones, Maria. 2010. "Toward a Decolonial Feminism." *Hypatia* 25 (4): 742–59.

Lukose, Ritty A. 2009. *Liberalization's Children: Gender, Youth, and Consumer Citizenship in Globalizing India.* Durham, NC: Duke University Press.

Marshall, David Jones. 2014. "Love Stories of the Occupation: Storytelling and the Counter-Geopolitics of Intimacy." *Area* 46 (4): 349–51.

Massey, Doreen. 1991. "A Global Sense of Place." *Marxism Today,* June, 24–29.

Mayer, Tamar. 2000. *Gender Ironies of Nationalism: Sexing the Nation.* New York: Routledge.

———. 2004. "Embodied Nationalisms." In *Mapping Women, Making Politics,* edited by Lynn Staeheli, Eleonore Kofman, and Linda Peake, 156–61. New York: Routledge.

McDuie-Ra, Duncan. 2012. "Cosmopolitan Tribals: Frontier Migrants in Delhi." *South Asia Research* 32 (1): 39–55.

McKinnon, Katharine. 2016. "The Geopolitics of Birth." *Area* 48 (3): 285–91.

McRae, Elizabeth Gillespie. 2018. *Mothers of Massive Resistance: White Women and the Politics of White Supremacy.* Oxford: Oxford University Press.

Megoran, Nick. 2008. "From Presidential Podiums to Pop Music: Everyday Discourses of Geopolitical Danger in Uzbekistan." In *Fear: Critical Geopolitics and Everyday Life*, edited by Rachel Pain and Susan Smith, 25–36. Burlington, VT: Ashgate.

Menon, R, and K. Bhasin. 1998. *Borders and Boundaries: Women in India's Partition.* New Brunswick, NJ: Rutgers University Press.

Mills, Amy. 2006. "Boundaries of the Nation in the Space of the Urban." *Cultural Geographies* 13: 367–94.

Mody, Perveez. 2008. *The Intimate State: Love-Marriage and the Law in Delhi.* New York: Routledge.

Mohan, Rao. 2011. "Love Jihad and Demographic Fears." *Indian Journal of Gender Studies* 18 (3): 425–30.

Mohanty, Chandra Talpade. 2003. *Feminism without Borders: Decolonizing Theory, Practicing Solidarity.* Durham, NC: Duke University Press.

Moore, Donald S. 2005. *Suffering for Territory: Race, Place, and Power in Zimbabwe.* Durham, NC: Duke University Press.

Morokvasic-Müller, M. 2004. "From Pillars of Yugoslavism to Targets of Violence: Interethnic Marriages in the Former Yugoslavia and Thereafter." In *Sites of Violence: Gender and Conflict Zones*, edited by Wenona Giles and Jennifer Hyndman, 134–51. Berkeley: University of California.

Morrison, Carey-Ann, Lynda Johnston, and Robyn Longhurst. 2013. "Critical Geographies of Love as Spatial, Relational and Political." *Progress in Human Geography* 37 (4): 505–21.

Moss, Pamela, and Isabel Dyck. 2003. "Embodying Social Geography." In *Handbook of Cultural Geography*, edited by Kay Anderson, Mona Domosh, Steve Pile, and Nigel Thrift, 58–73. London: Sage.

Mountz, Alison. 2010. *Seeking Asylum: Human Smuggling and Bureaucracy at the Border.* Minneapolis: University of Minnesota Press.

———. 2011. "The Enforcement Archipelago: Detention, Haunting, and Asylum on Islands." *Political Geography* 30 (3): 118–28.

Nagar, Richa. 1998. "Communal Discourses, Marriage, and the Politics of Gendered Social Boundaries among South Asian Immigrants in Tanzania." *Gender, Place and Culture: A Journal of Feminist Geography* 5: 117–39.

———. 2014. *Muddying the Waters: Coauthoring Feminisms across Scholarship and Activism.* Champaign: University of Illinois Press.

Nash, Catherine. 2005. "Geographies of Relatedness." *Transactions of the Institute of British Geographers* 30 (4): 449–62.

Nast, Heidi J. 1998. "Unsexy Geographies." *Gender, Place and Culture* 5 (2): 191–206.

———. 2000. "Mapping the 'Unconscious': Racism and the Oedipal Family." *Annals of the Association of American Geographers* 90: 215–55.

Nast, Heidi, and Steve Pile. 1998. "Introduction: Makingplacesbodies." In *Places through the Body*, edited by Heidi J. Nast and Steve Pile, 1–19. London: Routledge.

Nayak, Anoop. 2003. *Race, Place, and Globalization, Youth Cultures in a Changing World.* Oxford: Berg.

Nguyen, Nicole, Dan Cohen, and Alice Huff. 2017. "Catching the Bus: A Call for Critical Geographies of Education." *Geography Compass* 11 (8): 1–13.

Norberg-Hodge, Helena. 2000. *Ancient Futures: Learning from Ladakh*. New York: Random House.

Oza, Rupal. 2001. "Gender, Geography, and Globalization." *Signs* 26: 1067–95.

———. 2007. "The Geography of Hindu Right-Wing Violence in India." In *Violent Geographies: Fear, Terror, and Political Violence*, edited by Derek Gregory and Allan Pred, 153–74. New York: Routledge.

Ozer, Simon, Preben Bertelsen, Rashmi Singla, and Seth J. Schwartz. 2017. "'Grab Your Culture and Walk with the Global': Ladakhi Students' Negotiation of Cultural Identity in the Context of Globalization-Based Acculturation." *Journal of Cross-Cultural Psychology* 48 (3): 294–318.

Paasi, Anssi. 2011. "Borders, Theory and the Challenge of Relational Thinking." *Political Geography* 30: 62–63.

Pain, Rachel. 2015. "Intimate War." *Political Geography* 44: 64–73.

Pain, Rachel, and Lynn Staeheli. 2014. "Introduction: Intimacy-Geopolitics and Violence." *Area* 46 (4): 344–47.

Painter, J., 2006. Prosaic Geographies of Stateness. *Political Geography* 25 (7): 752–74.

Pande, Raksha. 2014. "Geographies of Marriage and Migration: Arranged Marriages and South Asians in Britain." *Geography Compass* 8 (2): 75–86.

Pandey, Gyanendra. 2006. *The Construction of Communalism in Colonial North India*. New Delhi: Oxford University Press.

Pasternak, Shiri. 2017. *Grounded Authority: The Algonquins of Barriere Lake against the State*. Minneapolis: University of Minnesota Press.

Perry, Imani. 2018. *Vexy Thing: On Gender and Liberation*. Durham, NC: Duke University Press.

Petech, Luciano. 1977. *The Kingdom of Ladakh*. Istituto italiano per il Medio ed Estremo Oriente.

Pigg, Stacy Leigh, and Vincanne Adams. 2005. "Introduction: The Moral Object of Sex." In *Sex in Development: Science, Sexuality, and Morality in Global Perspective*, 1–38. Durham, NC: Duke University Press.

Pilkington, Doris. 2002. *Follow the Rabbit-Proof Fence*. St. Lucia: University of Queensland Press.

Pinault, David. 2001. *Horse of Karbala: Muslim Devotional Life in India*. New York: Palgrave.

Pinsker, Joe. 2018. "How Well-Intentioned White Families Can Perpetuate Racism." *Atlantic*, September 4, 2018. https://www.theatlantic.com/family/archive/2018/09/white-kids-race/569185/.

Povinelli, Elizabeth A. 2002. *The Cunning of Recognition: Indigenous Alterities and the Making of Australian Multiculturalism*. Durham, NC: Duke University Press.

Puar, Jasbir K. 2007. *Terrorist Assemblages: Homonationalism in Queer Times*. Durham, NC: Duke University Press.

Puri, Jyoti. 1999. *Woman, Body, Desire in Post-Colonial India: Narratives of Gender and Sexuality*. New York: Routledge.

Qadeer, Imrana. 2005. Population Control in the Era of Neo-liberalism. *Journal of Health and Development* 1 (4): 31–48.

Rai, Mridu. 2004. *Hindu Rulers, Muslim Subjects: Islam, Rights, and the History of Kashmir*. Princeton, NJ: Princeton University Press.

Rajan, Rajeswari Sunder. 2003. *The Scandal of the State: Women, Law, and Citizenship in Postcolonial India*. Durham, NC: Duke University Press. http://www.bsos.umd.edu/gvpt/lpbr/subpages/reviews/Rajan03.htm.

Ramaswamy, Sumathi. 2010. *The Goddess and the Nation: Mapping Mother India*. Durham, NC: Duke University Press.

Rao, Mohan. 2004. *From Population Control to Reproductive Health*. Thousand Oaks, CA: Sage.

———.2010. "On Saffron Demography." *Economic and Political Weekly*, 27–29.

Rizvi, Janet. 1996. *Ladakh: Crossroads of High Asia*. New Delhi: Oxford University Press.

———. 1999. *Trans-Himalayan Caravans*. New Delhi: Oxford University Press.

Roberts, Dorothy. 2014. *Killing the Black Body: Race, Reproduction, and the Meaning of Liberty*. Vintage.

Robinson, Cabeiri deBergh. 2013. *Body of Victim, Body of Warrior: Refugee Families and the Making of Kashmiri Jihadists*. Berkeley: University of California Press.

Rose, Nikolas. 2001. "The Politics of Life Itself." *Theory, Culture & Society* 18: 1–30.

———. 2006. *The Politics of Life Itself*. Princeton, NJ: Princeton University Press.

Rose, Nikolas, and Carlos Novas. 2005. "Biological Citizenship." In *Global Assemblages: Technology, Politics, and Ethics as Anthropological Problems*, edited by Aihwa Ong and Stephen J. Collier, 439–463, Malden, MA: Blackwell.

Sabhlok, Anu. 2010. "National Identity in Relief." *Geoforum* 41 (5): 743–51.

———. 2017. "'Main Bhi to Hindostaan Hoon': Gender and Nation-State in India's Border Roads Organisation." *Gender, Place & Culture* 24 (12): 1711–28.

Said, Edward. 1979. *Orientalism*. New York: Vintage.

Saldanha, Arun. 2007. *Psychedelic White: Goa Trance and the Viscosity of Race*. Minneapolis: University of Minnesota Press.

———. 2008. "The Political Geography of Many Bodies." In *The Sage Handbook of Political Geography*, edited by Cox, Kevin R., Murray Low and Jennifer Robinson, 323–33. London: Sage.

Saldon, Stanzin. 2017. "I Am Saldon. I Am Shifah." *Indian Express*, September 19, 2017. http://indianexpress.com/article/opinion/columns/i-am-saldon-i-am-shifah-4850000/.

Sarkar, Tanika. 2018. "Who Rules India? A Few Notes on the Hindu Right." Revista Canaria de Estudios Ingleses 76 (April): 223–39.

Scheper-Hughes, Nancy, and Margaret M. Lock. 1987. "The Mindful Body: A Prolegomenon to Future Work in Medical Anthropology." *Medical Anthropology Quarterly* 1: 6–41.

Scott, James. 1998. *Seeing like a State: How Certain Schemes to Improve the Human Condition Have Failed*. New Haven, CT: Yale University Press.

Secor, Anna J. 2001. "Toward a Feminist Counter-Geopolitics: Gender, Space and Islamist Politics in Istanbul." *Space & Polity* 5: 191–211.

Shakspo, Nawang Tsering. 1995. "The Significance of Khuksho." In *Recent Research on Ladakh 4 & 5: Proceedings of the Fourth and Fifth International Colloquia on Ladakh*, edited by Henry Osmaston and Philip Denwood, 181–87. Delhi: Motilal Banarsidass.

Sharpe, Christina. 2009. *Monstrous Intimacies: Making Post-Slavery Subjects*. Durham, NC: Duke University Press.

———. 2016. *In the Wake: On Blackness and Being*. Durham, NC: Duke University Press.

Sheikh, Abdul Ghani. 1995. "A Brief History of Muslims in Ladakh." In *Recent Research on Ladakh 4 & 5: Proceedings of the Fourth and Fifth International Colloquia on Ladakh*, edited by Henry Osmaston and Philip Denwood, 189–92.

———. 2007. "Transformation of Kuksho Village." In *Recent Research on Ladakh 2007*, edited by John Bray and Nawang Tsering Shakspo, 163–69. Leh: Jammu & Kashmir Academy of Art, Culture and Languages.

Siddiqui, Kalim. 2017. "Hindutva, Neoliberalism and the Reinventing of India." *Journal of Economic and Social Thought* 4 (2): 142–86.

Simpson, Audra. 2007. "On Ethnographic Refusal: Indigeneity, 'Voice' and Colonial Citizenship." *Junctures: The Journal for Thematic Dialogue* 9: 67–80.

———. 2009. "Captivating Eunice: Membership, Colonialism, and Gendered Citizenships of Grief." *Wicazo Sa Review* 24 (2): 105–29.

———. 2014. *Mohawk Interruptus: Political Life across the Borders of Settler States*. Durham, NC: Duke University Press.

Singh, Bhrigupati. 2011. "Agonistic Intimacy and Moral Aspiration in Popular Hinduism: A Study in the Political Theology of the Neighbor." *American Ethnologist* 38 (3): 430–50.

Smith, Linda Tuhiwai. 1999. *Decolonizing Methodologies: Research and Indigenous People*. New York: Zed Books.

Smith, Sara. 2008. "Notes from the Field: The Geopolitics of Intimacy and Babies in Leh." *Ladakh Studies* 23: 20–25.

———. 2011. "'She Says Herself, "I Have No Future"': Love, Fate, and Territory in Leh District, India." *Gender, Place and Culture* 18 (4): 455–76.

———. 2012a. "Intimate Geopolitics: Religion, Marriage, and Reproductive Bodies in Leh, Ladakh." *Annals of the Association of American Geographers* 102 (6): 1511–28.

———. 2012b. "'In the Heart, There's Nothing': Unruly Youth, Generational Vertigo and Territory." *Transactions of the Institute of British Geographers* 38 (4): 272–85.

———. 2013. "'In the Past, We Ate from One Plate': Memory and the Border in Leh, Ladakh." *Political Geography* 35: 47–59.

———. 2016. "Intimacy and Angst in the Field." *Gender, Place & Culture* 23 (1): 134–46.

———. 2017. "Politics, Pleasure, and Difference in the Intimate City: Himalayan Students Remake the Future." *Cultural Geographies* 24 (4): 573–88.

Smith, Sara, and Mabel Gergan. 2015. "The Diaspora Within: Himalayan Youth, Education-Driven Migration, and Future Aspirations in India." *Environment and Planning D: Society and Space* 33 (1): 119–35.

———. 2017. "Life, Love and Activism on the Forgotten Margins of the Nation-State." In *Children, Young People and Critical Geopolitics*, edited by Matt Benwell and Peter E. Hopkins, 91–105. Burlington, VT: Ashgate.

Smith, Sara, and Pavithra Vasudevan. 2017. "Race, Biopolitics, and the Future: Introduction to the Special Section." *Environment and Planning D: Society and Space* 35 (2): 210–21.

Smith, Sara, Pavithra Vasudevan, Carlos Serrano, and Banu Gökariksel. 2019. "Editorial: Breaking Families: Whiteness, State Violence and the Alienable Rights of Kin." *Political Geography* 72: 144–46.

Spillers, Hortense J. 1987. "Mama's Baby, Papa's Maybe: An American Grammar Book." *Diacritics* 17 (2): 65–81.

Srinivas, Smriti. 1998. *The Mouths of People, the Voice of God: Buddhists and Muslims in a Frontier Community of Ladakh*. New York City: Oxford University Press.

Stoler, Ann Laura. 2002. *Carnal Knowledge and Imperial Power: Race and the Intimate in Colonial Rule*. Berkeley: University of California Press.

———. 2013. *Imperial Debris: On Ruins and Ruination*. Durham, NC: Duke University Press.

Storey, David. 2001. *Territory: The Claiming of Space*. New York: Prentice Hall.

Sultan, Parvez, and Sweta Goswami. 2017. "Delhi's Republic Day Tableaux: A Story of Rejection and Acceptance." *Hindustan Times*, January 26, 2017. https://www.hindustantimes.com/delhi/delhi-s-republic-day-tableaux-a-story-of-rejection-and-acceptance/story-oz1NBqA9bIaeZqGSHETHdJ.html.

Towghi, Fouzieyha, and Kalindi Vora. 2014. "Bodies, markets, and the experimental in South Asia." *Ethnos* 70 (1): 1–18.

Tyner, James A., and Donna Houston. 2000. "Controlling Bodies: The Punishment of Mul-
tiracialized Sexual Relations." *Antipode* 32 (4): 387–409.

Ul-Qamrain, Noor. 2015. "Buddhists in Ladakh Allege Love Jihad." *Sunday Guardian*, January 31, 2015. http://www.sunday-guardian.com/news/buddhists-in-ladakh-allege-love
-jihad.

Varagur, Krithika. 2018a. "Communal Tensions Rattle an Indian Himalayan Region." *Voice
of America: East Asia*, April 3, 2018. https://www.voanews.com/a/inter-faith-marriages
-create-tensions-in-india/4329930.html.

———. 2018b. "On the Run." *Caravan: A Journal of Politics and Culture*, June 1, 2018, 12–13.

Varma, Rashmi. 2017. "(Un)Modifying India: Nationalism, Sexual Violence and the Politics
of Hindutva." *Feminist Dissent*, no. 2: 57–82.

Varma, Saiba. 2016. "Love in the Time of Occupation: Reveries, Longing, and Intoxication
in Kashmir." *American Ethnologist* 43 (1): 50–62.

———. 2019. "Kashmir Has Become a Zone of Permanent, Limitless War." *The Nation*.
September 4.

Vasan, Sudha. 2017. "Being Ladakhi, Being Indian." *Economic & Political Weekly* 52 (14): 43.

Vasudevan, Alexander. 2015. "The Autonomous City: Towards a Critical Geography of Occupation." *Progress in Human Geography* 39 (3): 316–37.

Vasudevan, Pavithra. In Press. "An Intimate Inventory of Race and Waste." *Antipode.*

Vora, Kalindi. 2015. *Life Support: Biocapital and the New History of Outsourced Labor.* Minneapolis: University of Minnesota Press.

Wadi, Shahd. 2012. "Palestinian Women's Bodies as a Battlefield." In *Plots of War: Modern
Narratives of Conflict*, edited by Isabel Capeloa Gil and Adriana Martins, 2: 114–23. Ber-
lin: Walter de Gruyter.

Warner, Michael. 1991. "Introduction: Fear of a Queer Planet." *Social Text* 9: 3–17.

Weheliye, Alexander. 2014. *Habeas Viscus: Racializing Assemblages, Biopolitics, and Black Feminist Theories of the Human.* Durham, NC: Duke University Press.

Wells, Ida B. 1997. *Southern Horrors and Other Writings: The Anti-Lynching Campaign of Ida B.
Wells, 1892–1900.* Edited by Jacqueline Jones Royster. Boston: Bedford Books.

Williams, Jill, and Vanessa Massaro. 2013. "Feminist Geopolitics: Unpacking (In)Security,
Animating Social Change." *Geopolitics* 18 (4): 751–58.

Williams, Philippa. 2007. "Hindu–Muslim Brotherhood: Exploring the Dynamics of Communal Relations in Varanasi, North India." *Journal of South Asian Development* 2 (2):
153–76.

Williams-Oerberg, Elizabeth. 2016. "Educational Migration among Ladakhi Youth." In *Inter-
nal Migration in Contemporary India*, edited by D. Mishra, 154–79. New Delhi: Sage.

Wouters, Jelle J. P., and Tanka B. Subba. 2013. "The 'Indian Face,' India's Northeast, and 'the
Idea of India.'" *Asian Anthropology* 12 (2): 126–40.

Wynter, Sylvia. 2003. "Unsettling the Coloniality of Being/Power/Truth/Freedom: Towards
the Human, after Man, Its Overrepresentation—An Argument." *New Centennial Review*
3 (3): 257–337.

Yuval-Davis, Nira. 1989. "National Reproduction and the Demographic Race in Israel." In
Women-Nation-State, 92–109. London: Macmillan.

Zutshi, Chitralekha. 2003. *Languages of Belonging: Islam, Regional Identity, and the Making of
Kashmir.* New Delhi: Permanent Black.

INDEX

Note: *t* denotes a reference to a table; *f* denotes a reference to a figure.

ABOUT THE AUTHOR

SARA SMITH teaches geography at the University of North Carolina at Chapel Hill. She is a political geographer interested in territory, bodies, and the future, both in the context of the Ladakh region of North India and in relation to the U.S. and global context through attention to racialization and territory.